The Battle of Majuba Hill

The Transvaal Campaign, 1880-1881

John Laband

Helion & Company

Helion & Company Limited
26 Willow Road
Solihull
West Midlands
B91 1UE
England
Tel. 0121 705 3393
Fax 0121 711 4075
Email: info@helion.co.uk
Website: www.helion.co.uk
Twitter: @helionbooks
Visit our blog http://blog.helion.co.uk/

Published by Helion & Company 2017
Designed and typeset by Farr out Publications, Wokingham, Berkshire
Cover designed by Paul Hewitt, Battlefield Design (www.battlefield-design.co.uk)
Printed by Henry Ling Limited, Dorchester, Dorset

Text © John Laband 2017
Illustrations © as individually credited
Maps drawn by George Anderson © Helion & Company 2017

Cover: The Boer assault on the British positions on the summit of Majuba Hill on 27 February
1881, painted in 1881 by Otto Heinrich Landsberg (1803–1905). (MuseumAfrica, Johannesburg)

ISBN 978-1-911512-38-7

British Library Cataloguing-in-Publication Data.
A catalogue record for this book is available from the British Library.

For details of other military history titles published by Helion & Company Limited
contact the above address, or visit our website: http://www.helion.co.uk.

We always welcome receiving book proposals from prospective authors.

Contents

List of Abbreviations

AAG	Assistant Adjutant-General
BPP	*British Parliamentary Papers*
Bt	Baronet
BV	Argief Boeren Voormannen, NARP
CB	Companion of the Most Honourable Order of the Bath
CMG	Companion of the Most Distinguished Order of St Michael and St George
DAAG	Deputy Assistant Adjutant-General
DAG	Deputy Adjutant-General
DD	Department of Defence, Cape Colony, papers, WCPA
DQMG	Deputy Quartermaster-General
GCB	Knight Grand Cross of the Most Honourable Order of the Bath
GCMG	Knight Grand Cross of the Most Distinguished Order of St Michael and St George
GH	Government House, Cape Colony, papers, WCPA
GOC	General Officer Commanding
ILN	*Illustrated London News*
JC	P.J. Joubert Collection, NARP
KCB	Knight Commander of the Most Honourable Order of the Bath
KCMG	Knight Commander of the Most Distinguished Order of St Michael and St George
KCSI	Knight Commander of the Most Exalted Order of the Star of India
KDG	1st (King's) Dragoon Guards
KG	Knight of the Most Noble Order of the Garter
NARP	National Archives Repository, Pretoria
NCO	non-commissioned officer
NFF	Natal Field Force
OVS	Oranje-Vrijstaat (Orange Free State)
PAR	Pietermaritzburg Archives Repository
QMG	Quartermaster-General
RA	Royal Artillery
RE	Royal Engineers
RML	Rifled Muzzle Loader
TNA	The National Archives, Kew
TNLS	The National Library of Scotland
VC	Victoria Cross

WC	Sir Evelyn Wood Collection, PAR
WCPA	Western Cape Provincial Archives and Records Service
WO	War Office papers, TNA
ZAR	Zuid-Afrikaansche Republiek (South African Republic)

Preface

A 'Small War'

The battle of Majuba Hill on 27 February 1881 in which Major General Sir George Pomeroy Pomeroy-Colley lost his life was deplored by the British as a strategically ill-conceived and tactically mismanaged disaster.[1] The victorious Boers, on the other hand, celebrated it as a glorious manifestation of God's favour and saw themselves in biblical terms as the puny David overcoming the giant Goliath through divine intervention. Be that as it may, Majuba was the spectacular climax of the singularly unsuccessful campaign of 1880–1881 which British forces in South Africa waged against the rebellious Boers of the recently annexed Transvaal Territory. Yet, for all its symbolic importance, Majuba was an entirely unnecessary battle, forced on by Major General Colley when the British government had already initiated the negotiations that would concede the Transvaal its independence.

Reflecting differing viewpoints concerning the war that culminated in the battle of Majuba, there has always been uncertainty about what it should be called.[2] To name it the Boer War made some sense until that title was usurped by the far greater conflict of 1899–1901, the Second Boer War, subsequently known as the Second Anglo-Boer War or the South African War. With that, the earlier war of 1880–1881 began to be termed the First Boer War. This made particular sense to many Afrikaner historians who had long insisted on a close continuity between the two wars of rising Afrikaner nationalism against British imperialism, and who revered it as *die Eerste Vryheidsoorlog* or the First War of Independence. This sectarian nomenclature has unsurprisingly failed to find favour among British historians, some of whom have begun calling the conflict the Anglo-Transvaal War which echoes the contemporary appellation of Transvaal War employed by some of the British military. Far more widespread, however, was the term adopted by contemporary British loyalists in South Africa who dubbed the war the Transvaal Rebellion. To refer to the war as a rebellion is to abandon any pretence of impartiality, yet the word most accurately describes the real nature and extent of the war of 1880–1881. When the Boers of the Transvaal took up arms against established British rule it was indeed technically a rebellion because their political

---

1 For an explanation of Colley's unusual surname, see chapter 2.
2 For a full discussion on what to call the war, see Laband, John, *The Transvaal Rebellion: The First Boer War 1880–1881* (Harlow: Longman Pearson, 2005), pp. 4–7.

objective was the restoration of the independence they had reluctantly forfeited in 1877. Negotiations around that goal before, during and after the uprising were thus closely bound up with—and determined by—the fortunes of military operations.

As for the military operations of 1880–1881, they are best comprehended under the definition of a 'small war'. In 1896 Major Charles E. Callwell, a Royal Artillery officer with extensive experience in colonial campaigns of the Victorian era, including the final stages of the Transvaal Rebellion, brought out *Small Wars: Their Principles and Practice*.[3] The book went through revised and updated editions in 1899 and 1906, and was taken up internationally as the standard manual on colonial warfare. In the work Callwell elaborated the concept of a 'small war' which he believed was "an art by itself" if it were to be conducted successfully. While admitting that the term was "somewhat difficult to define," he nevertheless concluded it encompassed " … all campaigns other than those where both the opposing sides consist of regular troops." Consequently, while for Callwell the expression 'small war' did not refer to the actual scale of a campaign, it was useful in denoting " … operations of regular armies against irregular, or comparatively speaking irregular, forces … which in their armament, their organization, and their discipline are palpably inferior."[4]

In Callwell's eyes, therefore, the Transvaal Rebellion was a regular 'small war' to which he referred repeatedly in his book.[5] His comments were hardly complimentary, however. The very reverse of a successful campaign from the British perspective, it offered many pointers to what should be avoided or improved on in the future. As in any 'small war' it was fought by contrasting military systems, but in this case it provided a devastating demonstration of the effects of modern fire and movement tactics as successfully practised by mounted Boer irregulars against far less agile British professional soldiers. And although the British and the white Boer settlers were similarly armed and shared many assumptions and practices which set them distinctly apart from the traditional Africans societies of South Africa, they had very different expectations of how a war between them should be fought. In other

Studio photograph taken in 1874 of Col. George Pomeroy Colley wearing the tropical dress Sir Garnet Wolseley had designed for the Asante campaign of 1873–1874. Subsequently, in 1880 as Maj. Gen. Sir George Pomeroy Pomeroy-Colley, KCSI, he would be appointed H.M. High Commissioner for South-East Africa, Governor of Natal, and Commander-in-Chief of Natal and the Transvaal. (Collection of Ian Castle)

---

3   Callwell landed with his battery in Durban in January 1881. Established as a leading military theorist, he rose to the rank of major general and was appointed Director of Military Operations and Intelligence at the War Office (1914–1916). He was created KCB in 1917. See Moreman, T.R., 'Callwell, Sir Charles Edward (1859–1928)', *Oxford Dictionary of National Biography* (Oxford University Press, 2004; online ed., January 2008) <http://www.oxforddnb.com..ibproxy.wlu.ca/view/article/32251> (accessed 20 August 2015).

4   Callwell, Colonel C.E., *Small Wars: Their Principles and Practice*, 3rd ed. (London: His Majesty's Stationary Office, 1906), pp. 4, 21–23.

5   See Callwell's detailed index references in *Small Wars*.

words, as was typical of a 'small war', this was a clash of military cultures—although Callwell would not have expressed it thus.

John Lynn has persuasively argued that a military culture is deeply rooted in the wider cultural assumptions and values of any particular society so that soldiers' choices concerning appropriate military bearing, rituals, uniforms, the exploitation of new military technologies, drill, and tactics may depend more upon aesthetic and social preferences rather than upon concrete advantages in the field. Conceptions of what properly constitute the codes of honourable conduct in war and the rules of fair combat are also determined by a society's prevailing culture. When a society's ideal military norms are flouted by an enemy fighting by culturally alien methods, the response is to condemn such aberrant warfare as duplicitous and dishonourable and, in many cases, to seize on it to justify the adoption of less restrained warfare in response.[6]

During the Transvaal Rebellion the British never sank to extreme military measures against the Boers but, condemning the alien rules they fought by, they could not but tend to regard them as typical of the 'savages' normally encountered in 'small wars'. As even a Boer apologist, William Garrett Fisher, would write of them, " ... the tactics of untrained volunteers like the Boers can scarcely be judged by the same standard that we apply to professional soldiers ... The Boers had learned their savage fighting from more than a hundred years of savage warfare ... and in such a warfare none of the rules which govern civilized campaigns were likely to be developed."[7]

Paradoxically, it was comforting for the British to believe that the Boers had despicably placed themselves outside the norms of 'civilized warfare' (as the British understood them). That way they could attribute their military debacle in the Transvaal to dishonourable Boer conduct. It was far worse to admit that the British defeat as exemplified at Majuba was the consequence of shortcomings in training and leadership in the late-Victorian army.

---

6   Lynn, John A., *Battle: A History of Combat and Culture* (Boulder, Col. and Oxford: Westview Press, 2003), pp. xx–xxi, xvi–xviii, 115, 121, 124, 232, 245, 249, 280, 303, 306, 314.
7   Garrett Fisher, William E. *The Transvaal and the Boer: A Short History of the South African Republic, with a Chapter on the Orange Free State* (London: Chapman & Hall, 1900), pp. 206–207.

Acknowledgements

I am especially grateful to Ian Knight, Ian Castle and Martin Boswell for so generously allowing me to raid their invaluable collections of illustrative material for this book. Ian Knight was especially helpful with his suggestions. I also wish to thank the following for their obliging and professional assistance: Erica le Roux of the Western Cape Archives and Records Service, Cape Town; Melanie Geustyn of the National Library of South Africa, Cape Town Campus; Pieter Nel, the Assistant Director of the Pietermaritzburg Archives Repository; Michelle Looke, the Photographic Archivist at the National Archives and Records Service of South Africa, Pretoria; and Dudu Madonsela, the Curator of the Bensusan Museum and Library of Photography, MuseumAfrica, Johannesburg. And here I must express my appreciation for the unfailing assistance I have received from the staff of the various archives and libraries where I have researched over the years.

I am particularly indebted to Christopher Brice, the editor of the Warfare in the Victorian Age series, for his painstaking care, assistance and comradely advice throughout the gestation of this book. I must also thank the production team at Helion & Company, especially George Anderson, the cartographer, who transformed my sketches into elegant maps, and Ann Farr who was responsible for the stylish design and typesetting.

As has been the case with all my previous books, this one would never have been pushed to completion without the love, understanding and forbearance of my wife, Fenella.

Greyton
Western Cape
South Africa

1

The British Annexation of the Transvaal

The presence of Dutch-speaking settlers on the vast plains of the highveld of the South African interior was the consequence of their organised migration—the Great Trek—from the British-ruled Cape Colony to the south. During the Napoleonic Wars Britain had occupied the Dutch-ruled Cape of Good Hope to secure the strategic sea route to India, and formally annexed it in 1814. The 27,000 or so white colonists living in the Cape were descended from Dutch, Flemish, German, and French Huguenot settlers and were developing a sense of their own Afrikaner identity and increasingly speaking their local dialect, Afrikaans. They did not readily accept British rule, especially when it interfered with their firmly held views of racially-based mastery over black people. Some resolved that if they moved north into the distant interior they could establish their own independent republics and live their lives free of British interference. By 1836 a series of parties of *voortrekkers* (pioneers) were on the move, taking with them all their livestock and goods and chattels, as well as their many thousands of black dependents. It is thought that by 1845 as many as 14,000 emigrant Boers (or farmers) had abandoned the Cape, violently displacing the African societies they encountered or relegating those who remained to labourers on the immense farms they laid out for themselves.[1]

The independently-minded Boers found cooperation difficult and splintered into several precarious republics, chronically at war with abutting African states and with each other. The British feared this instability in the interior would impact the Cape, but were uncertain how best to impose their will beyond the Orange (Garieb) River, the colony's northern frontier. Lord John Russell's Whig administration first attempted a forward policy and in February 1848 established the Orange River Sovereignty between the Orange River and the Vaal River to the north. However, the government

---

1   Etherington, Norman, *The Great Treks: The Transformation of Southern Africa, 1815–1854* (London: Longman Pearson, 2001), pp. xix–xxv, 1–9, 340–44 makes the vital point that the Boer exodus was not unique and but one of many 'treks' during the early nineteenth century by other indigenous peoples in southern Africa.

The first official raising of the Union Flag in Pretoria on 25 May 1877 following the British annexation of the Transvaal Territory on 12 April 1877. (NARP, TAB 32813)

rapidly backtracked and resolved that British paramountcy could be exerted indirectly without the costs and difficulties of formal rule.[2]

The first step in this direction was to reach agreement with the Boers settled north of the Vaal River whose wrangling republics had decided in 1849 to unite under a single *volksraad,* or parliament. By the Sand River Convention of 17 January 1852, the British recognised the full independence of the Boers north of the Vaal and undertook not to interfere in their affairs. In September 1853 these Boers officially named their fledgling state the Zuid-Afrikaansche Republiek (ZAR) or South African Republic, commonly known as the Transvaal. The British completed their retreat from the interior when, by the Bloemfontein Convention of 23 February 1854, they also recognised the independence of the former Orange River Sovereignty as the Oranje-Vrijstaat (OVS) or Orange Free State.[3]

The OVS retained its existing economic, cultural, and social ties with the Cape, but the ZAR went its own way in isolation. It was not easy. In particular, the Transvalers were hard pressed to subdue the still-independent African polities along all their borders except their southern one. Military action was hamstrung by the logistical difficulties of transporting ammunition and essential equipment over enormous distances from the coast, and by a critical

---

2   Saunders, Christopher, and Smith, Iain R., 'Southern Africa, 1795–1910' in Porter (ed.), Andrew, *The Oxford History of the British Empire*, vol. 3, *The Nineteenth Century* (Oxford: Oxford University Press, 2001), p. 602.

3   Heydenrych, D.H., 'The Boer Republics, 1852–1881', in Cameron (ed.), Trewhella, and Spies (ed.), S.B., *An Illustrated History of South Africa* (Johannesburg: Jonathan Ball, 1986), p. 150.

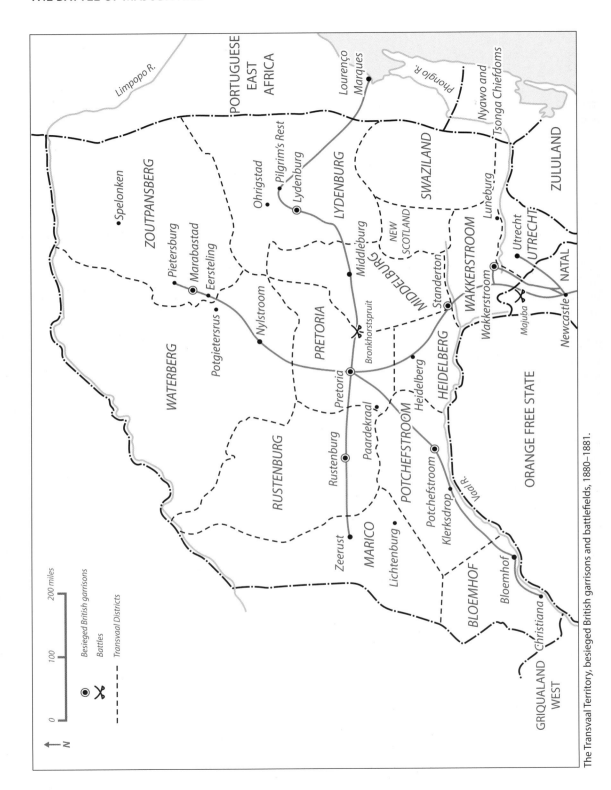

The Transvaal Territory, besieged British garrisons and battlefields, 1880–1881.

lack of manpower.[4] Regarding the latter, the British reckoned that at the time of the Transvaal Rebellion the Boer population was only 36,000 strong, with some estimates going up to 45,000.[5] Boer farmers in their rudimentary homesteads were sparsely sprinkled across the countryside on their 6,000-acre farms tenuously connected by execrable roads (wagons made their own tracks through the veld, only converging at drifts and passes). There they lived self-sufficient lives, cut off from most social and cultural amenities. Boers were strict Calvinists with a fundamentalist faith in the Word of the Bible, though fractious in their faith in a way common to many Protestant sects. Even so, religion was the great cement of Boer society, and ministers of religion the most influential individuals in society.[6]

There were also some 5,000 non-Dutch white aliens, or *uitlanders*, settled in the Transvaal in the late 1870s.[7] Two-thirds of them lived in the sparse scattering of little villages which usually consisted of no more than a small church, courthouse, market square, and a few dozen houses, and which lacked anything on the scale of a town hall or hospital. Potchefstroom and Pretoria were the two largest towns, but even the latter which, as capital, was the administrative, military, legal, and commercial hub with the buildings to match, had a civil population of around only 2,250.

The majority of the *uitlanders* were of British stock, though there were other "foreign adventurers"—Irish, Jews, Americans, Hollanders, Germans, Belgians and Portuguese—whom the British liked to deprecate as "rarely men of high character and disinterested aims."[8] Initially, *uitlanders* settling in the ZAR before British annexation had been predominantly missionaries, traders, and prospectors, but those who arrived later during the period of British rule were generally the artisans and clerks required in a society where modern skills and commercial practices were increasingly in demand. This small 'English' element disproportionally controlled almost all mercantile and commercial business, and made it an object of suspicion and dislike in a society dominated by rural Boers still resolutely pre-industrial in outlook.

For their part, in the countryside the Boers lorded it over an African population estimated at between 700,000 and 800,000 and which outnumbered them 20 to 1. The ZAR's boundaries remained only loosely defined, and in this opaque frontier zone lands under African rule shaded off into farms occupied by Boers where Africans were required to perform tribute labour (*opgaaf*) for the proprietor, whether as agricultural workers,

---

4   Stapleton, Timothy J., *A Military History of South Africa from the Dutch-Khoi Wars to the End of Apartheid* (Santa Barbara, Calif.: Praeger, 2010), p. 46.

5   *Blue Book for the Transvaal Province 1879* (Pretoria: Coppen, Deecker, 1879), pp. 8–9; Great Britain, War Office Intelligence Department, *Précis of Information Concerning South Africa. The Transvaal Territory* (London: Harrison and Sons, 1878), pp. 50–3; *British Parliamentary Papers* (BPP) (C. 2950), Appendix II: Sketch Map of the Transvaal Territory, published in March 1880 by the British Intelligence Branch of the Quartermaster-General's Department, gives the unrealistically precise population figures of 33,739 "Dutch", 5,316 "Non-Dutch" and 774,930 "Kaffirs" (the now pejorative term for Africans).

6   For a detailed description of Boer society in the Transvaal, see Laband, *Transvaal Rebellion*, pp. 26–40.

7   For the "Non-Dutch" in the Transvaal, see Laband, *Transvaal Rebellion*, pp. 48–49.

8   Sir Bartle Frere, quoted in Garrett Fisher, *Transvaal*, p. 179.

Sir Theophilus Shepstone, KCMG, Administrator of the Transvaal, 1877–1879. (PAR, C. 418)

domestics or as bearers in the great hunts so essential for the Boer rural economy. These labourers were subject to ZAR law, which forbade Africans to possess firearms, ammunition or horses (the means of war), and were required to carry a pass which tied them to their farm.[9]

In the second half of the 1870s the Conservative administration led by Benjamin Disraeli, Earl of Beaconsfield, resolved to adopt a forward policy in South Africa once more and assert British interests. In January 1877 Sir Theophilus Shepstone, British Special Commissioner in the Transvaal, entered the ZAR with a small escort of 25 Natal Mounted Police. He carried in his valise secret instruction entrusted to him by the Earl of Carnarvon, the Secretary of State for Colonies from 1874 to 1878, to annex the republic to the Crown with or without popular consent—a commission in flat contravention of the Sand River Convention of 1852 committing Britain never to interfere in the affairs of the ZAR.[10]

Shepstone's *démarche* had its roots in the anxieties of Tory imperial strategists. They regarded the intensifying jostling among the rival European powers to acquire new territories abroad as a perilous moment for Britain, urgently requiring them to consolidate and defend the Empire.[11] To their way of thinking, India, rather than Africa, was central to British commercial interests and her status as an imperial power. Nevertheless, India's security depended on the Royal Navy's control of the African sea routes through the Suez Canal and around the Cape. It was essential, therefore, to secure South Africa as a strategic link, and Carnarvon argued that this could best be achieved through knitting together a politically stable British confederation of the subcontinent's white settler states. Thanks to the discovery of diamonds in 1867 in the northern Cape and the enormous wealth being generated at the Kimberley diggings (what historians call the 'mineral revolution'), the whole region was being sufficiently transformed economically to support the edifice of the envisaged confederation.

Even so, Carnarvon understood that confederation could never go forward without the Cape Colony, the largest and richest territory in South Africa with more than twice the number of white colonists of the Colony

---

9   Laband, *Transvaal Rebellion*, pp. 38–42.

10 Gordon, Peter, 'Herbert, Henry Howard Molyneux, fourth earl of Carnarvon (1831–1890)', *Oxford Dictionary of National Biography* (Oxford University Press, 2004; online ed., January 2011) <http://www.oxforddnb.com.libproxy.wlu.ca/view/article/33859> (accessed 20 August 2015).

11 The following discussion on Carnarvon's confederation scheme is based on Cope, Richard, *Ploughshare of War: The Origins of the Anglo-Zulu War of 1879* (Pietermaritzburg: University of Natal Press, 1999), pp. 80–85 and 257–264 and on Goodfellow, C.F., *Great Britain and South Africa Confederation (1879–1881)* (Cape Town: Oxford University Press, 1966), pp. 49–59.

of Natal and the two Boer republics combined. In June 1872 the Cape had been granted responsible government which gave it much greater control over its own administration, finances and defence obligations, so its prickly legislative assembly would have to be wooed.[12] The OVS and the ZAR had also to be part of the confederation because they acted as powerful magnets for disaffected Afrikaners living under British rule elsewhere in South Africa, and to leave them out would have grave political repercussions. Moreover, they stood across the vital trade routes to the African interior. But how could Carnarvon draw them in? The isolationist ZAR posed a greater problem than the OVS with its existing ties to the Cape. Not only was the landlocked ZAR intending to build a railway line to Portuguese Delagoa Bay to reduce its dependence on British ports, but it was engaged— as was the OVS—in endemic wars with African neighbours which threatened to destabilize the whole region. So it was clear to Carnarvon that in the interests of the confederation of southern Africa's white-ruled states it was imperative that he also break the military power of the remaining independent African kingdoms, disarm them and impose some form of British supremacy over them.

Henry Herbert, 4th Earl of Carnarvon, Secretary of State for the Colonies, 1874–1878. (Collection of Ian Knight)

The Boer-Pedi War of 1876–1877 gave Carnarvon the lever he was seeking for. When he learned that the Bapedi of the Maroteng paramountcy ruled by Sekhukhune woaSekwati bordering the eastern ZAR had inflicted a decided reverse on the inept forces of the anarchic and bankrupt republic, he seized on the Boer military debacle as an excuse to annex the ZAR preparatory to dealing conclusively with the recalcitrant Bapedi. [13] Requiring parliamentary sanction before taking action, in December 1876 Carnarvon instructed the Colonial Office to draft enabling legislation—the South Africa Act of 1877— very similar to the British North America Act of 1867 which had created the self-governing federal Dominion of Canada out of three separate British colonies. To bring off his political coup, Carnarvon turned to the recently knighted Sir Theophilus Shepstone, who had framed and driven Natal's 'native policy' from 1846 to 1875, to use his famed diplomatic skills to annex the ZAR without bloodshed.

Nor did Shepstone disappoint. The 'English' community was only too eager to be taken over; ordinary Boers were resentful of their government's faltering administration and military defeat; while the *volksraad*,

---

12 Davenport, Rodney, and Saunders, Christopher, *South Africa: A Modern History*, 5th ed. (London: Macmillan, 2000), pp. 199–203.
13 For the Boer-Pedi War, see Great Britain, *Transvaal Territory*, pp. 67–74; Laband, John, *Zulu Warriors. The Battle for the South African Frontier* (New Haven and London: Yale University Press, 2014), pp. 64–68.

Sir Bartle Frere, Bt, H.M. High Commissioner for South Africa and Governor of the Cape, 1877–1880. (Collection of Ian Knight)

overwhelmed by the burden of the national debt, was paralysed by divisions between political factions. So when at 11: 00 a.m. on 12 April 1877 Shepstone proclaimed the ZAR the British Transvaal Territory and ran up the Union Flag in Church Square in Pretoria, Boer opposition was muted. The *volksraad* did resolve to send a delegation abroad to make its objections to annexation widely known, but meanwhile appealed to citizens to refrain from violence so as not to prejudice their mission.[14]

Shepstone, now the Administrator of the Transvaal Territory, did not find it an easy task to mollify his new subjects. Nevertheless, in his efforts he had the full support of Her Majesty's new High Commissioner for South Africa and Governor of the Cape, Sir Bartle Frere—famous as a statesman in India—whom Carnarvon had selected in March 1877 to consummate South African confederation.[15]

Frere's task was not easy. He found himself embroiled in the Ninth Cape Frontier War of 1877–1878 and the Northern Border War of 1878 in the Crown Colony of Griqualand West. These campaigns, although ultimately successful, alarmed the Cape government, especially since the Bapedi were proving reluctant to accept Shepstone's authority. When Shepstone finally sent troops against them in the First Anglo-Pedi War of October 1878 the Bapedi successfully resisted their advance, dealing British credibility in the Transvaal a severe blow.[16]

In February 1878 Sir Michael Hicks Beach succeeded Carnarvon as colonial secretary.[17] Distracted by the Russo-Turkish War of 1877–1878 and the Second Afghan War of 1878–1880 which threatened to pit Britain against Russia in the Mediterranean and in Central Asia, Hicks Beach was inclined to leave the experienced Frere to his own devices in South Africa. For Frere's part, the recent concatenation of wars involving three British colonies had convinced him that confederation hinged on finally solving the 'native question'. To his mind and to Shepstone's too, this meant breaking the military might of the Zulu kingdom ruled by Cetshwayo kaMpande which they believed to be at the epicentre of a 'black conspiracy' dedicated to overthrowing white power in South Africa. Going to war against the amaZulu possessed an additional advantage. Since 1848 a border dispute

14 Schreuder, Deryck M., *The Scramble for Southern Africa, 1877–1895* (Cambridge: Cambridge University Press, 1980), pp. 61–4; Laband, *Transvaal Rebellion*, pp. 17–18; Laband, *Zulu Warriors*, pp. 70–73.

15 Benyon, John, *Proconsul and Paramountcy in South Africa: The High Commission, British Supremacy and the Sub-Continent 1806–1910* (Pietermaritzburg: University of Natal Press, 1980), pp. 144–148; Benyon, John, 'Frere, Sir (Henry) Bartle, first baronet (1815–1884)', *Oxford Dictionary of National Biography* (Oxford University Press, 2004; online ed., January 2011) <http://www.oxforddnb.com.libproxy.wlu.ca/view/article/10171> (accessed 20 August 2015).

16 For these three campaigns, see Laband, *Zulu Warriors*, pp. 111–149, 166–182, 187–194.

17 Pugh, Martin, 'Beach, Michael Edward Hicks, first Earl St Aldwyn (1837–1916)', *Oxford Dictionary of National Biography* (Oxford University Press, 2004; online ed., January 2011) <http://www.oxforddnb.com.libproxy.wlu.ca/view/article/33859> (accessed 20 August 2015).

had been smouldering between the Transvalers and the amaZulu, periodically threatening to break into flame. By crushing the amaZulu Frere would resolve the border dispute and thereby demonstrate the advantages of British rule and win over unreconciled Boers.[18]

Sir Garnet Wolseley, KCMG, KCB, GCMG, H.M. High Commissioner for South-East Africa and Governor of Natal, 1879–1880, photographed prior to being appointed GCB in 1880. (Collection of Ian Knight)

Indeed, the Boers required winning over since Shepstone, whose administration of the Transvaal was proving a disappointed on many fronts, seemed quite unable to appease them.[19] In early 1878 he was faced by widespread disturbances following the failure of the delegation the Boers had sent to London to protest annexation. A series of increasingly stormy mass gatherings culminated in a second, and equally unsuccessful, delegation going to London in late 1878 to present a strongly-supported petition against British sovereignty. Turned down flat by Hicks Beach, the disappointed delegation reported back to a public meeting on 10 January 1879 at Wonderfontein. The meeting agreed to step up anti-British agitation and to establish what amounted to a shadow administration.[20]

At that critical juncture, on 11 January 1879, British troops invaded Zululand. Hicks Beach, already involved in enough difficulties abroad, had belatedly attempted to halt Frere's determined march to war, but the High Commissioner, anticipating a short, decisive campaign that would solve so many problems simultaneously and clinch confederation, had pushed on regardless. Frere's insubordination would have been condoned if successful, but the humiliating disaster at Isandlwana on 22 January 1879, followed by a costly campaign that limped on until September 1879, destroyed his career. On 28 May 1879 the government sidelined him by dividing the high commissionership and leaving him only as Governor of the Cape. General Sir Garnet Wolseley was sent to South Africa to replace him with Frere as H.M. High Commissioner for South- East Africa, Governor of Natal and the Transvaal, and Commander-in-Chief of the Forces in those theatres.[21]

Shepstone went to the wall even earlier, and on 4 March 1879 Colonel Owen Lanyon (who had previously been the Administrator of Griqualand

18 Laband, *Zulu Warriors*, pp. 76–77, 198–199.

19 For Shepstone's lack-lustre administration of the Transvaal, see Theron, Bridget, 'Theophilus Shepstone and the Transvaal Colony, 1877–1879', *Kleio*, 34 (2002), pp. 104–127.

20 Scott, Louis, 'Boereweerstand teen Gedwonge Britse Bestuur in Transvaal, 1877–1880', in Van Jaarsveld (ed.), F.A., Van Rensburg (ed.), A.P.J., and Stals (ed.), W.A., *Die Eerste Vryheidsoorlog van Verset en Geweld tot Skikking deur Onderhandeling 1877–1884* (Pretoria and Cape Town: Haum, 1980) (henceforth *Eerste Vryheidsoorlog*), pp. 15–27.

21 Laband, John, '"The Danger of Divided Command": British Civil and Military Disputes over the Conduct of the Zululand Campaigns of 1878 and 1878', *Journal of the Society for Army Historical Research*, 81:328 (Winter 2003), p. 347.

Former Vice-President Paul Kruger of the ZAR and member of the Boer Triumvirate, photographed in 1881 during the course of the Transvaal Rebellion. (NARP, TAB 36951)

West) replaced him as Administrator.[22] A tough soldier, Lanyon's style of administration proved unbending and authoritarian and did nothing to win over the Boers who were growing increasingly restive under British rule. Shortly before his supersession, Frere had thrice met the Boer leaders in April 1879 when they turned down his offer of self-government within a British confederation and insisted on independence. They were encouraged by Britain's halting military performance in the Anglo-Zulu War to believe that it if came to open resistance they might well be able to defeat the British war machine. For the moment, though, they were willing to try other means, including a widespread refusal to pay taxes.[23]

The ambitious and energetic General Wolseley, despite strenuous efforts, was no more successful than Frere in reconciling the dissident Boers to British rule, not least because he made his sophisticated contempt for them all too obvious.[24] Even his crushing of the Bapedi in the brutal Second Anglo-Pedi War of November-December 1879 did not help because the elimination of the longstanding Zulu and Pedi threats removed the Boers' most pressing security problems and allowed the republican leaders to focus on anti-British agitation.[25] Disaffection throughout the Transvaal became more pronounced, and in October 1879 Lanyon had to despatch troops to the village of Middelburg to compel compliance with the laws.[26]

The next mass meeting of *burghers* (citizens) was held at Wonderfontein from 10 to 15 December 1879. This time, the Queen's sovereignty was publicly denounced and it was agreed to boycott all things 'English' in the Transvaal. Paul Kruger emerged as the dominant figure during the meeting. Born in the Eastern Cape in 1825, he had taken part in the Great Trek as a boy and grew up a true frontiersman, gaining a considerable reputation as a dauntless hunter and a brave and resourceful military commander in the ZAR's wars against its African neighbours. At only seventeen he had been elected a field cornet, and in from 1863 to 1873 he had held the post of commandant-general of the ZAR. In 1877, on the eve of the British annexation, Kruger had been elected vice-president of the ZAR and had become an unfaltering

22 Lanyon was confirmed in the post only on 4 June 1880. See Theron-Bushell, B.M., 'Puppet on an Imperial String: Owen Lanyon in South Africa, 1875–1881', (unpublished D.Litt. et Phil. thesis, University of South Africa, 2002), p. 135, n. 1; Stearn, Roger T., 'Lanyon, Sir (William) Owen (1842 –1887)', *Oxford Dictionary of National Biography* (Oxford University Press, 2004; online ed., January 2011) <http://www.oxforddnb.com.libproxy.wlu.ca/view/article/16060> (accessed 20 August 2015). .

23 Le May, G.H.L., *Afrikaners: An Historical Interpretation* (Oxford: Blackwell, 1995), pp. 73–78. For Frere in the Transvaal and his three meetings with the Boer leaders, see Worsfold, Basil, *Sir Bartle Frere. A Footnote to the History of the British Empire* (London: Butterworth, 1923), pp. 213–225.

24 For Wolseley in the Transvaal, see Theron-Bushell, 'Lanyon', chapters V and VI.

25 For the Second Anglo-Pedi War, see Laband, *Zulu Warriors*, pp. 265–277.

26 Theron-Bushell, 'Lanyon', pp. 222–223.

activist against British rule.[27] He was a *Dopper*, as the extremely conservative members of his fundamentalist Calvinist sect were known, and took the Bible literally. He believed that he possessed a special understanding of God's purpose and undertook always to do His will lest he invite divine punishment. Although less extreme in their beliefs, the majority of Boers who were members of more orthodox denominations of the Calvinist Church shared the ingrained theological assumption that they were the elect, the chosen people of God, whose hand was visible in the history of the nation. [28]

To the dismay of colonial officials, the Afrikaner press in both the Cape and the OVS came out in virulent solidarity with their blood-brothers of the Transvaal. In the OVS strong public pressure began to mount for the government to abandon its official policy of strict neutrality and to go to the aid of its sister republic in restoring its independence. Encouraged by this wave of sympathy, in April 1880 Paul Kruger began an extensive speaking and fundraising tour of

William Ewert Gladstone, British Prime Minister, 1880–1885. (Author's collection)

the Cape and OVS to mobilise Afrikaner opinion against confederation. He was accompanied by Piet Joubert who (like him) had taken part as a child in the Great Trek and who had entered politics at an early age to become one of the ZAR's most prominent leaders, acting as its president in 1875–1876.[29] So successful were Kruger and Joubert that in June 1880 the Cape parliament flatly rejected a motion for confederation. British officials were left in no doubt that the agitation among Afrikaners the length and breadth of South Africa spelled the rejection of confederation.[30]

In April 1880 the Liberals under William Gladstone won the British general election. Their victory gave the Transvaal Boer leaders renewed hope because the Liberals had campaigned against the Conservatives' confederation policy in South Africa. But Gladstone's government did not live up to its rhetoric. It was a fractious administration with radical and conservative wings which Gladstone held together through compromise and astute political juggling. Gladstone himself sympathised with Boer demands

---

27 Davenport, T.R.H., 'Kruger, Stephanus Johannes Paulus [Paul] (1825–1904)', *Oxford Dictionary of National Biography* (Oxford University Press, 2004; online ed., May 2006) <http://www.oxforddnb.com.libproxy.wlu.ca/view/article/41290> (accessed 20 August 2015). .

28 In 1859 the Nederduits Hervormde Kerk broke from the mainstream Calvinist Nederduits Gereformeerde Kerk van Suid Africa. See Templin, J. Alton, *Ideology on a Frontier: The Theological Foundations of Afrikaner Nationalism, 1652–1910* (Westport, Conn. and London: Greenwood Press, 1984), pp. 149–152, 183 n. 23; and Le May, *Afrikaners*, pp. 78–82.

29 Nöthling, Cmdt. C.J., 'Military Commanders of the War (1880–1881)', *Scientia Militaria: South African Journal of Military Studies*, 11: 1 (1981), p. 78.

30 Heydenrych, 'Boer Republics', pp. 158–159; Saunders (ed.) Christopher, *Reader's Digest Illustrated History of South Africa: The Real Story*, 3rd ed. (Cape Town: the Readers' Digest Association, 1994), pp. 194–195.

for self-determination. But the self-contained and efficient Earl of Kimberley, who, as Colonial Secretary from April 1880 to December 1882, was directly responsible for the Transvaal, went against him—despite his reputation as a Gladstonian loyalist—by urging a strong hand to uphold the imperial image in southern Africa.[31] On 12 May 1880 the new cabinet decided not to scrap the policy of confederation. Gladstone wrote to Kruger and Joubert on 8 June to confirm he would not let the Transvaal go, citing his government's obligation to the British settlers in the Transvaal and its duties to the Africans.[32]

Nevertheless, despite their official position, the Liberals had actually abandoned confederation. Frere, confederation's discredited champion who was lingering on in living reproach as Governor of the Cape, was finally recalled on 1 August 1880. Gladstone replaced him as H.M. High Commissioner for South Africa and Governor of the Cape with the experienced technocrat, Sir Hercules Robinson. Sir George Strahan was to act for Robinson until he arrived from New Zealand in January 1881.[33]

Meanwhile, British officials in South Africa, who were becoming increasingly paranoiac about the alarming spectre of a general Afrikaner uprising against British hegemony, were taken off-guard by two African revolts in late 1880 against Cape rule. In Basutoland, which the Cape had administered since 1871, a full-scale rebellion known as the Gun War broke out in October 1880 under Chief Lerotholi. The Basotho took every advantage of their mountainous terrain and used their illegal firearms to deadly effect in ambushes.[34] Brigadier General C.M. Clarke found the Cape military forces he commanded inadequate to quell the Basotho. He had in any case to suspend operations when faced with a new rebellion in the Cape's neighbouring Transkei Territory where in late October 1880 the Mpondomise under Chiefs Mhlonhlo and Mditshwa took up arms. Cape forces managed to put this rebellion down by late December 1880.[35] However, in Basutoland the conflict became a stalemate. It would not be until February 1881 that the two sides concluded a ceasefire.[36]

---

31 Powell, John, 'Wodehouse, John, first earl of Kimberley (1826 –1902)', *Oxford Dictionary of National Biography* (Oxford University Press, 2004; online ed., May 2009) <http://www.oxforddnb.com.libproxy.wlu.ca/view/article/36987> (accessed 20 August 2015).

32 *BPP* (C. 2676), enc. 2 in no. 24a: W.E. Gladstone to S.T. Kruger and T.C. Joubert, 8 June 1880. See Schreuder, Deryck M. *Gladstone and Kruger. Liberal Government and Colonial 'Home Rule', 1880–1885* (London: Routledge and K. Paul; Toronto: University of Toronto Press, 1969), pp. 81–85.

33 Goodfellow, *Confederation*, pp. 193–195.

34 For the Gun War, see Eldredge, Elizabeth A., *Power in Colonial Africa: Conflict and Discourse in Lesotho, 1870–1960* (Wisconsin: University of Wisconsin Press, 2007), pp. 71–117; Burman, Sandra, *Chiefdom, Politics and Alien Law: Basutoland under Cape Rule, 1881–1884* (New York: Africana Publishing Company, 1981), pp. 132–91; Storey, William Kelleher, *Guns, Race, and Power in Colonial South Africa* (Cambridge: Cambridge University Press, 2008), pp. 287–318.

35 For the Transkei Rebellion, see Saunders, Christopher, 'The Transkeian Rebellion of 1880: A Case Study of Transkeian Resistance to White Control', *South African Historical Journal*, 8 (1976), pp. 32–39; Stapleton, *Military History*, pp. 73–74.

36 In April 1881 an agreement was reached by which the Basotho accepted colonial rule, but were allowed to retain their firearms under license. In 1884 Basutoland was removed from Cape administration and the Crown Colony of Basutoland became the first of the High Commission Territories with considerable internal autonomy under its own chiefs.

The Gun War and the Transkei Rebellion shook colonial confidence, but because the Cape government suppressed them with its own forces and did not call on imperial troops for assistance, Gladstone's government believed it could afford to disregard the two conflicts. In any case, its attention was grimly focused on the hugely intractable Irish question closer to home where the protracted Land War remained unresolved. So the Liberals allowed the Transvaal issue to drift, and permitted themselves to be reassured by Lanyon (who was made a KCMG in May 1880) that the Boers were becoming reconciled to British rule.[37] Lanyon was far off the mark, however. Bitterly disappointed with the uncompromising position maintained by Gladstone's government, Kruger and his close associates came to the conclusion that further meetings and protests were useless. Instead, as Kruger put it, the "best course appeared to be to set quietly to work and to prepare for the worst by the purchase of arms and ammunition."[38]

37 Theron-Bushell, 'Lanyon', pp. 239–244
38 Kruger, Paul, *The Memoirs of Paul Kruger, Four Times President of the South African Republic, Told by Himself* (London: T. Fisher Unwin, 1902), p. 165.

2

The Transvaal Garrison

The Transvaal *uitlanders*, although aware of intensifying Boer discontent, believed they were secure under the protection of the British garrison with its headquarters in Pretoria. The experienced Officer Commanding the Transvaal District was Colonel William Bellairs. He had served in the West Indies, Ireland, Canada, and Gibraltar, and fought in the Crimean War (1854–1855), the Ninth Cape Frontier War, and the Anglo-Zulu War.[1] In November 1880 he had about 1,800 regular troops under his command distributed in garrisons across the Transvaal. The Pretoria garrison consisted of five companies and a mounted troop of the 2nd Battalion, 21st Regiment (Royal Scots Fusiliers), N Battery, 5th Brigade, Royal Artillery (RA), and a detachment of Royal Engineers. Two further companies of the Fusiliers were stationed in Rustenburg. Two companies of the 94th Regiment were posted in Lydenburg, with two more companies of the same regiment in Marabastad, a company at Standerton, and another company and a mounted troop in Wakkerstroom.[2]

Britain relied primarily on the Royal Navy to maintain its overseas supremacy, but naval bases still needed to be defended by land-based troops. So too did British colonies around the world, but garrisons were expensive to maintain. Since the 1840s succeeding British governments had spasmodically attempted to reduce the colonies' dependence on British troops by prompting them to take on more of the burden of their own defence by raising and training volunteer units from the local settlers, supported by auxiliaries drawn from the indigenous population. However, the problem of imperial garrisons was first addressed with determination only when Edward Cardwell, Secretary of State for War in William Gladstone's first cabinet (1868-1874),[3] undertook his sweeping army reforms.[4]

---

1   Nöthling, 'Commanders', p. 76.
2   Bellairs (ed.), Lady, *The Transvaal War 1880 –81*(Edinburgh and London: William Blackwood and Sons, 1885), p. 43.
3   See Bond, Brian, 'Cardwell, Edward, first Viscount Cardwell (1813–1886)', *Oxford Dictionary of National Biography* (Oxford University Press, 2004; online ed., January 2008) <http://www.oxforddnb.com.libproxy.wlu.ca/view/article/4620> (accessed 20 August 2015).
4   The description below and in subsequent chapters of the British Army in 1880—reform, organisation, recruitment, dress, weaponry, tactics, communications and logistics—is

British headquarters staff during the Boer siege of Pretoria, 1880–1881. Standing, left to right: Capt. M. Churchill, DAAG, and G.Y. Lagden, Private Secretary. Seated left to right: Lt. Col. Fred. Gildea, commander of the garrison, Sir Owen Lanyon, KCMG, Administrator of the Transvaal (1879 –1881), and Col. William Bellairs, Officer Commanding the Transvaal District. On the ground: Lt. the Hon. A.S. Hardinge, ADC. (WCPA, E3091)

Cardwell aimed to withdraw troops from colonies of white settlement and to scale down garrisons elsewhere, except for India. The introduction of short service in 1870— whereby recruits spent six years in the regular army and six more in the reserve—was designed to create a large pool of trained reservists, to reduce unhealthy service abroad and to save money. The Localisation Bill of 1872 established 66 territorial districts in Britain with two linked battalions attached to each brigade depot.[5]

based, unless otherwise specified, on the following sources: Bailes, H. ,'Technology and Tactics in the British Army, 1866–1900' , in Haycock (ed.), R., and Neilson (ed.), K., *Men, Machines. and War* (Waterloo, Ontario: Wilfrid Laurier University Press, 1988), pp. 35–47; Haythornthwaite, Philip J., *The Colonial Wars Source Book* (London: Caxton Editions, 2000), pp. 17–45, 48–60; Knight, Ian, *Go to Your God like a Soldier: The British Soldier Fighting for Empire, 1837–1902* (London: Greenhill Books, 1996), pp. 12–32, 132, 138–52, 155–72, 182–202, 204–6, 247–9; Laband, John, *The Atlas of the Later Zulu Wars 1883-1888* (Pietermaritzburg, University of Natal Press, 2001), pp. 9–19; Laband, *Transvaal Rebellion*, pp. 59–85; Laband, John and Paul Thompson, *The Illustrated Guide to the Anglo-Zulu War* (Pietermaritzburg: University of Natal Press, 2000), pp. 21–30; Spiers, E., 'The Late Victorian Army 1868–1914' , in Chandler (ed.), D.G., and Beckett (ed.), I., *The Oxford History of the British Army* (Oxford: Oxford University Press, 2003), pp. 187–200; and Strachan, Hew, *European Armies and the Conduct of War* (London and New York: Routledge, 1983), pp. 76–89.

5　It should be noted that soon after the conclusion of the Transvaal campaign in 1881 the recommendations of the Ellice Committee on the Formation of Territorial Regiments came into effect, so that the old regimental numbers and county affiliations, which had previously characterised individual battalions, were changed to territorial titles in the new regiments. Confusingly, contemporary commentators and later historians have often used the new territorial titles to describe battalions engaged in the Transvaal campaign, so that, for example, the 2nd Battalion, 21st Regiment (Royal Scots Fusiliers)

A company of the 2nd Battalion, the Northamptonshire Regiment, which formed part of the imperial garrison stationed at Fort Napier in the Colony of Natal, in parade dress at the unveiling of the Anglo-Zulu War memorial in Pietermaritzburg on 11 October 1883. Until 1881 the battalion was designated the 58th (Rutlandshire) Regiment and as such had fought in the Anglo-Zulu War of 1879 and had formed part of the Natal Field Force in 1880–1881 when it had been present at the battles of Laing's Nek, Ingogo and Majuba. (PAR, C. 111)

Cardwell's intention was that the linked battalions would alternate in recruiting at home and serving abroad, thus ensuring that the Empire would by guarded only by seasoned troops. However, it would rapidly become apparent that chronic demands for imperial defence required a stronger presence overseas than Cardwell had envisaged. Minor colonial campaigns could only be provided for by calling upon regular and reserve units for volunteers, and by draining standing garrisons, as became necessary in South Africa in 1880–1881. All too often imperfectly trained and untested battalions had to be posted to the colonies.[6]

The Cardwell reforms failed to raise either the quantity or quality of recruits who still came from the poorest sectors of society and whose status—even if they were the guardians of Empire—remained questionable in a society traditionally wary of soldiers.[7] Pay at a shilling a day was uncompetitive and more than half of this meagre sum was deducted for extra food, laundry services and so on. The conditions of service life (though improved) remained harsh with unvarying and unpalatable staple rations of bread and meat. Discipline was rigid and punishment by flogging, though abolished in 1872 in time of peace, was permitted for wartime service until 1881. Except when on campaign, service life in garrison was a monotonous round of drill, parades, fatigues and gymnastic exercises, with recreational activity centred on regimental canteens and local brothels. Consequently, it remained difficult to attract recruits and the army had to lower physical standards. Moreover, as experienced soldiers now left the ranks earlier on account of short-term enlistment, the number of young, 'unblooded' men in the ranks rose proportionally, thus compromising military effectiveness.

Despite these negatives, some elements of the life of soldiers in the ranks were improving in this period. Many late-Victorian officers, infused with gentlemanly and Christian evangelical virtues, showed increasing concern

---

is anachronistically referred to as the Royal Scots Fusiliers, and the 94th Regiment as the 2nd Battalion, The Connaught Rangers. For detailed descriptions of the new territorial regiments, see Richards, Walter, *Her Majesty's Army: A Descriptive Account of the Various Regiments Now Comprising the Queen's Forces, from their First Establishment to the Present* (London: H. Virtue, n.d. [c.1888]), volumes 1–2.

6   For an analysis of Cardwell's reforms, see Spiers, Edward M., *The Army and Society 1815–1914* (London and New York: Longman, 1980), pp. 177–203; and Spiers, Edward M., *The Late Victorian Army, 1868–1902* (Manchester: Manchester University Press, 1992), pp. 2–28.

7   See Spiers, *Army and Society*, pp. 35–71; Spiers, *Late Victorian Army*, pp. 118–151.

about their men's conditions, some attempting to stamp out drunkenness and encouraging alternatives like team sports and further study. Indeed, soldiers had to attend school for five hours each week, and promotion to non-commissioned officer required a basic certificate of education. It is reasonable to estimate that by the 1870 about half the NCOs and private soldiers were literate, and were writing expressive (and uncensored) letters home while on active service.[8]

Despite Cardwell's attempt to professionalise the officer corps through the abolition of the purchase of commissions in 1871 and the opening of promotion to merit, its social composition remained resistant to change, as did the requirement of a private income to supplement pay in order to meet the cost of expensive uniforms and mess traditions.[9] In the regiments stationed in South Africa in 1880 most officers still came mainly from the younger sons of the gentry, clergy, and the professional middle classes, often from families with long traditions of military service. The majority had received a public school education with its cult of team games that were intended to develop health, strength, coordination, and quickness of eye essential for an officer, as well as moral virtues like self-discipline and team spirit. And officers from public schools did indeed tend to cleave to an honorific and gentlemanly code which encompassed calm resolve under fire and chivalrous conduct towards the enemy.

If a career in the army still allowed most officers to indulge their passion for manly sports, especially field sports, a consequence of the Cardwell reforms was to require that they attain a higher level of military education too. A good number passed through either the Royal Military Academy, Woolwich, founded in 1741 to train gentleman cadets for the RA and Royal Engineers (RE), or through the Royal Military College, Sandhurst, founded in 1801 to train gentleman cadets for the cavalry and infantry.[10] Military periodicals and works on strategy and tactics were increasingly available, and ambitious or more intellectual officers regularly contributed to them. How many of their fellow officers read them is naturally another matter. What contributed to an amateurish gentleman-ideal prevalent among many officers and the persistence of a certain prejudice against intellectuals and bookworms was the expectation that they would likely see military service only in 'small wars'. These simply did not demand the same degree of technical knowledge and complex managerial expertise deemed essential for officers in the mass armies of continental Europe. Nor was it necessary. Colonial campaigns required initiative, dash, tactical adaptability, and flair honed by frequent experience under fire. And since promotion was grudging and usually by

8   Emery, Frank, *Marching over Africa: Letters from Victorian Soldiers* (London: Hodder and Stoughton, 1986), pp. 14, 18.

9   For late Victorian officer, see Spiers, *Army and Society*, pp. 1–34; Spiers, *Late Victorian Army*, pp. 89–117; Clayton, Anthony, *The British Officer: Leading the Army from 1660 to the Present* (Harlow, United Kingdom: Pearson Longman, 2006), pp. 100–102, 106–107, 109–114; Brice, Christopher, *The Thinking Man`s Soldier. The Life and Career of General Sir Henry Brackenbury 1837–1914* (Solihul, England: Helion, 2012), pp. 23–24.

10   The military academies at Woolwich and Sandhurst were amalgamated in 1947 as the Royal Military Academy Sandhurst. See Heathcote, Tony, 'Academies, Military', in Holmes (ed.), Richard, *The Oxford Companion to Military History* (Oxford: Oxford University Press, 2001), p. 4

Men of the 2/21st Regiment (Royal Scots Fusiliers) drawn up in 1881 in front of Fort Commeline, built to cover the western approaches to Pretoria during the Boer siege of the town, 1880–1881. Note their helmets dyed brown on campaign.

seniority, ambitious officers knew that the quickest and surest way to scamper up the ladder was through plucky and distinguished service in one of those fortunately quite frequent 'small wars'.[11]

The soldiers of the British garrison stationed in the Transvaal in 1880 would have stood out from the drably apparelled Boer population on account of their distinctive uniforms. The standard overseas field dress for British soldiers was the undress uniform of a single-breasted five-buttoned unlined serge frock which was scarlet for infantry and RE, and blue for all others except the Rifles, who wore dark green. Officers wore either a scarlet tunic or a dark blue patrol jacket which was the preferred choice in the field. In November 1880 the two regiments in the Transvaal still wore their traditional facing colours on cuffs and collar, blue for the 21st Fusiliers and Lincoln green for the 94th Regiment. Trousers were dark blue with a red welt down the seam for infantry or a wide red stripe for RA and were tucked into black leather boots—all too often of poor quality. Mounted infantry wore their regimental frocks with dark buff corduroy trousers tucked into their boots. Scarlet as a battledress would only be officially discredited by the Colour Committee of 1883, and it was not until 1897 that khaki was finally adopted as service wear on all overseas postings.[12]

The infantry were fitted with accoutrements of the Valise pattern introduced in 1871 consisting of a black waterproofed canvas sack, or valise, supported in the small of the back by white shoulder straps. The straps were attached to a waist belt to which were fitted three ammunition pouches holding in total 70 rounds. The rolled greatcoat and mess-tin were secured above the valise and the wooden water bottle attached to the belt. Mounted infantry carried their ammunition in leather bandoliers. Headgear was the light cork sun helmet, adopted for overseas service in 1877. The brass shako-

---

11 Brice, *Brackenbury*, pp. 29–30.
12 See The National Archives, Kew (TNA) WO 33/39: Report of the Colour Committee, 1883. The last time scarlet was worn on campaign was in Zululand in 1888. See Laband, *Later Zulu Wars*, p. 16.

Royal Engineers during the siege of Pretoria, 1880–1881. (WCPA, E4459)

plate badge was usually removed on active service, and the white helmet stained light brown with tea, coffee, or mud, as were the white equipment straps and pouches. Indeed, on active service uniforms hardly met the requirements of the parade ground. They were seldom replaced, and a regiment like the 94th, which had gone through both the Anglo-Zulu War and the Second Anglo-Pedi War of 1879, was wearing a tattered assortment of garments by 1880, some of them civilian clothes, and everything patched and worn, including accoutrements which were missing straps and other elements. Soldiers' scarlet frocks were faded to the colour of brick-dust and their helmets were misshapen from having been slept in throughout months of campaigning.[13] Officers in the field tended in any case to adopt an idiosyncratic assortment of non-regulation dress, drab civilian shooting tweeds being especially favoured. Many of the officers and men also sported beards on campaign, completing their wild appearance.

British infantry in South Africa were armed with the Martini-Henry Mark II rifle, introduced in 1874 when it replaced the Snider-Enfield.[14] It was a single-shot, centre fire weapon, with a falling block mechanism operated by a lever. (The British Army did not adopt a magazine rifle until 1888, when

---

13 Butterfield (ed.), Paul .H., *War and Peace in South Africa 1879–1881: The Writings of Philip Anstruther and Edward Essex* (Melville, South Africa: Scripta Africana, 1987), p. 134: Anstruther to his wife, Zaida, 14 November, 1880.

14 Von Moltke, Kaptein R., 'Wapentuig van die Eerste Vryheidsoolog', *Scientia Militaria, South African Journal of Military Studies* , 11: 1 (1981), pp. 11–14; Machanik, Felix, 'Firearms and Firepower, First War of Independence, 1880–1881', *South African Military History Journal*, 5: 1 (December 1980) < samilitaryhistory.org/journal.html > (accessed 25 August 2015). Although the Martini-Henry Mark III was accepted into service in August 1879, it was designed for the British Volunteers, Militia, and the troops of dominion governments rather than for British regulars.

Officers and men of N/5 Brigade, RA under the command of Lt. E.H. Hare, photographed in 1881 during the siege of Pretoria. (PAR, C. 103/2)

the Martini-Henry was replaced by the bolt-action Lee-Metford Mark I.) The Martini-Henry weighed 9 lbs, and fired a .450 calibre hardened lead bullet of 1.1 ounces. The propellant was black powder which gave off dense white smoke on detonation. It was fitted with a triangular socket bayonet, 22 inches long, which had been universal issue since 1876 and was known as the 'lunger'. When combined with the four-foot-long rifle it gave a formidable reach of over six feet in hand-to-hand combat, but was of poor quality and too often bent or broke. Mounted infantry were equipped with the Martini-Henry carbine. Officers carried privately-owned swords and double-action .45 revolvers (usually the Mark II Adams or the Webley Royal Irish Constabulary model of 1867) which were not accurate at more than 25 yards at best. The artillery deployed in the Transvaal consisted of 9-pounder Rifled Muzzle Loaders (RMLs) sighted between 1,690 and 2,780 yards, and light, 7-pounder RML Mark IV steel mountain guns, mounted on light carriages. The mountain gun's low muzzle-velocity rendered shrapnel-shot ineffective.[15]

The forces in the Transvaal under Bellairs' command were organised—on paper at least—in a clear-cut fashion.[16] The standard infantry tactical unit was the battalion which on service was made up of a headquarters and eight companies, with a nominal complement of 30 officers and 866 men. A battery of six guns, each with its own limber, ammunition-wagon and crew, was the RA's usual tactical unit, but was often broken up if necessary into three divisions of two guns, each worked by two officers and 45 men. No regular

15 Hall, Major D.D., 'The Artillery of the First Anglo-Boer War 1880 –1881', *Military History Journal*, 5:2 (December 1980) < samilitaryhistory.org/journal.html > (accessed 27 August 2015); Hall, Major Darrell, 'Field Artillery of the British Army 1860–1960', *Military History Journal*, 5:1 (December 1980) < samilitaryhistory.org/journal.html > (accessed 25 August 2015); Von Moltke, 'Wapentuig', pp. 18–20.

16 For British military organisation, see Laband, John, *Historical Dictionary of the Zulu Wars* (Lanham, Md., Toronto and Oxford: The Scarecrow Press, 2009), p. 163.

cavalry was stationed in the Transvaal, but mounted infantry was instead. A squadron of mounted infantry, made up of two troops, usually consisted of three officers and 110 men. Experience had taught the British of the need to combine the mobility of cavalry with the infantry's firepower for scouting and fighting, a combination (as we shall see) basic to the Boer commando. The first dedicated mounted rifle unit was raised in the Cape Colony in 1827. Thereafter, mounted infantry were regularly raised from volunteers among the infantry battalions, and it was accepted even by conservative soldiers that they were particularly suited to colonial warfare.[17]

On 24 April 1880 Colonel Bellairs and the Transvaal garrison came under the overall command of Major General Sir George Pomeroy Pomeroy-Colley who succeeded Wolseley as H.M. High Commissioner for South-East Africa, Governor of Natal and Commander-in-Chief of Natal and the Transvaal. Heavily bearded, balding and slight in build, Colley was born in Dublin in 1835, the youngest son of a commander in the Royal Navy, the Hon. George Francis Colley.[18] The latter was the third son of the fourth Viscount Harberton and carried the family surname Pomeroy. But in 1830 he assumed the surname Colley as a condition for inheriting the estate of his grandmother, the first Viscountess Harberton, who had been born a Colley of Castle Carbery. On 8 May 1880, just before taking up his South African command, General Colley added Pomeroy to Colley to form a double-barrelled surname that sat oddly alongside his retained middle name Pomeroy.

Colley entered Sandhurst in 1849, and after passing out first three years later was as a result commissioned without purchase into the distinguished 2nd (the Queen's Royal) Regiment. After postings abroad to the Cape Colony in 1854 and to China in 1860 where he fought in the Second Anglo-Chinese War, in 1862 he entered the Staff College established at Camberley in 1858 to turn out select officers better prepared than previously for strategic intelligence and other staff duties. With unprecedented brilliance Colley passed out first in less than half the usual time with the highest aggregate of marks ever obtained. Understandably, he was counted among those reforming officers who prized intellect over athletic prowess, and who understood that for the army to perform its duties effectively across the Empire it had to embrace new technologies such as the submarine telegraph cable, and to be constantly prepared to adopt the latest armaments and to reassess tactical doctrine.[19] Colley, on the strength of his intellectual excellence, took up a

---

17   See Bou, Jean, 'Modern Cavalry: Mounted Rifles, the Boer War, and the Doctrinal Debates', in Dennis (ed.), Peter, and Grey (ed.), Jeffrey, *The Boer War: Army, Nation and Empire* (Canberra: Army History Unit, Australian Department of Defence, 2000), pp. 99–105.

18   The standard authority for Colley's life up to taking up his South African command in 1880 remains Butler, Lt. Gen. Sir William F., *The Life of Sir George Pomeroy-Colley, KCSI, CB, CMG Including Services in Kaffraria—in China—in Ashanti and in Natal* (London: John Murray, 1899), chaps I–XII. See also Beckett, Ian F.W., 'Colley, Sir George Pomeroy Pomeroy- (1835–1881)', *Oxford Dictionary of National Biography* (Oxford University Press, 2004; online ed., January 2008) <http://www.oxforddnb.com.libproxy.wlu.ca/view/article/5910> (accessed 20 August 2015); and Beckett, Ian F.W., 'George Colley', in Corvi (ed.), Steven J., and Beckett (ed.), Ian F.W., *Victoria's Generals* (Barnsley, South Yorks: Pen & Sword Military, 2009), pp. 74–80.

19   Beckett, Ian F.W., *The Victorians at War* (London: Hambledon, 2003), pp. 179–190.

H.R.H. Prince George, Duke of Cambridge, KG, Field Marshal Commanding-in-Chief. (Giles St Aubyn, *The Royal George,* New York: Alfred A. Knopf, 1964)

series of military academic posts. While serving as Professor of Military Law and Administration at the Staff College, a position he held from 1871 to 1873, he joined Sir Garnet Wolseley's staff in the First Asante (Ashanti) War of 1873–1874. During this campaign he demonstrated his superior administrative skills in the field.

Sir Garnet Wolseley was the most influential reforming soldier of his time, and firmly supported the Cardwell reforms.[20] However, he and other reformers came up directly against the Queen's militarily conservative cousin, HRH Prince George, Duke of Cambridge who between 15 July 1856 and 31 October 1895—when he finally retired under pressure—was the Field Marshal Commanding-in-Chief, elevated by royal patent in 1887 to Commander-in-Chief.[21] His position was a somewhat anomalous one. By the War Office Act of 1870 the War Office held responsibility for financing the army, for the disposition of troops and for political decisions concerning their deployment. Cambridge was therefore technically subordinate to the secretary of state for war and it was his duty to implement the military decisions of the government. However, he held office at the pleasure of the Crown, and doggedly maintained his grip on matters of command, discipline, appointments and promotions. He was extremely jealous of these prerogatives and furiously resisted the interference of civilians—including cabinet members—in military affairs. Conservative military circles, who deplored reform and advanced military ideas as epitomised by Cardwell's reforms, gravitated around the reactionary Duke and encouraged him in his propensity to judge the army's efficiency in terms of spit-and-polish, parades and field days rather than on effectiveness on campaign.

Wolseley was convinced that although the Duke and his fellow conservatives could no longer resist the inauguration of the new system, they would nevertheless do their best to undermine it.[22] He saw it as his mission, therefore, to demonstrate that the reforms did work, and on his

---

20 See Beckett, Ian F.W., 'Wolseley, Garnet Joseph, first Viscount Wolseley (1833–1913)', *Oxford Dictionary of National Biography* (Oxford University Press, 2004; online ed., May 2009) <http://www.oxforddnb.com.libproxy.wlu.ca/view/article/33372> (accessed 20 August 2015).

21 The fullest account of Cambridge as Field Marshal Commanding-in-Chief is to be found in St. Aubyn, Giles, *The Royal George, 1819–1904. The Life of H.R.H. Prince George Duke of Cambridge* (New York: Alfred A. Knopf, 1964), pp. 112–259, 300–338. See too Spiers, Edward M., 'George, Prince, second Duke of Cambridge (1819–1904)', *Oxford Dictionary of National Biography* (Oxford University Press, 2004; online edn, January 2008) <http://www.oxforddnb.com.libproxy.wlu.ca/view/article/36995> (accessed 20 August 2015).

22 Preston (ed.), Adrian, *The South African Journal of Sir Garnet Wolseley 1879–1880* (Cape Town: A.A. Balkema, 1973), p. 304, Appendix C: Wolseley, Memoir: the Boer command, 27 May 1881.

Mounted Infantry of Col. Evelyn Wood's personal escort during the Anglo-Zulu War recruited from the 90th Light Infantry. (Collection of Ian Knight)

various campaigns assembled a staff equally committed to that end. This select coterie of officers, first formed for the Asante (Ashanti) expedition of 1873–1874, was known subsequently as the 'Ashanti Ring' (or 'Mutual Admiration Society', as its detractors dubbed it). Its members were either decorated veterans of distinguished service, or Staff College graduates who, like Colley, showed promise.[23] They, in turn, benefited from their successful service with Wolseley which helped them gain public recognition and rapid promotion. The Duke was probably correct, however, in his disapproving concern that the elite 'Ashanti Ring' depressed morale elsewhere by denying excluded officers of promise the opportunity to shine. It also encouraged emulation. Sir Frederick Sleigh Roberts's rival ring in India formed a similar coterie of favoured officers grouped around a charismatic commander who was particularly concerned by the evils of short service, and campaigned determinedly and fruitlessly against it.[24] The ambitions of these rival military factions—the Duke's, Wolseley's and Roberts's— prevented the emergence of a common military doctrine. Moreover, they accentuated the inevitable divisions and rivalries within the army which were played out in the immensely complex internal manoeuvring concerning command—never more so than in South Africa in the period of the Transvaal Rebellion.[25]

23 Beckett (ed.), Ian W.F., *Wolseley and Ashanti. The Asante War Journal and Correspondence of Major General Sir Garnet Wolseley 1873–1874* (Stroud, Glocs.: The History Press for the Army Records Society, 2009), pp. 38–44.

24 Farwell, Byron, *Eminent Victorian Soldiers: Seekers of Glory* (New York and London: W.W. Norton, 1985), p. 177.

25 Beckett, Ian F.W., 'Military High Command in South Africa, 1854–1914', in Boyden (ed.), Peter B., Guy (ed.), Alan J., and Harding (ed.) Marion, *'Ashes and Blood'. The British Army*

As Wolseley's protégé, Colley was made colonel and appointed CB in 1874 for his service in Asante. He rejoined Wolseley's staff on his special mission to Natal in 1875 to further the cause of confederation, and familiarized himself with the surrounding territories, including the ZAR. In April 1876 he was appointed the military secretary to Lord Lytton, the Viceroy of India, and in February 1878 became his private secretary. As such he exercised considerable influence on policy in India. He strongly advocated a 'forward policy' into Afghanistan to forestall Russia's territorial ambitions which led to the Second Anglo-Afghan War in November 1878. In 1878 he was appointed CMG and created KCSI in July 1879.

An opportunity for a field command arose in early 1878 when he was recommended for General Officer Commanding (GOC) Her Majesty's Forces in South Africa to replace General Sir Arthur Cunynghame who was making heavy weather of the Ninth Cape Frontier War. But the Duke of Cambridge considered him too junior and in March 1879 the post went instead to Lieutenant General Sir Frederic Thesiger, later Lord Chelmsford. Indeed, Cambridge was suspicious of Colley as one of the intriguers in the 'Ashanti Ring' and only reluctantly permitted Wolseley to appoint him his chief of staff with the rank of brigadier general when Wolseley superseded Chelmsford in the final stages of the Anglo-Zulu War of 1879. Colley's influence on his chief was apparent in the settlement Wolseley imposed on the defeated Zulu on 1 September. Certainly, by breaking up the Zulu kingdom into thirteen impotent fragments under compliant 'kinglets', Wolseley was apparently following the blueprint Colley had once proposed for Afghanistan.[26]

Colley did not serve with Wolseley in the Second Anglo-Pedi War because with the renewal of the Second Anglo-Afghan War in September 1879 he was recalled to India. Nevertheless, as we have seen, Wolseley succeeded in having him appointed as his successor in South Africa with the rank of major general. Colley took up his command in June 1880 having expressed the hope to Wolseley that he would "do my master credit."[27] Military and civil powers in South East Africa were thus effectively combined in his person, which meant that the disputes between competing civil and military authorities which had marred the conduct of operations in the Ninth Cape Frontier War and the Anglo-Zulu War were avoided in the Transvaal Rebellion.[28] As high commissioner, Colley was the imperial agent in southern Africa outside of Cape Colony, which had its own governor and high commissioner. Colley was directly responsible to the secretaries of state both for the colonies and

in South Africa 1795–1914 (London: National Army Museum Publication, 2001). pp. 60–3.

26 Laband, John and Thompson, Paul, 'The Reduction of Zululand, 1878 –1904', in Duminy (ed.), Andrew, and Guest (ed.) Bill, *Natal and Zululand from Earliest Times to 1910: A New History* (Pietermaritzburg: University of Natal Press and Shuter & Shooter, 1989), p. 203.

27 Quoted in Beckett, 'George Colley', p. 79.

28 See Laband, John, "'The Direction of the Whole of the Forces Available': The Disputed Spheres of the Military and Civil Authorities in the Eastern Cape (1877–1878), Natal (1879) and Zululand (1888)," *Scientia Militaria: South African Journal of Military Studies*, 41: 2 (2013), pp. 60–69.

Maj. Gen. Sir Garnet Wolseley, Administrator of Natal in 1875, with his staff at Government House, Pietermaritzburg. Left to right: Sir Henry Brackenbury, Capt. Barker, Wolseley, Viscount Mandeville, Sir William Butler, Frederick Gifford, 3rd Baron Gifford, and Col. George Pomeroy Colley in the tropical dress he is wearing in the studio photograph of 1874. (PAR, C. 1305/1)

for war, and superior to Sir Owen Lanyon, the Administrator of the Transvaal (who nevertheless also reported to the colonial secretary).

As Commander-in-Chief of Natal and the Transvaal, the framing and implementation of defence policy in South Eastern Africa were Colley's preserve alone, and overrode the inferior authority of other administrators as well as allowing him to act independently of the GOC South Africa with his headquarters in Cape Town. In any case, the relative smallness of the imperial garrison, and the subordination of military to civil authority, meant that South Africa was not a significant or highly prized military command, and late-Victorian GOCs were seldom officers of high calibre or ambition. Lieutenant General the Hon. Leicester Smyth, an old Etonian and veteran of the Anglo-Basotho War of 1852 and the Crimean War, who was appointed GOC in November 1880, was no exception.[29] Major General Redvers Buller contemptuously wrote him off as a "feeble creature" who did not know "his own mind for five minutes together,"[30] but Smyth nevertheless possessed sufficient authority to thwart Colley by rationing his military assistance, even if he could not dictate military policy.

---

29 Lloyd E.M., revised by Lunt, Rev. James, 'Smyth [formerly Curzon-Howe], Sir Leicester (1829–1891)', Oxford Dictionary of National Biography (Oxford University Press, 2004; online ed., May 2009) <http://www.oxforddnb.com.libproxy.wlu.ca/view/article/25955> (accessed 20 August 2015). Smyth remained in command at the Cape until November 1885.

30 Pietermaritzburg Archives Repository (PAR) WC III/2/5: Maj. Gen. Buller to Brig. Gen Wood, 15 December 1880.

Colley came with the reputation of being the brightest star in the 'Ashanti Ring' and his strong brow, accentuated by his receding hairline, seemed to verify his widely acknowledged superior intellect. Armed as he was with extensive civil and military authority great things were expected of him. But observers also noted that the new Governor of Natal's eyes were unexpectedly soft, and that he seemed both shy and modest. Nor did it go unnoticed among hard-boiled colonists that he was a bird-watching enthusiast and that he played the flautino, a high-pitched cousin of the baroque recorder. So just how effectively he would cope with the simmering Transvaal crisis remained a matter for some speculation.

3

The Boers take up Arms

Colley's broad authority over the Transvaal as High Commissioner for South-East Africa suited Lanyon in Pretoria. Already the distracted Colonial Office tended to let its Administrator go his own way in the Transvaal without much interference, and Lanyon realised that Colley in Pietermaritzburg (whom he disdained as his junior in experience) could exert little supervision over him. The implementation of a workable tax-collection system was the key to Lanyon's policy in the Transvaal, but for the Boers, who had baulked at paying taxes even to their own republic, shelling out taxes to the British symbolised more than anything else their submission to alien rule.[1] Lanyon nevertheless persisted in bringing tax evaders to book, only to stir simmering discontent into open rebellion.

In the Potchefstroom District in the south-western Transvaal, which was proving particularly recalcitrant, Lanyon determined to make an example of one of the tax evaders, P.L. (Piet) Bezuidenhout, and took him to court. Bezuidenhout won his case, but refused to pay the costs. The *landdros* (magistrate), A.M. Goetz, thereupon confiscated his wagon in execution and put it up for auction in Potchefstroom on 11 November 1880. On the day of the auction P.A. (Piet) Cronjé, who had been taken as a baby on the Great Trek and was a well-known activist in the district, rode into town with about 100 armed companions.[2] They seized the wagon to return to Bezuidenhout and then provocatively encamped outside Potchefstroom. Lanyon ordered the arrest of the ringleaders, and when they defied the local special constables, he ordered up troops. By 20 November a force of 180 men of the 2/21st Fusiliers and two 9-pdr guns of N/5 Brigade, RA under the command of Major C. Thornhill, RA were entrenched outside Potchefstroom and manned various strong-points in the town itself. The Boers were not to be intimidated, and a stand-off ensued.[3] Then 111 *burgers* (citizens) of the Wakkerstroom District

---

1   Theron-Bushell, 'Lanyon', pp. 258–259, 299–302.
2   Cronjé later commanded the commando that forced the surrender of the Jameson raiders in 1896. In the Anglo-Boer War of 1899–1902 he was given command of the western front where he failed to capture Mafeking. He finally surrendered at Paardeburg in February 1900. See Nöthling, 'Commanders', pp. 77–78.
3   *BPP* (C. 2740), enc. 1 in no. 60: Goetz to Hudson, 11 November 1880; no. 61: Lanyon to Kimberley, 14 November 1880; enc. 2 in no. 61: Lanyon to Bellairs, 14 November 1881; enc. 3 in no. 61: Morcom to Public Prosecutor, Potchefstroom, 13 November 1880; and

in the southern Transvaal also challenged the British administration by declaring that they would only pay taxes under protest.[4] Lanyon simply could not credit that the Boers were in earnest in their resistance and delayed calling on Colley for reinforcements until 25 November. Even then he failed to communicate any sense of real urgency.[5]

As for Colley, who was Commander-in-Chief of Natal as well as of the Transvaal, the possible threat posed to Natal's western and southern borders by the concurrent Gun War and by the Transkei Rebellion seemed of far greater concern than the situation in the Transvaal, and he was not prepared to deplete the Natal garrison to any great extent.[6] The most he most was prepared to do was to order up four companies of the 58th (Rutlandshire) Regiment to relieve the companies of the 94th Regiment currently stationed at Newcastle in northern Natal and at Wakkerstroom in the Transvaal. Once relieved, these companies would join other companies of the 94th Regiment at Pretoria so that Lanyon had enough troops concentrated there to overawe seditious gatherings.[7] But this redeployment came too late, and on 16 December there were only 1,759 British soldiers in the Transvaal, still parcelled out among seven garrisons.

Grasping the political potential of events in Potchefstroom and Wakkerstroom, the Boer leaders called a mass meeting for 8 December 1880. About 5,000 *burgers* duly turned up at Paardekraal, situated between Pretoria and Potchefstroom, for an emotion-charged and decisive rally which lasted until 15 December. On Monday, 13 December the gathering resolved to reconstitute the old *volksraad*, and in the absence of former President T.F. Burgers (who had left the Transvaal on annexation to live in retirement in the Cape), elected a triumvirate to lead it consisting of Kruger, the former vice-president, Piet Joubert, a former acting president and Marthinus Wessel Pretorius, a former president. On 16 December—the anniversary of the symbolically charged victory of the *voortrekkers* over the amaZulu at the battle of Blood River (Ncome) in 1838—the provisional Boer government approved a proclamation announcing the restoration of the ZAR which was described as being in a state of siege and under the rule of martial law.[8] The assembled *burgers* gathered around a flagpole where the *Vierkleur* (the old republican flag with its red, white and blue horizontal stripes and green perpendicular stripe next to the pole) was unfurled.[9] Exhorted by Piet Joubert, they erected a cairn around the flagpole, each stone a symbol

Hudson to Goetz, 14 November 1880; (C. 2783), enc. in no. 12: report by P.A. Cronjé. See Bennett, Ian, *A Rain of Lead: The Siege and Surrender of the British at Potchefstroom* (London: Greenhill Books, 2001), pp. 45–48.

4   *BPP* (C. 2740), enc. in no. 68: Declaration by Wakkerstroom burghers, 16 November 1880.

5   *BPP* (C. 2783), enc. 1 in no. 14: Lanyon to Colley, telegram, 25 November 1880; Theron-Bushell, 'Lanyon', pp. 268–273.

6   *BPP* (C. 2783), enc. 3 in no. 14: Colley to Lanyon, 3 December 1880; *BPP* (C. 2866), no. 3: Colley to Kimberley, 26 December 1880.

7   *BPP* (C. 2783), enc. 3 in no. 14: Colley to Lanyon, 3 December 1880; no. 25: Colley to Kimberley, 13 December 1880; no. 37: Colley to Kimberley, 19 December 1880.

8   *BPP* (C. 2838), enc. 7: Proclamation, South African Republic, 16 December 1880.

9   The *Vierkleur* was hoisted for the first time on 6 January 1857 at Potchefstroom at the inauguration of the first President of the ZAR, M.W. Pretorius, and subsequently approved by the *volksraad* on 13 February 1858. See Conradie, D., 'The Vierkleur and the

that the *burgers* had sworn loyalty to each other to fight to the death in the republic's defence.[10]

To fulfil such an oath required military organisation. The British thought they understood the Boer military system and its apparent shortcomings.[11] Prior to 1880 they had faced the Boers in battle on a number of occasions. True, the Boers had worsted the British in a night skirmish at Congella in 1842 during the struggle to control Natal, but the British had soon retrieved the situation and the Boers had capitulated.[12] More recently, the supposed superiority of British regulars over Boer irregulars had been confirmed in the skirmishes at Zwartkopjes in 1845 and Boomplaats in 1848 which had temporarily established British control over the territory north of the Orange River.[13] During the course of the nineteenth century regular British forces had fought side-by-side with Boer militia in no less than seven of the nine Cape Frontier Wars.[14] However, any notion of the effectiveness of the Boer military system had been offset by the fluctuating successes of the Boers of the OVS against the Sotho kingdom in the wars of 1858, 1865–1866 and 1868.[15] Most recently, the British had witnessed the poor Boer morale, disorganisation and abject military failure in the Boer-Pedi War of 1876–1877.[16] For the British—and most English-speaking settlers likewise—that military debacle confirmed their scornful assumption that the Boers could never prevail against British regulars. This prejudice was reinforced by a metropolitan bias against country bumpkins who did not fight in uniform like proper soldiers but in disreputable civilian clothes, even if these were often specially adapted with ammunition pockets and pouches attached to shirts, waistcoats and jackets. The only common features of Boer dress on campaign were their unmilitary but comfortable corduroy trousers and distinctive wide-brimmed felt hats.

Union Jack in the 1880–1881 War between the Zuid-Afrikaansche Republiek and Britain', *Scientia Militaria: South African Journal of Military Studies*, 1: 11 (1981), p. 58.

10 Grobler, J.E.H., 'Paardekraal: Eensydige Herstel van die Onafhanklikheid', in *Eerste Vryheidsoorlog*, pp. 104–106.

11 This section draws heavily on a fine work of synthesis on the Boer military system by van der Waag, Ian, 'South Africa and the Boer Military System', in Dennis (ed.) Peter, and Grey (ed.), Jeffrey, *Boer War*, pp. 49–51, 53–62, 64, 67; and on the classic analysis by Tylden, George, 'The Development of the Commando System in South Africa, 1715 to 1922', *Africana Notes and News*, 13 (March 1958–December 1959), pp. 303–13. See also Trapido, Stanley, 'Reflections on Land, Office and Wealth in the South African Republic, 1850-1900 ' in Marks (ed.), Shula, and Atmore (ed.), Anthony, *Economy and Society in Pre-Industrial South Africa* (London: Longman, 1980), particularly pp. 352, 356, 361; Duxbury, George R., *David and Goliath: The First War of Independence, 1880 –1881* (Saxonwold, South Africa: South African National Museum of Military History, 1981) , pp. 2-3, 24-6; Machanik, 'Firearms'; and Laband, *Transvaal Rebellion*, pp. 59 –67.

12 Laband, John, *The Rise and Fall of the Zulu Nation* (London: Arms and Armour Press, 1997), pp. 124–125.

13 Walker, Eric A., *The Great Trek*, 3rd ed. (London: Adam and Charles Black, 1948), pp. 350, 373–4.

14 Laband, *Zulu Warriors*, pp. 94–108, 113–145.

15 Laband, John, 'War and Peace in South Africa', in Boyden (ed.), Peter B., Guy (ed.), Alan J., and Harding (ed.) Marion, *'Ashes and Blood'. The British Army in South Africa 1795–1914* (London: National Army Museum Publication, 2001), pp. 14–15; Stapleton, Tim, *A Military History of South Africa from the Dutch-Khoi Wars to the End of Apartheid* (Santa Barbara, California: Praeger, 2010), pp. 41–6.

16 Laband, *Zulu Warriors*, pp. 63–71.

The Boer commanders in the war of 1880–1881. Top row, left to right: *Veldkornet* L. Pieter Bezuidenhout (Potchefstroom); *Kmdt.* S.P. Grové (Middleburg); *Assistent Kmdt. Generaal* Hendrik Schoeman (Pretoria); *Kmdt.* Henning Pretorius (Pretoria); *Kmdt.* Lewis Fourie (Laing's Nek). Second row, left to right: *Kmdt.* H.R. Lemmer (Potchefstroom); *Kmdt.* J.D. Weilbach (Potchefstroom and Laing's Nek); *Weesheer* [Member of Orphanage Board]) J.S. Joubert; *Kmdt.* J. du Plessis du Beer (Wonderboom and Pretoria); *Kmdt.* Diederik J. Muller (Lydenburg) Centre: *Kmdt. Generaal* J.Petrus Joubert .Third row, left to right: *Kmdt.* Hans Erasmus (Pretoria); *Assistent Kmdt. Generaal* J.P. Steyn (Lydenburg); *Kmdt.* Hans Botha (Zwartkop and Pretoria); *Kmdt.* Gert Engelbrecht (Standerton). Bottom row, left to right: *Veggeneraal* J.H.M. Kock (Potchefstroom); *Veggeneraal* Frans Joubert (Bronkhorstspruit); *Veld Kmdt. Generaal* Nicolaas Smit (Bronkhorstspruit, Schuinshoogte and Majuba); *Assistent Kmdt. Generaal* Pieter A. Cronje (Potchefstroom) (NARP, TAB 18009)

What made it so difficult from the British perspective to acknowledge Boer military capability was the alien nature of their military system. The Boer republics lacked conventional military forces or standing armies and their forces were a militia in which no structured military training or parade-ground drill took place. The outspokenness and informality of the men, even towards their officers, led the British to believe the Boer forces were entirely undisciplined. And it was indeed the case that the lax discipline of *burgers* could adversely affect the outcome of operations. The practice of holding a council of war before going into action was always a potential weakness because battle plans were freely discussed by all present, though only officers had the vote. Those whose preferred plan was not adopted had no compunction in packing up and abandoning their comrades to their misguided devices. In general, *burgers* on campaign thought little of absenting themselves and riding home for a while, because they knew that if they decided to come back there was no machinery for punishing them for desertion.

It was easy for the British to deride such indiscipline, but it has to be understood in terms of Boer military culture. Boer military structure and style of combat were suited to their particular environment and reflected their notions of a burgher's obligations to the community. If properly motivated—as they were in the Transvaal Rebellion, but had not been in the Boer-Pedi War—the Boers could mount a determined and skilful campaign capable of probing the manifest weaknesses inherent in the British military system.

The *kommando* (commando) system was the organisational basis of the Boer military system. It had first been formalised in 1715 on the Cape frontier when the Dutch East India Company, whose urban-based Burgher Militia and garrison of soldiers were designed to repel a sea-borne attack on Cape Town by European foes, looked to an alternative and more mobile mode of border defence against African raiding. The commando system became a central feature of *burger* society, and continued in the Cape when British rule was established. As both a military and an economic institution it—together with the Calvinism of the *burgers*—created a web of social relations essential in holding together and ensuring the survival of the community. It is no surprise, therefore, that the *voortrekkers* perpetuated the commando system once they established their republics on the highveld.

With certain exceptions—members of the *volksraad*, state employees, clergymen and school-teachers—every able-bodied free *burger* between 16 and 60 was required to serve without pay in time of need as part of his civil responsibility.[17] Young men under 18, however, and men over 50 were only called out in an emergency. In 1876 the number of *burgers* in the ZAR capable of bearing arms was recorded with unrealistic precision as 7,326.[18]

The selection of Boer officers was by open, popular vote. For the British, whose officer caste (with very few exceptions) remained socially distinct, this indicated an alien and unworkable military egalitarianism. Yet, in fact,

---

17 Those exempt from service had to contribute financially towards the campaign; while owners of land residing outside the ZAR had to find a substitute to serve, or pay a fine.

18 Great Britain, *Transvaal Territory*, p. 51.

Boer officers, although elected, also came from the elite of society and were among the large landowners who controlled labour, hunting and trade, and were closely connected through their common economic interests, political alliances, and ties of kinship. This oligarchy exerted considerable pressure on the rest of Boer society which consisted mainly of lesser farmers with a few professionals, ministers of religion, and government officials thrown in. Needless to say, wealth, influence, popularity—or even the apparent wisdom associated in Boer society with the wearing of a long, white beard—did not guarantee effective or sophisticated military leadership among these elected oligarchic officers.

The most important official in the commando system was the *veldkornet* (or field cornet), invariably elected from a family of local notables. For electoral and administrative purposes the resuscitated ZAR was divided in 1880 into 13 districts, in each of which there were between two or six *veldkornette* depending on the number of wards.[19] Every *veldkornet* was responsible in his duties to the *landdros*, or magistrate, and through him to the *Krijgsraad*, or state war council. It was the *landdros's* duty to ensure that the *burgers* in his ward were always combat-ready. In time of war he mustered them within 48 hours into their district commando under its *kommandant*, or commanding officer, whom the *veldkornette* had previously chosen. *Veldkornette* were empowered to commandeer wagons, trek oxen, slaughter cattle, horses and whatever else was necessary to supply the commando.

The *burger* on commando was expected to provide himself with a rifle and 50 rounds of ammunition. Requiring his firearm for hunting and defence, the Boer farmer bought the best weapon he could obtain. In 1880 a variety of breech-loading, falling block or bolt action rifles and carbines were available for purchase in southern Africa such as the American-made Winchester model 1876, the Swiss-made Vetterli model 1869, the British-made Calisher-Terry, and—a great favourite—the Snider-Enfield (known familiarly as '*die Snyter*'), which had been adopted by the British Army in 1866 until superseded by the Martini-Henry in 1874. However, the most popular firearm of all was the British-made 1866 pattern Westley Richards rifle which the Boers personalised as 'Wessel Rykaard' or 'Wessel Riekert'. It was a .450 calibre, falling block, single action breech-loading rifle firing a no. 2 cartridge, and which was very accurate up to 600 yards. Although similar in manufacture, sighting, calibre, weight and ammunition to the Martini-Henry Mk II carried by the British troops, like the Snider-Enfield its hammer and firing pin were situated on the right exterior of the barrel which meant that the hammer had to be cocked for firing and half-cocked for loading. Along with their rifle, Boer officers often carried an Adams revolver—but never a sword as did their British counterparts. Some Boers still preferred the old muzzle-loading hunting musket, or *roer*, because the slow, round bullet produced more shock to tissue than did the swifter, conical rifle bullet.

Besides his weapon, the *burger* was expected to provide his own horse and saddlery. The Boers generally rode the Cape Horse or *Boereperd*, a distinct breed that was a cross between horses imported to the Cape from Europe and Indonesia (horses were not indigenous to southern Africa) and which

---

19 *Blue Book Transvaal*, pp. 116–117.

was accustomed to local conditions. An even hardier variant of horse was the tough little Basuto Pony, much favoured for patrolling and skirmishing on commando.[20] Boer ponies were trained to stand without being held, which allowed every rifle to be put into the firing line. The Boers were easy on their ponies, not usually pushing them more than six miles an hour, and rode light, not carrying much more than a blanket, saddlebag, tin mug and haversack.

On being called out, *burgers* were supposed to carry eight days' rations. After that, they relied on whatever supplies the commando carried in its wagons, or lived off the countryside. Boer ponies and the draft animals on commando were put out to graze, herded by *oorlamse kaffers* (civilised or sophisticated blacks), Africans whom the Boers had seized as children from neighbouring communities, reared as 'apprentices', socialised into Boer culture and kept on in adulthood as skilled labourers or domestics. In a real sense they were akin to military slaves elsewhere in Africa and technically contravened the Sand River Convention which had forbidden slavery in the ZAR.[21] These black 'servants' carried out all the behind-the-line services including driving the wagons and managing the teams of oxen, grooming horses, slaughtering livestock, collecting firewood, cooking, guarding ammunition, digging trenches and emplacements for the *burgers*, and helping with the sick and wounded because there were no Boer ambulance or hospital services to speak of. Known as *agterryers* ('after-riders' or lackeys who accompanied their masters on horseback on a journey, a hunting expedition, or to war), they had been an inseparable part of the commando system since its inception in the Cape, and the institution had moved inland with the Boers during the Great Trek. Before the British annexation of 1877 *agterryers* had taken part in the campaigns of the ZAR, performing both their customary menial tasks and sometimes taking a direct military role. Unfortunately, because their presence on campaign was so much taken for granted, there is little specific reference to *agterryers* in the sources. Their familiar presence on the battlefields of 1880–1881 must consequently be largely inferred, and it must be presumed that their participation was almost entirely confined to a support role (unlike the war of 1899–1902, where they often became directly involved militarily) and that they took little part in the actual fighting.[22]

On 13 December 1881 the *burgers* assembled at Paardekraal elected Piet Joubert *Kommandant Generaal* (Commandant General) over their

Petrus Lefras Uys, a prominent farmer in the Utrecht District of the Transvaal, photographed in 1879 during the Anglo-Zulu War with his four sons in front of their wagon. They are dressed and armed in typical fashion for Boers on campaign. Note their *agterryers* on the right.

(Collection of Ian Knight)

20 Swart, Sandra, *Riding High: Horses, Humans and History in South Africa* (Johannesburg: Wits University Press, 2010), pp. 18–37, 80–87.

21 Laband, *Transvaal Rebellion*, p. 41.

22 Labuschange, Pieter, *Ghostriders of the Anglo-Boer War (1899–1902): The Role and Contribution of Agterryers* (Pretoria: University of South Africa, 1999), pp. ix, 4–5, 7–9, 14, 25–6; Warwick, Peter, *Black People and the South African War 1899–1902* (Johannesburg: Ravan Press, 1983), pp. 11, 25–6; Nasson, William, 'Africans at War', in Gooch, John, *The Boer War: Direction, Experience and Image* (London, Portland, Or: Frank Cass, 2000), pp. 126–140. For the ambiguous status of *agterryers* in the context of African military slavery, see Laband, John, 'The Slave Soldiers of Africa', *Journal of Military History*, 81: 1 (January 2017), pp. 20–1.

forces. This post gave him supreme military command and control over the distribution of arms and ammunition. Joubert protested he was no general and not suited to the job.[23] Nonetheless, he took energetic action and, in terms of the martial law proclaimed on 16 December, sent out far and wide to appoint further military commanders and to mobilise the approximately 7,000 mounted burghers he believed available to him.[24] The Boer leaders knew they must move rapidly, and on 14 December they resolved to send a commando of 400 men under Piet Cronjé to Potchefstroom to seize the printing press (the only other one in the Transvaal was in Pretoria) to print the proclamation of the republic.

Since the 1870s communication between British headquarters and military units and posts had been by field telegraph line which was much more rapid than by the traditional mounted dispatch rider and superior to heliograph (which transmitted Morse code flashes) or flag signalling.[25] However, the telegraph line was always vulnerable to enemy action. On 15 December Cronjé's commando cut the wires, ending communication between Lanyon in Pretoria and Colley in Pietermaritzburg, and then rode into Potchefstroom.[26] There on 16 December shots were exchanged between Cronjé's men and the British troops holding the town—both sides accused the other of firing first—and inflicted the initial casualties of the rebellion.[27]

Meanwhile, to forestall a possible British sortie by the Pretoria garrison, Field Cornet D.J.E. Erasmus set off for the capital with a commando of 200 men. It was decided meanwhile to make Heidelberg, a village situated halfway between Pretoria and the Natal border and without a British garrison, the ZAR's temporary capital. On 16 December the members of the provisional government, followed by a commando of 800 men, occupied the place.[28] The Triumvirate sent at once to Lanyon enclosing a copy of their proclamation and warning him that they would fight if he did not hand the administration of the Transvaal over to them "within twice 24 hours."[29] Lanyon's unequivocal response to this challenge was to issue a proclamation on 18 December calling on Colonel Bellairs and the imperial garrison "to vindicate the authority of Her Majesty's Government, and to put down insurrection wherever it may be found to exist."[30] Force of arms would now decide the issue.

23 Meintjes, Johannes, *The Commandant-General: The Life and Times of Petrus Jacobus Joubert of the South African Republic 1831–1900* (Cape Town: Tafelberg, 1971), p. 74.

24 Grobler, 'Paardekraal', pp. 106, 108.

25 The British employed the Mance pattern heliograph, devised in 1869. Its flashes could be seen up to 50 miles away through a telescope, but visibility depended on the amount of sunlight. See Laband, *Historical Dictionary*, p. 111.

26 *BPP* (C. 2783), enc. 2 in no. 49: Bellairs to DAG, Pietermaritzburg, 17 December 1880; Grobler, 'Paardekraal', pp. 105, 107–108.

27 Bennett, *Rain of Lead*, pp. 71–75.

28 See *BPP* (C. 2959), enc. 4 in no. 4: Report of Acting Landdrost of Heidelberg, 16 December 1880.

29 *BPP* (C.2838), enc. 7: Kruger, et al. to Lanyon, 16 December 1880.

30 TNA: WO 32/7812, enc. 2 in no. 079/3975: Proclamation by Lanyon, 18 December 1880.

4

Bronkhorstspruit

Colonel Bellairs, Commanding the Transvaal District, considered Lanyon's detachment of a considerable portion of the Pretoria garrison to Potchefstroom sheer folly. He urged that it made better strategic sense to concentrate the scattered British garrisons in Pretoria in order to have an effective field force of about 700 regulars in hand.[1] On 23 November Lanyon compounded his strategic weakness by finally accepting the need for concentration while remaining unwilling to abandon any post entirely. He consequently ordered elements of the Wakkerstroom, Marabastad and Lydenburg garrisons to make hazardous marches through an increasingly hostile countryside to Pretoria while leaving the three outposts to be held by drastically reduced garrisons.[2]

Telegraphic information that the Boers had declared the restored ZAR on 16 December only reached Colley in Pietermaritzburg on 19 December because the Boers had cut the lines north of Standerton. This intelligence prompted Colley to push ahead with embryonic plans to form a column preliminary to an advance into the Transvaal, and he ordered Lanyon to avoid any clashes before his arrival.[3] The problem with this response was that the forces earmarked for the relief column were dispersed and meagre, and it continued to concern Colley that when he advanced into the Transvaal, Natal would be left dangerously denuded of troops while the Gun War and the Transkei Rebellion were still unresolved. He therefore applied to the government in London to despatch another regiment to garrison Natal and act as a reserve.[4]

In this regard, it should be noted that in 1880–1881 Colley was less free to exercise his own political and military judgment than previous wartime commanders in South Africa because he was in direct telegraph contact with the British government. Pietermaritzburg had been linked to Durban

---

1   *BPP* (C. 2866), enc. in no. 77: Bellairs to DAG, 14 November 1880; *BPP* (C. 2783), enc. in no. 49: Bellairs to Lanyon, 16 November 1880; Bellairs, *Transvaal War*, p. 51.
2   *BPP* (C. 2838), enc. 2: Lanyon to Kimberley, 23 January 1881.
3   TNA: WO 32/7797, no. 079/3492: Colley to QMG, London, telegram, 9 December 1880; *BPP* (C. 2783), enc. 1 in no. 49: Colley to Lanyon, 19 December 1880.
4   *BPP* (C. 2783), no. 37: Colley to Kimberley, 19 December 1880; enc. 1 in no. 41: Colley to Childers, 19 December 1880.

by overland cable since 1864 and Durban with Cape Town since April 1878, but it had still taken a steamer at least 16 days from Cape Town to reach the nearest international telegraph station on the Cape Verde Islands or Madeira. But since December 1879 a submarine cable had linked Durban via Delagoa Bay, Zanzibar and Aden to London permitting the government to respond to Colley's every communication with disconcerting despatch.[5]

While Colley began his preparations, the Boers were already seizing the military initiative. They knew that the British garrisons were busy preparing their defences against possible Boer attacks, and anticipated that Colley must march from Natal to secure Pretoria, the seat of the administration. The Triumvirate's strategy was not to storm the posts held by the British since they were short of rifle ammunition, and possessed only a strange and ineffective assortment of muzzle-loading artillery pieces for siege-work: a couple of ship's guns and carronades and three amateur muzzle-loaders (only one of which saw action) constructed by Marthinus Ras, a blacksmith who lived near Rustenburg. Besides, those *burgers* who volunteered to work this handful of questionable artillery pieces had never undergone any formal training in handling them.[6] So rather than conduct a regular siege, the Boers investing the British posts were ordered to blockade the garrisons, repel any sorties and starve them into submission. In that way the British forces caught in their various outposts would be prevented from concentrating to form a field force—such as Bellairs had envisaged—strong enough to relieve Potchefstroom, threaten Heidelberg, or take the main Boer forces disputing Colley's advance from the rear.[7] As Acting Commandant General H.P. Malan would write rather deflatingly to Cronjé, who was engaging the garrison at Potchefstroom much more energetically than elsewhere,[8] the mountain pass to Natal was where the war would be decided and not around any of the beleaguered British outposts.[9]

In accordance with the strategy they had adopted, it was essential for the Boer Triumvirate to intercept those British forces ordered to concentrate on Pretoria. They had already missed their chance with the company of the 94th Regiment ordered to vacate Marabastad in the northern Transvaal, for it had promptly begun its march on 30 November and had safely reached Pretoria on 10 December, six days before the opening of hostilities.[10] That left a company of the 58th Regiment and two companies of the 94th Regiment under Captain G. Froom still making their way to Pretoria from Wakkerstroom, and a force under Lieutenant Colonel Philip R. Anstruther on the road from Lydenburg in the eastern Transvaal.

---

5   Laband, *Historical Dictionary*, p. 283.
6   Hall, 'Artillery'; Von Moltke, 'Wapentuig', pp. 17–19, 25; Friend, D., 'Training Doctrines of the Staatsartillerie of the Zuid-Afrikaansche Republiek', *Military History Journal*, 11: 5 (June 2000) < samilitaryhistory.org/journal.html> (accessed 27 August 2015).
7   Grobler, J.E.H, 'Die Beleëring van die Britse Garnisoene', in *Eerste Vryheidsoorlog*, p. 130.
8   For the early stages of the siege of Potchefstroom, see Bennett, *Potchefstroom*, chapters 4–7.
9   National Archives Repository, Pretoria (NARP) BV 17, p. 48: H.P. Malan to P.A. Cronjé, 6 January 1881.
10 Laband, *Transvaal Rebellion*, pp. 90, 116.

Lydenburg was garrisoned by the Headquarters and two companies of the 94th Regiment. On 27 November Anstruther received his orders to retire on Pretoria 188 miles away, but he was slow in setting off. It took him over a week to assemble the train necessary to move out an established garrison with all its baggage: 30 transport wagons, two mule carts, an ox-drawn ambulance, the ox-drawn regimental canteen, and a water cart. With the wagons were three women and two children along with about 60 black wagon drivers and *voorlopers*.[11] All were under the charge of two officers of the Commissariat and Transport Department (formed in 1876) and of four or five men of the under-staffed and over-worked Army Service Corps (created in 1870) which provided the NCOs and other ranks of the commissariat.[12] Also with the column were an officer of the Army Medical Department, created in 1873 when doctors were transferred there from the regimental strength, and three men of the Army Hospital Corps created in 1857 to provide orderlies and

bearers. As with the commissariat, this was an unwieldly administrative arrangement.[13]

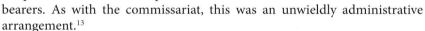

When Anstruther finally began his march on 5 December, the troops escorting the baggage train numbered six officers and 246 men of the 94th Regiment. About 60 men were left behind to hold the fortified post at Lydenburg named Fort Mary after the wife of its commander, 2nd Lieutenant Walter Long, who gamely remained by his side.[14] Because of the incessant rain and thick mist typical of summers in the eastern Transvaal, the progress of Anstruther's already delayed column was particularly slow. On 17 December, while held up at the Olifants (Lepelle) River which was in spate, Anstruther received an urgent warning from Bellairs that Boer forces were on the move in his direction, and that he should take every precaution against being

Lt. Col. Philip Anstruther, commander of the 94th Regiment in Lydenburg, was defeated at Bronkhorstspruit on 20 December 1880 while marching to Pretoria. (*Illustrated London News*, 26 February 1881)

11 *BPP* (C. 2866), enc. F in no. 76: Bellairs to Lt. Col. Anstruther, 23 November 1880; enc. G in 76: Anstruther to Bellairs, 30 November 1880; enc. H in no. 76: Anstruther to Bellairs, 5 December 1880: 94th Regiment Marching-Out State; enc. T in no. 76: Surgeon Ward to the senior Medical Officer, Transvaal, 22 December 1880; enc. S in no. 76: Anstruther to DAAG, Transvaal, 26 December 1880: notes in margin. Note that there are slight discrepancies between these tallies. A *voorloper* led the front pair of oxen drawing a wagon by a thong attached to their yoke, and the rest followed. See Laband, *Historical Dictionary*, p. 212.

12 Following an overhaul in 1880–1881 the Commissariat and Transport Department was re-designated the Commissariat and Transport Staff, and the Army Service Corps the Commissariat and Transport Corps. Only in 1888 would there be a full integration of the two branches into the Army Service Corps. See Laband, *Historical Dictionary*, p. 51.

13 These two branches were only finally combined in 1898 into the Royal Army Medical Corps. See Laband, *Historical Dictionary*, p. 7.

14 *BPP* (C. 2866), enc. H in no. 76: Anstruther to Bellairs, 5 December 1880; Long, Mrs W.H.C., *Peace and War in the Transvaal: An Account of the Defence of Fort Mary, Lydenburg* (London: Low's, 1882), chapter II.

The battlefield of Bronkhorstspruit photographed soon after the lifting of siege of Pretoria at the end of March 1881. The bones of draft-oxen still litter the road. Note the two flattened British helmets. (PAR, C. 104/2)

ambushed on the road to Pretoria. Yet Anstruther, who had fought in the Anglo-Zulu War and in the Second Anglo-Pedi War, was unwilling to take the danger too seriously. Bluff, good natured and unfussed, he held the Boers in amiable contempt and discounted their ability to take effective action.[15]

Once the Olifants River had fallen enough to cross, the column resumed its march on Monday, 20 December. The bulk of the troops led the way, followed by the wagon train and a rearguard of 20 men. In contravention of regulations for a column on the march, there were no outlying flank guards to give early warning of enemy movements. Many of the men had their tunics unbuttoned and the band continued playing a medley of popular tunes. Its firearms—along with those of some of the soldiers—were nonchalantly stowed on the wagons.[16]

The Boer commando shadowing the British with orders to prevent it from reinforcing Pretoria was under the command of Commandant Frans Joubert (1827–1904), uncle of Commandant General Piet Joubert.[17] Contemporary

15 *BPP* (C. 2866), enc. L in no. 76: Bellairs to Anstruther, 15 December 1880; enc. K in no. 76: Anstruther to AAG, Pretoria, 16 December 1880; enc. M in no. 76: Anstruther to Bellairs, 17 December 1880; enc. in no. 76: Bellairs to DAG, Pietermaritzburg, 30 December 1880: Remarks on the defeat experienced by Lt.-Col. Anstruther on the 20th December 1880; Butterfield, *War and Peace*, p. 140: Lt. J.J. Hume's account.

16 *BPP* (C. 2866), enc. Q in no. 76: Cpl. Stewart's and Pvt. Weston's statements; Butterfield, *War and Peace*, pp. 141–142: Lt. Hume's account; Great Britain, War Office, *Field Exercise and Evolution of Infantry*, pocket edition (London: Her Majesty's Stationary Office, 1877), pp. 305–310.

17 NARP: JC 26, no. 2451: P.J. Joubert to J.H.G. van der Schyff, 22 December 1880. Joubert's victory at Bronkhorstspruit would earn him the nickname of 'Frans Held' or Frans the

British reports greatly exaggerated the size of this commando to explain away defeat, but it probably numbered only about 300 men.[18]

Joubert's handling of his commando was typical of Boer tactics as they had developed by 1880. They were based on several interconnected elements: horses that gave his mounted men the advantages of mobility and surprise and permitted swift tactical withdrawals; and small-arms that, expertly handled, laid down a devastatingly heavy and accurate fire. The third classic element was the laager of ox-wagons which, when drawn up in an all-round defensive position, allowed Boers to maximise their fire-power and avoid being out-flanked. They had made the Boer military machine almost unbeatable against Africans armed with traditional sharp-edged weapons or clubs, especially when they persisted in mass attacks in the open as the amaNdebele had at Vegkop in 1836 and the amaZulu at Veglaer and Blood River (Ncome) in 1838.[19] However, while wagon-laagers might still act as effective strongholds against enemies with small-arms—and the British had employed them as such in the Anglo-Zulu War of 1879—once the enemy entered the field with artillery, as the British did in 1880, laagers lost their usefulness except as base camps.

In any case, the Boers of the ZAR and OVS had long before been forced to make adjustments to their tactics in their frequent wars against African states along their borders. Instead of fighting pitched battles in the open, as against the amaZulu, the Boers found themselves having to storm Sotho and Pedi mountain fastnesses determinedly held by warriors armed with the modern rifles which from the 1860s were becoming increasingly available to them, especially at the diamond diggings where they engaged in migrant labour. Africans such as the Basotho also adopted the pony and became as mobile as any Boer commando.[20] Consequently, the Boers in the interior began operating like mounted infantry, for to storm a defended position on high ground meant leaving horses in the rear and employing coordinated infantry fire and movement tactics in which well-aimed covering fire by selected marksmen made it difficult for the defenders to show themselves to fire back at their assailants.

In operating against an enemy not holed up in a defensive position, but on the move as was Anstruther's column, the Boer used their efficient forward scouting to track the foe. The commando would then approach under cover of dead ground (even if this meant a wide detour) in order to bring the striking force unseen to within effective rifle range. Accordingly, when Joubert's scouts reported that Anstruther's British convoy was directly north of him on the road, he ordered his men who had been riding as was normal practice in a solid column, to shake themselves out into line at intervals of ten paces. They then advanced through the sparsely scattered thorn trees

---

Hero. See Nöthling, 'Commanders', p. 78.

18 For a full discussion on all aspects of the Boer commando at Bronkhorstspruit, see Grobler, J.E.H., 'Die Sege by Bronkhorstspruit', in *Eerste Vryheidsoorlog*, pp. 118–120.

19 See Laband, *Zulu Nation*, pp. 80, 96–101.

20 See Stapleton, *Military History*, pp. 41–50, 53–4; Laband, *Zulu Warriors*, pp. 43–5.

down the gentle forward slope of the low hills parallel to the road where the ground levelled out 200 yards to its south. [21]

A mile short of the Bronkhorstspruit, and still 38 miles from Pretoria, the tootling British band was shocked into silence at about 1:20 p.m.by the menacing sight of Boer horsemen lined up on their left flank. Anstruther ordered the column to halt, the wagons to close up, and the men to get into formation with their arms. The soldiers responded with military precision but made no attempt to take cover behind the wagons. Absurdly, the band recommenced playing.

Joubert's despatch-rider, Paul de Beer, approached within 100 yards of the head of the column under a flag of truce and handed Anstruther a despatch written in English and dated 17 December. It was signed by the Boer Triumvirate. Anstruther proceeded to read it out aloud to his staff. It informed him that while the Triumvirate was still uncertain if a state of war actually existed between them and the British, it would construe any further " … movement of troops" as a " … declaration of war."[22]

Anstruther replied with some heat that he had his orders to proceed to Pretoria and would do so. But before his reply could be delivered to Joubert, Nicolaas Smit, a hardened fighter who had distinguished himself in the numerous campaigns and punitive expeditions waged by the ZAR against neighbouring African communities, including the recent Boer-Pedi War,[23] took it on himself to give the signal to attack before the advantage of surprise was frittered away. The Boers galloped forward in approved style, flung themselves off their horses about 140 yards from the road, and opened a devastating fire at close range standing, kneeling or lying spread out behind what little natural cover they could find. However, they would have been quite prepared to remount their horses and withdraw before they became too decisively engaged in a fire-fight that was going against them. Boer manpower was too precious and limited to risk taking unnecessary casualties. There was consequently no shame in withdrawing to live and fight another day and Boers, unlike the British, discounted the pointless virtue of dying in a glorious last stand.

The seasoned men of the 94th Regiment knew how they should respond to the Boer assault. During the late-Victorian era, tactical practices in the British Army were being transformed. 'Bush-fighting', with its emphasis on marksmanship, had been encouraged through accumulated experience in Victorian 'small wars' and was pushed along further by the advent of breech-loading rifles that made it possible to load and fire more rapidly, and to do so while kneeling or lying down. The 1877 edition of *Field Exercise and*

---

21 There are many recorded eye-witness accounts of the ensuing battle and its immediate aftermath. These are referred to in the secondary literature. See Bellairs, *Transvaal War*, pp. 73–91; Carter, Thomas Fortescue, *A Narrative of the Boer War: Its Causes and Results*, new ed. (Cape Town: J.C. Juta; London: John Macqueen, 1896), pp. 129–146; Lehmann, Joseph, *The First Boer War* (London: Jonathan Cape, 1972), pp. 114–130; Duxbury, *David and Goliath*, pp. 9–16; Laband, *Transvaal Rebellion*, pp. 93–100.

22 *BPP* (C. 2838), annexure 3: Kruger, M.W. Pretorius, P.J. Joubert and W. Edward Bok to the Commander-in-Chief of Her Majesty's Troops on the Road between Lydenburg and Pretoria, 17 December 1880.

23 Nöthling, 'Commanders', p. 80.

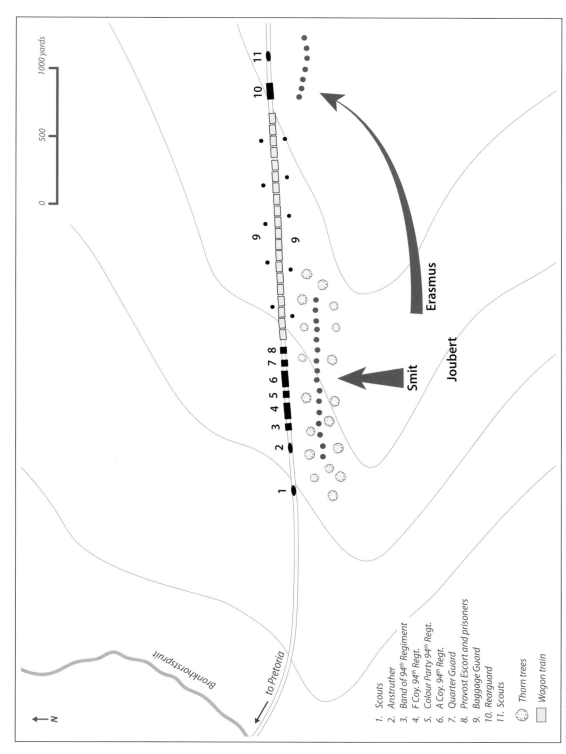

（map labels）

1000 yards
500
0

N

Bronkhorstspruit

to Pretoria

Erasmus

Smit

Joubert

1. Scouts
2. Anstruther
3. Band of 94th Regiment
4. F Coy. 94th Regt.
5. Colour Party 94th Regt.
6. A Coy. 94th Regt.
7. Quarter Guard
8. Provost Escort and prisoners
9. Baggage Guard
10. Rearguard
11. Scouts

Thorn trees

Wagon train

The battle of Bronkhorstspruit, 20 December 1880

49

Evolution of Infantry incorporated all the new tactical ideas accepted by the War Office, and this was the manual with which the officers serving in the Transvaal war ought to have been familiar, especially as it came in a convenient pocket edition. A section on 'Extended Order' replaced the regulations on skirmishing, and allowed for an interval of at least three paces between each file, and increased extension depending on circumstances. When a company was extended as a fighting line, another was supposed to act in support about 150 yards to the rear with the company commander in front. Any part of the extended line could be reinforced by throwing forward supports, with the senior officer taking command of both companies. If forced to retire, the extended firing line would fall back through the supporting line, and the two would continue falling back by alternate portions, each company covering the retreat of the other.[24]

Unfortunately for the British troops at Bronkhorstspruit, the unexpectedness and characteristic speed of the Boer attack allowed them no time to complete their regulation deployment and they had to fling themselves down in the grass to return fire while still only partly extended. To make matters worse for them, the Boers followed their usual tactics of outflanking their foes. So while the main Boer force engaged the head and centre of the British column, Commandant Erasmus led some horsemen to fall on the wagons to the rear, killing most of the rearguard and shooting or driving away the terrified African wagon drivers.

Nevertheless, all might have been well and the Boers repulsed if British marksmanship had been up to standard. The Martini-Henry bullet flattened on impact, causing massive tissue damage and splintering bones lengthways, stopping its victim in his tracks. However, the rifle depended for its effect on both range and volume. It was sighted up to 1,450 yards, but was most effective at less than 400 yards. Yet even at point-blank range (below 100 yards) a skirmishing line, with intervals of at least three paces and as many as ten, could not develop the necessary volume of fire at six shots a minute to stop a determined charge. However, at Bronkhorstspruit the troops were not facing a charge but were engaged in a fire-fight.

By 1880 marksmanship was taught and encouraged in the British army, although not practised regularly enough, and insufficient emphasis was given to individual fire. Firing from medium to long range (300 to 1,400 yards) continued to be delivered in volleys by section, and independent fire, with the men selecting their own target, was usually only ordered from close range (100 to 300 yards). Whatever the circumstances, it was vital to avoid premature firing until the enemy was within sufficient range, and to maintain fire discipline, as slower, deliberate, better-aimed fire was more effective. Obviously, an accurate estimation of range was crucial for the full effectiveness of fire. Rifles sights were calibrated, but the men relied upon their officer's orders to set them correctly—an assessment which in any case the officer might easily make incorrectly.

When the firing began at Bronkhorstspruit the British rifle sights were set to a regulation 400 yards, but when the Boers moved forward the troops failed to re-sight their rifles correctly and their fire generally went high over

---

24 Great Britain, *Field Exercise*, pp. 53–54, 97–9.

the heads of the Boers. The likely reason for this was the Boers' deliberate picking off all the officers and NCOs in the first minutes of the battle so that no orders were given to adjust sights.

By contrast, Boer musketry was excellent. *Burgers* raised on isolated farms in a harsh environment grew up tough and self-reliant with a rifle in their hands and a horse between their thighs. As habitual hunters by the age of 10 or so, they knew how best to use terrain, had learned when stalking game not to waste ammunition (which was both expensive and scarce) through inaccurate fire, and had developed an ability to judge distance precisely. These engrained skills resulted in accurate individual fire in combat and in the initiative essential in irregular warfare when men were widely scattered and not in close communication with their leaders. Ironically, the eradication of much game through effective hunting meant that by 1880 younger Boers were getting less shooting practice, and their relative 'de-skilling' meant that middle-aged men were on the whole better shots.[25]

Be that as it may, at Bronkhorstspruit the Boers set up stone range markers to assist the accuracy of their fire, and demonstrated just how deadly modern breech-loading rifles could be when handled correctly. They completely pinned down the British who were unable to collect arms or reserve ammunition from the wagons. Anstruther, although repeatedly wounded, rode up and down the ranks to encourage his men, but saw within 15 minutes that the situation was hopeless and that he must surrender to save further life. He ordered his troops to throw up their hats and wave handkerchiefs as a signal of surrender, and firing finally ceased when a soldier climbed onto a wagon and showed a white flag.

Joubert himself was appalled at the scale of the slaughter, the precise extent of which is not quite clear.[26] It would seem that during the battle one officer was killed and another eight wounded. Two of these died the same day and two more (of whom Anstruther was one) within the next three weeks. Fifty-six men were killed during the fight and 92 wounded, of whom at least another seven died within the month. As a testimony to the accuracy of Boer shooting, each casualty had received on average five wounds. In stark contrast, only one Boer was killed in the battle and four others lightly wounded.

In short supply of every kind of war *matériel,* the Boers comprehensively looted the stricken column of firearms, ammunition, boots, jackets, officers' swords, wagons and horses, rejoicing in what they literally regarded as a godsend.[27] Although mortally wounded, Anstruther wrote in pencil to Joubert the day after the battle invoking " … the custom of every civilized nation" to furnish the wounded with shelter, care, food and transport.[28] Joubert needed little prompting, and left 20 tents, blankets, the hospital wagon, water cart and rations to establish a camp for the British wounded in a well-watered glade of gum trees near Bronkhorstspruit. Humane Boers

---

25 Storey, *Guns, Race, and Power*, pp. 133–143; Machanik, 'Firearms'; Von Moltke, 'Wapentuig', pp.9-16.

26 NARP: BV 3, p. 90: P.J. Joubert to Kruger and M.W. Pretorius, 21 December 1880.

27 See NARP: JC 26, no. 2452: P.J. Joubert to J.H.G. van der Schyf, 22 December 1880.

28 NARP: JC 26, no. 2460: Anstruther to Joubert, 21 December 1880.

The head of the staff of the Bandmaster of the 94th Regiment which the Boers retrieved from the Bronkhorstspruit battlefield. (NARP, TAB 32625)

in the neighbourhood succoured the wounded in many ways. Joubert also allowed 20 unwounded men to remain to bury the dead and aid the wounded, but one unwounded officer and 62 men were taken prisoner to Heidelberg. Most were subsequently released over the border into the OVS.

In his official communiqué reporting the battle, Bellairs sought to ameliorate the humiliation of defeat and surrender by laying the responsibility squarely on the "negligent" Anstruther's shoulders. The debacle could thus be attributed not to a failure in the British military system, nor to the officers and soldiers who had exhibited "gallantry and endurance," but rather to an individual commanding officer's failure to exercise leadership according to laid down military principles.[29]

The only redeeming action the British took that wretched day was the saving of the Colours of the 94th Regiment. Each regiment of infantry carried two colours: the Sovereign's Colour which was the Union flag with the regimental number, and the individual Regimental Colour inscribed with its battle honours. Both were made of silk measuring three feet, nine inches by three feet, and were attached to a pike of eight feet, seven inches. The Colours were of great symbolic significance to the regiment, and to lose them was an appalling disgrace.[30] At least the 94th regiment was spared that. Some of the men tore the Colours off their pikes and hid them under the dangerously wounded Mrs Anne Fox as she lay on her stretcher. They were then passed to Conductor Richard Egerton who wound them around his waist under his civilian coat and got them safely to Pretoria.[31]

If Bronkhorstspruit came as a quite unanticipated shock to the British requiring to be explained away, it was greeted with rejoicing by the insurgent Boers of the Transvaal. Further afield, the news flared through the Afrikaner populations of the OVS, the Cape, and Natal, stimulating their nationalist aspirations and support for their gallant blood-brothers in the Transvaal. Commandant General Joubert published a proclamation in which he " … bowed down in the dust before Almighty God" who had given the victory to the heroic *burgers* in their " … war of self-defence."[32]

Joubert concluded his proclamation by blaming the British for starting the war and conducting it " … contrary to all the rules of war accepted by civilized nations." To Bellairs, however, it was the Boers who had egregiously broken the rules of war, not his troops. He responded to Joubert's provocation in his District Orders of 28 December 1880 which detailed the cautious

---

29 *BPP* (C. 2866), enc. U in no. 76: Capt. M. Churchill, DAAG: District Orders, 28 December 1880. When Bellairs initially wrote to the War Office explaining the debacle he referred to Anstruther's 'culpable negligence', a phrase the War Office thought prudent to omit from the published *British Parliamentary Papers*. See TNA: WO 32/7801, enc. in no. 079/3752: Bellair's report on Bronkhorstspruit, 21 December 1880.

30 Laband, *Historical Dictionary*, p. 48.

31 Laband, *Transvaal Rebellion*, p. 99.

32 *BPP* (C.2866) enc. V in no. 76: Proclamation by Cmdt.-Gen. Joubert and the Triumvirate, 23 December 1880; brought to Lanyon on Christmas day.

The Colours of the 94th Regiment saved at Bronkhorstspruit displayed in Pretoria in 1881 crossed with those of the 2/21st Fusiliers. (MuseumAfrica)

procedures his troops were to follow in future to guard against the Boers again carrying out their " … cunning, but savage designs" of advancing to battle stations under the cover of parlaying under a flag of truce.[33] And there is no doubt that the apparent treachery associated with the Boer attack at Bronkhorstspruit did irreversible damage to their image in the eyes of the British public.[34]

Colley was still in Pietermaritzburg while these events unfolded in the Transvaal. He was ever more conscious that animosity between the Boers and British throughout South Africa was waxing more bitter and unforgiving with every incident. He understood that it was becoming imperative to move as swiftly as he could with his relief force, not only to rescue the beleaguered garrisons in the Transvaal and restore the British administration, but also to bring the war to a rapid and successful termination before the entire subcontinent was dragged into the maelstrom.

33 *BPP* (C. 2866), enc. U in no. 76: Capt. M. Churchill, DAAG: District Orders, 28 December 1880.

34 See Lehmann, *Boer War*, pp. 122–124 for the popular denigration of the Boers in the British press.

5

The Blockaded Garrisons

When explaining Boer strategy in the Transvaal to Lord Kimberley, Colley characterised it as " … surprising and attacking in detail our troops while spread in peace garrisons."[1] To combat this, he ordered all Transvaal *landdroste* and *veldkornette* to enrol loyalists as volunteers to defend their homes and government laagers. While he was concentrating a relief column in northern Natal these defenders were to hold out as best they could but—and here Colley expressed his deep-seated decency—they were permitted to capitulate if the odds against them seemed irresistible.[2]

In Pretoria, Potchefstroom, Standerton and Wakkerstroom many of the loyalist civilians took refuge from the besieging Boers with the British garrisons in their forts, or behind hastily erected defences where they suffered considerable privations. Their menfolk organised themselves into volunteer units to support the regular troops, and saw incessant military action. Elsewhere, in Rustenburg, Lydenburg, and Marabastad, where the forts were rudimentary and the garrisons small, the civilians prudently decided to remain neutral.[3] In other villages without a British garrison civilians made no attempt to resist the Boers. On 23 December 120 Boers under Commandant Grové took formal possession of Middelburg in the eastern Transvaal without a shot being fired. His men seized the government weapons and ammunition, commandeered goods from all the stores and imposed a curfew on the inhabitants. The leading loyalists were arrested and the Boers levied a war contribution in cash and livestock on those whom they suspected might consider resistance. They then mounted guards on the town and effectively cut it off from the rest of the world for the duration. Zeerust in the western Transvaal fell to a Boer commando on Christmas day, and Utrecht in the southern Transvaal to another commando three days later. These two villages suffered much the same fate as Middelburg.[4]

On 20 December, the same day that Anstruther's column surrendered at Bronkhorstspruit, Captain G. Froom and his two companies of the 94th

---

1   *BPP* (C.2866), no. 74: Colley to Kimberley, 10 February 1881.
2   *BPP* (C. 2866), enc. 5 in no. 3: Colley to Landdrosts, Field Cornets, &c., of the Transvaal, n.d. [December 1880].
3   Laband, *Transvaal Rebellion*, pp. 107–108.
4   Laband, *Transvaal Rebellion*, pp. 113–114.

Artillerymen of N/5 Brigade, RA photographed in the Ordnance Depot during the siege of Pretoria. To the left is a 9-pounder gun and to the right an obsolete muzzle-loading ship's cannon dug out of stores. (WCPA, E3097)

Regiment and one company of the 58th Regiment from the Wakkerstroom garrison were also on the road to Pretoria. Commandant van der Schyff was mustering a commando to attack him on the march, but Froom did not share Anstruther's fate. Unencumbered by a large baggage train, he made a dash to Standerton, a small town of some 50 houses on the north bank of the Vaal River where a company of the 94th was in garrison.[5] Froom decided to halt there and help defend the town. The joint garrison under Major W.E. Montague of the 94th Regiment mustered 333 infantry and 75 Mounted Infantry, and volunteers. Together they held the military camp and the hastily constructed earthwork dubbed Fort Alice.[6]

In Heidelberg on Christmas day Commandant-General Joubert learned that the British were fortifying Standerton. His prime strategic intention remained to hold the Transvaal-Natal border against Colley, and on 27 December he set off for the border with a commando of 800 men. However, he could not permit Montague's large force to operate freely in his rear while he occupied the border passes, so he detached 100 men under Commandant Lombard to help blockade the garrison.[7]

---

5   For Froom's dash to Standerton, see Bellairs, *Transvaal War*, pp. 91–96.
6   For the defence of Standerton until the end of January, see PAR: WC III/2/13: Maj W.E. Montague to Wood, 27 March 1881: Report on the siege of Standerton; TNA: WO 32/7833, no. 079/4715: Maj W.E. Montague to Wood, 29 March 1881: Report and enclosures of the siege of Standerton.
7   NARP: BV 16, p. 11: Joubert to Kruger, 25 December 1880; NARP: BV13, p. 423: Joubert to Kruger, 21 February 1881.

The six companies of the volunteer Pretoria Rifles, the garrison of the Convent Redoubt during the siege of Pretoria, with their commandant (centre foreground), Maj. Frederick LeMesurier, RE, who was responsible for planning the defence of Pretoria. (WCPA, E3098)

News of Bronkhorstspruit reached Wakkerstroom on 24 December.[8] Captain J.M. Saunders's command comprised approximately 120 men of the two companies 58th Regiment and about 40 volunteers from among the townspeople. He disposed them in makeshift defences about the town and prepared to hold it against a Boer commando under Commandant van Staden. The Boers formed a loose cordon around Wakkerstroom, but made no serious attempt to capture it. It was otherwise in Lydenburg where the siege was prosecuted with determination. Assistant Commandant General J.P.Steyn's commando of about 200 men entered the village on 6 January 1881 and demanded that Lieutenant Long surrender Fort Mary. Long stoutly refused, and valiantly repelled many assaults by the Boers who kept up an incessant small-arms fire on the fort and bombarded it with round-shot from an old ship's cannon.[9]

On 27 December some 200 Boers forces under Commandant M.A. van der Walt occupied Rustenburg and disarmed the townspeople. The investment of the small earthwork fort began the same day when the garrison of a single company of the 2/21st Fusiliers under Captain Daniel Auchinleck refused the Boer demand to surrender. The Boers brought up one of their home-made Ras guns on 8 January 1881 and it fired ever more effectively until it

8   For the defence of Wakkerstroom until the end of January, see TNA: WO 32/7883, no. 079/4814: Capt J.M. Saunders to Wood, [?] April 1881: Report of Officer Commanding Troops at Wakkerstroom from 14 December 1880 to 24 March 1881; Laband, *Transvaal Rebellion*, pp. 110–111.

9   See TNA: WO 32/7820, no. 079/4665: 2/Lt. W. Long's report on the defence of Fort Mary, Lydenburg, n.d. [recd. 10 April 1881]; Mrs Long, *Fort Mary*, chaps. III–VIII; Laband, *Transvaal Rebellion*, pp. 114–115.

Lt. Col. Gildea debriefing an African scout during the siege of Pretoria. (WCPA, M701)

blew its breech. Van der Walt was replaced as commander on 11 January by Kruger's son-in-law, Sarel Eloff who squeezed the loyalists in town for money.[10]

Word of Bronkhorstspruit reached Marabastad on 29 December and the garrison of one company of the 94th Regiment in the fort under Captain E.S. Brook, along with 30 loyalist volunteers and 43 black Transvaal Mounted Police prepared for an attack. The 100 or so Boers investing Marabastad under Commandant Barend J. (Swart Barend) Vorster were quartered in four laagers seven or eight miles distant from the fort, and skirmished constantly with the garrison's patrols.[11]

Close to a quarter of the total of 2,000 or so Boers blockading the British garrisons was committed under Cronjé to the siege of Potchefstroom.[12] As the main commercial link with the OVS and the only outside source for ammunition it was essential to seize it, but an even greater incentive was the capture of the British garrison's two 9-pdr guns. The Boers believed the guns were essential to neutralise the British artillery in Pretoria. Then, if both Potchefstroom and the capital fell, it would be possible to reinforce Joubert with both artillery and with men released from the sieges for his

---

10   For the siege of Rustenburg up to the end of January 1881, see WO 32/7833, no. 079/4722: Capt. D. Auchinleck to DAAG, Pretoria, 7 April 1881: Defence of Rustenburg and enclosures; Laband, *Transvaal Rebellion*, pp. 90, 115.

11   See WO 32/7833, no. 079/4724: Capt. E.S. Brook to DAAG, Pretoria, 7 April 1881: Diary of siege of Marabastad; Laband, *Transvaal Rebellion*, pp. 115–116.

12   NARP: BV 13, p. 423: Joubert to Kruger, 21 February 1881.

Lt. Carden and men of the 94th Regiment, along with volunteers of the Transvaal Artillery and their Krupp 4-pounder gun, while on picquet duty outside Pretoria during the siege. (Collection of Ian Knight)

decisive encounter on the border. But the 200 British soldiers in the fort under Lieutenant Colonel R.W.C. Winsloe, who had assumed command on 12 December, along with 50 civilians, held firm over the succeeding weeks despite unremitting Boer fire and the severe shortage of rations. Boer animosity towards the loyalist commercial and administrative community in Potchefstroom was given free rein under Cronjé who severely punished any captured civilians who had taken service with the British, or who did not defer satisfactorily to the new regime.[13]

Important as Potchefstroom was, Pretoria, the military and administrative capital of the British occupation, was naturally the greatest prize to be won. In the early hours of the morning of 21 December intelligence of Bronkhorstspruit reached Pretoria. Deeply shocked, Bellairs abandoned not only his previous plans to send out flying columns to break up the Boer commandos gathering to attack Pretoria, but gave up his intention to defend the town itself.[14] All civilians in Pretoria, including the hastily recruited volunteers, were ordered to move into the established military camp about half a mile to the south-west of the town, or into what became known as the Convent Redoubt about 600 yards north-east of the camp. Bellairs reckoned he had 590 infantry of the Headquarters and four companies of the 2/21st Fusiliers, the company of the 94th Regiment that had marched in from Marabastad, and the troop of Mounted Infantry raised from the

---

13 For the siege of Potchefstroom from late December 1880 until mid-January 1881, see Bennett, *Rain of Lead*, chaps. 7–12; Laband, *Transvaal Rebellion*, pp. 111–113.

14 For accounts of the siege of Pretoria, see Bellairs, *Transvaal War*, pp. 97–171; Davey, A.M., 'The Siege of Pretoria 1880–1881', in *Archives Year Book for South African History*, Nineteenth Year, Vol. 1 (Parow, South Africa: The Government Printer, 1956), pp. 277–300, 305–7; Van Jaarsveldt, Capt A.E., 'Pretoria Gedurende die Eerste Vryheidsoorlog', *Scientia Militaria: South African Journal of Military Studies*, 1: 11 (1981), pp. 48–56; Laband, Transvaal Rebellion, pp. 117–122.

same regiment. In addition, he had the gunners of the N/5 Brigade, RA who serviced his two 9-pdr guns along with the eight lighter pieces of artillery and an old Mitrailleuse (a French volley gun with multiple barrels) which the British had taken over from the ZAR when they annexed the Transvaal, as well as the bandsmen of the 2/21st Fusiliers who took charge of a rocket with its explosive head. Taken along with some Royal Engineers and Army Service and Army Hospital Corps personnel, Bellairs probably commanded in total close to 650 British regulars. And although only a third of the civilian men in Pretoria capable of bearing arms initially volunteered for service, the number of volunteers steadily grew as the siege progressed. Eventually Bellairs had 150 men of D'Arcy's Horse (or Pretoria Carbineers), 100 Nourse's Horse (including Melvill's Scouts who were Africans attached to Nourse's Horse), and the 500 infantry of the Pretoria Rifles. In total, then, some 1,400 men were available to hold Pretoria—double the number of Boers investing them. Furthermore, the 1,000 or so Africans in Pretoria provided labour for building defences and also acted as scouts, messengers and scavengers for food.

Lanyon proclaimed martial law on 21 December now that " … certain of the inhabitants" of the Transvaal were self-evidently " … in open rebellion."[15] Bellairs, as military commander of the Transvaal, took precedence over Lanyon in the defence of Pretoria, much to the frustration of the Administrator who was in any case neutralised since he was cut off from Colley and his directives as high commissioner for most of the siege. Bellairs, with the often reluctant civilians under his control, set about strengthening his defences. Pretoria was situated in a basin encircled by hills, and in order to cover the main routes into the town, Bellairs erected four fortified posts at strategic points on these roads.

Bellairs was reasonably certain that by 6 February 1881 the Boers had established ten wagon laagers across the main approaches to Pretoria within an average radius of 10 miles of the town, and that Commandant D.J.E. Erasmus was directing operations from the Doornkloof Laager.[16] However, he greatly over-estimated the investing forces which likely numbered no more than 800 men.[17] Lieutenant Colonel George Gildea, the spirited officer commanding the 2/21st Fusiliers, was determined to mount an 'active defence' and lead out sorties against these laagers. But they were so skilfully sited that it was easy for the Boers to take any British column sallying out in the flanks or rear. Gildea nevertheless led out major sorties on 29 December 1880 and 6 January 1881 which failed to shake the Boer encirclement. During the latter sally against 40 Boers under Field Cornet Hans Botha holding the Venter's Farm Laager, a young *burger* raised a white flag without Botha's authorization. The British ceased firing and two officers, carrying white flags, went forward to negotiate. But Botha furiously tore down the Boer token of surrender, firing resumed and the two officers were shot down. The British, already infuriated by the 'treachery' of the Bronkhorstspruit ambush, chose

---

15   TNA: WO 32/7812, enc. 2 in no. 079/3974: Proclamation by Lanyon, 21 December 1880.
16   TNA: WO 32/7814, enc. 1 in no. 079/4352: Bellairs to DAG, Pietermaritzburg, 6 February 1881.
17   NARP: BV 13, p. 423: Joubert to Kruger, 21 February 1881

Boer Prisoners in Pretoria taken in the Zwartkop action on 6 January 1881. Of the 17 captured, two were mortally wounded and their commander, Hans Botha, spent weeks in the British camp hospital recovering from a number of rifle and shell-splinter wounds. (Collection of Ian Knight)

to regard this incident as another indication of Boer perfidy, and Bellairs indignantly warned his troops against similar Boer subterfuges in future.[18]

Following this unfortunate affair, the dynamic Boer Assistant Commandant General Hendrik J. Schoeman, who had been prominent in the agitation leading to the rebellion, replaced Commandant Erasmus. He was responsible for the Boer success on 16 January in repulsing the third, and largest sally led out by Gildea. Bellairs henceforth lost faith in even limited sorties and decided it was his primary duty to keep the Pretoria garrison sufficiently up to strength to offer material aid to Colley's advancing column—should it ever succeed in breaking into the Transvaal.[19]

The Boer leaders never forgot that the reduction of the British garrisons was secondary to their main strategic concern, which was to hold Colley at the Transvaal border. Now that it seemed increasingly unlikely that any of the British posts would fall to their investing forces, the blockades were firmly reduced to a strategic side-show. On 31 January Kruger ordered the Boer forces investing the British to use ammunition sparingly, and to take no offensive action against the forts unless first attacked.[20] This was a victory of sorts for the British garrisons, whether less or more closely and uncomfortably invested, for they had succeeded in their passive objective of

18   TNA: WO 327812, enc. 2 in no. 079/3974: District Orders by Colonel Bellairs, 9 January 1881; Davey, 'Siege of Pretoria', p. 289.
19   TNA: WO 32/7812, enc. 3 in no. 079/3974: Bellairs to Lanyon, 17 January 1881; TNA: WO 32/7816, enc. in no. 079/4391: Bellairs to DAG, Pietermaritzburg, 4 March 1881.
20   NARP: BV 19, pp. 273–4: Kruger to Cronjé, 31 January 1881.

standing fast and tying down Boer forces which might otherwise have been deployed more effectively on the Natal front.

All now depended on whether Colley could break through Joubert's forces holding the pass from Natal to the Transvaal and proceed to relieve the Transvaal garrisons. It was by no means certain that he would succeed. Gildea, from hard experience gained in his unsuccessful sorties out of Pretoria, had learned to know and respect the effective Boer way of war. He observed how:

> … the Boers will never attack in the open; they are most tenacious to stones and cover, and it is very hard to get them out. Their principal tactics are traps, and as they are all well mounted, and have a thorough knowledge of the country, they can travel fast, and take up positions wherever they like. Cavalry with light Artillery are the only troops that can be used with any effect against the Boers. Infantry are only useful for holding positions, as the Boers will never let them come near enough to them in the open.[21]

It remained to be seen how quickly Colley would reach an equally perceptive appraisal of the foe and, if he did, how effectively he would put it into practice.

---

21   TNA: WO 32/7812, enc. 3 in no. 079/3974: Lt. Col. Gildea to DAAG, Pretoria, 7 January 1881.

6

Assembling the Natal Field Force

On first learning on 19 December 1880 of the Boer uprising in the Transvaal, Colley (as we have seen) commenced cobbling together what troops he had available for a relief column.[1] One company of the 58th Regiment was already stationed at the village of Newcastle in the far northern apex of Natal which he intended as his forward base. This remote, untidy little settlement with its scattering of houses and stores built of corrugated iron lay on the main road north to the Transvaal along which transport riders and their wagons carried trade goods into the interior.[2] Additional troops were available from the Natal garrison whose headquarters and remount centre were at Fort Napier, established on 31 August 1843 on the hill overlooking Pietermaritzburg, the capital of Natal. The garrison, besides protecting the port of Durban and Natal itself, served as a strategic reserve for other parts of southern Africa where British interests were at stake—such as the Transvaal Territory.[3] However, for reasons of imperial economy and to encourage colonial self-defence, the garrison was always maintained at the lowest possible strength. Consequently the infantry available to Colley amounted only to four more companies of the 58th Regiment and five of the 3rd Battalion, 60th Regiment (King's Royal Rifle Corps) scattered at various posts around Natal. Two additional companies of the 3/60th Rifles were stationed far to the south

---

1   Unless otherwise specified, details concerning the operations of the Natal Field Force are taken from the official Journal of the Natal Field Force. It was initially kept from 19 December 1880 by an experienced staff officer and veteran of the Anglo-Zulu War, Brevet Maj. Edward Essex, 75th Regiment, whom Colley first appointed DAAG and QMG, South Africa on 9 December 1880, and subsequently on 2 January 1881 Staff Officer to the NFF. Maj. Hart relieved Essex on 12 March 1881. The Journal is printed in Butterfield, *War and Peace*. The entries from 19 December up to the eve of the battle of Laing's Nek on 28 January 1881 are to be found on pp. 170–192.

2   Laband, John, and Thompson, Paul, with Henderson, Sheila, *The Buffalo Border 1879: The Anglo-Zulu War in Northern Natal* (Durban: Department of History, University of Natal, Research Monograph No. 6, 1983), pp. 4–5, 8–10.

3   Dominy, Graham. *Last Outpost on the Zulu Frontiers: Fort Napier and the British Imperial Garrison* (Urbana, Chicago and Springfield: University of Illinois Press, 2016), pp. 2–3, 34–43; Spiers, Edward M., 'The British Army in South Africa: Military Government and Occupation, 1877–914', in Boyden, et al., '*Ashes and Blood*', p. 6.

in Pondoland at Fort Harrison (now Port St John's) at the mouth of the Mzimvubu River, proclaimed British territory in August 1878 to secure the natural harbour.[4] However, these troops fell under the Cape Command, and on account of the nearby Transkei Rebellion General Smyth hung onto them despite all of Colley's efforts to prise these two precious companies loose.[5]

Colley put together the mounted portion of his relief column from 25 time-expired men drawn from detachments of the 1st (King's) Dragoon Guards (KDG) and from No. 7 Company of the Army Service Corps who had been waiting at Fort Napier to proceed back to England, as well as from 60 men drawn from the 58th Regiment and 3/60th Rifles. This nascent mounted infantry still had to be suitably equipped and mounted (there was difficulty in procuring horses because of the drain of the Gun War and additional horses had to be purchased from the Cape). Colley also had at his disposal the 140 men of the Natal Mounted Police (NMP), a small standing body of quasi-military police created in 1874 and under the command of their experienced commandant Major J.G. Dartnell.[6] The NMP was the only military force maintained by the Natal government on a permanent basis because, unlike the Cape, Natal was financially incapable of taking on more for its own defence.[7] The NMP's uniform consisted of a black tunic and breeches with a white helmet. By the end of the war this dashing uniform was destined to have become so dilapidated that scarcely two men were still dressed alike. Half of them still wore battered helmets, while the rest sported peaked forage caps or smasher hats.[8]

Colley knew that mounted infantry such as these were essential for his relief column, and was concerned that he had not recruited enough of them. Mounted settler volunteer units had fought in all the recent British campaigns in South Africa, yet Colley firmly turned down all offers to raise some. As he explained on 26 December to Lord Kimberley, the Colonial Secretary:

> My greatest anxiety at present is lest this rising should turn into a war between
> the two white races in South Africa, an internecine war the results of which I
> hardly dare to contemplate. There is undoubtedly strong sympathy with the Boers
> throughout the Dutch population of Natal and the Cape Colony; and in the Free
> State it is rumoured that it has taken the form of active assistance.[9]

---

4   *BPP* (C. 2220), enc. 1 in no. 72: Lt. Gen. Thesiger to Frere, 2 September 1878.
5   Western Cape Provincial Archives and Records Service (WCPA) GH 30/17: Sir Hercules Robinson to Lt. Gen. the Hon. Sir Leicester Smyth, 17 February 1881.
6   *BPP* (C. 2783), enc. 1 in no. 41: Colley to Childers, 19 December 1880; enc. 2 in no. 49: Colley to Childers, 26 December 1880; (C. 2866), enc. 1 in no. 20: Colley to Childers, 10 January 1881.
7   Laband and Thompson, *Anglo-Zulu War*, pp. 22–23; Dominy, *Last Outpost*, pp. 145–147; Paterson, Hamish, 'The Military Organisation of the Colony of Natal, 1881–1910' (unpublished MA thesis, University of Natal, 1985), pp. 36–40, 52–54, 56–61. It was impossible for the Natal administration to contribute much more than 10 per cent of the total imperial expenditure required to maintain the garrison at Fort Napier, and during the crisis of 1880–1881 this dropped to a derisory 0.6 per cent.
8   Holt, H.P., *The Mounted Police of Natal* (London: John Murray, 1913), pp. 109–110. A 'smasher' is a felt slouch hat with the wide brim turned up on the left side.
9   *BPP* (C. 2866), no. 3: Colley to Kimberley, 26 December 1880.

Panoramic view of the field of operations from the heliograph station above Fort Amiel in Newcastle: (1) Schuinshoogte; (2) Inkwelo Mountain; (3) O'Neill's cottage; (4) Majuba; (5) Mount Prospect Camp; (6) Laing's Nek. (*Illustrated London News*, 9 April 1881)

Colley had therefore to nurse his precious mounted men carefully. He reminded them that their principal functions were scouting and guarding the column against surprise when it advanced and that in action they were to act as cavalry, supporting and covering the flanks of an infantry attack, and charging and pursing only when the opportunity arose. Revealing that he had indeed studied Boer military practices, he advised his mounted troops to avoid becoming involved in a prolonged skirmish with the Boers (whom he acknowledged were more accurate shots and better trained at mounting and dismounting quickly), and proposed that they should rather charge at the Boer horses which were left in the rear when the Boers dismounted to take up position. Boers, Colley reasoned, were not used to hand-to-hand fighting and feared being left dismounted, so such an attack would force them to abandon their position. Accordingly, he optimistically armed his mounted men with swords, as well as carbines. They would never use them. In practice, the main function of Colley's mounted men became that of patrolling along the borders of Natal, which meant watching the drifts over the Buffalo (Mzinyathi) River to the east, the passes over the Drakensberg to the west, and the main road from the Transvaal over Laing's Nek to the north, as well as acting as mounted escorts to important officers. This left few mounted men to guard the lines of communication, one of the main functions of mounted troops, and consequently supplies usually had to be brought up without a mounted escort.[10]

Nor could Colley be confident that the artillery component of the column was sufficiently strong. He had only the two 9-pdr guns of the division of N/5 Brigade, RA stationed in Natal, along with the two 7-pdr mountains guns he could requisition from the Fort Napier garrison. So he urgently requested any artillery that could be spared from the Cape Command. Commodore F.W. Richards, commanding H.M.'s Vessels, Cape of Good Hope and West Coast of Africa, who had his naval base at Simon's Town, understood Colley's need. He took it on himself to convince the cautious General Smyth to release a naval detachment from the garrison battery in Cape Town. There was nothing unusual in this since Royal Navy crews were routinely trained

---

10   Holt, *Mounted Police*, pp. 97–98.

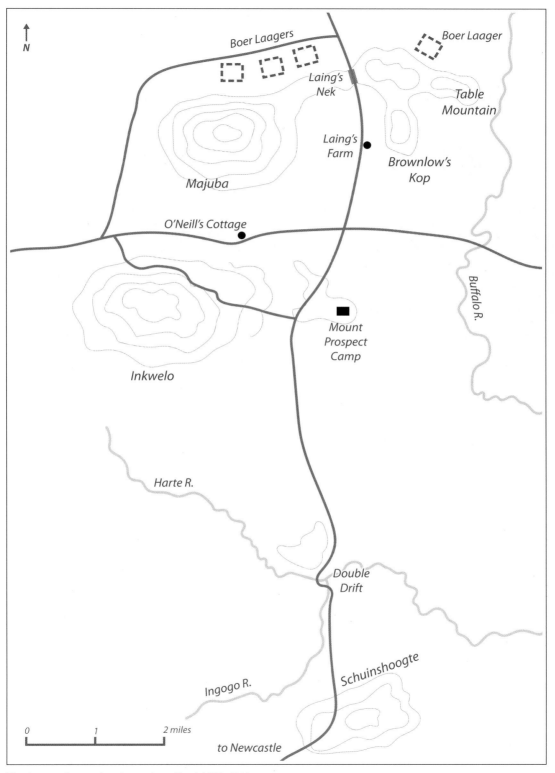

The theatre of operations in northern Natal, 1880–1881

A Gatling gun of 10/7 Brigade, RA that went into action at the battle of Ulundi on 4 July 1879 during the Anglo-Zulu War. Identical Gatling guns served with the Natal Field Force in 1880–1881. (KwaZulu-Natal Museum, Pietermaritzburg: the Ogilvie Collection)

in the use of small arms and light artillery to serve as landing parties in coastal areas when regular troops were not available. On 30 December 1880 Richards was able to offer Colley a Naval Brigade of 120 men from H.M.S. *Boadicea*. They would man serve two 9-pdr guns along with two Gatling guns. This early form of machine-gun, brought into service in 1871, could fire 200 .450 rounds a minute from ten rifled barrels rotated by a manually operated crank fed by gravity from a revolving upright case holding 40 cartridges. The Gatling could cause terrible casualties but it unsurprisingly had a tendency to jam and was normally confined to defensive action.

The Naval Brigade was also equipped with three 24-pounder Hale's rocket-tubes, approved in 1867, which fired rockets with explosive heads. The flanged rockets, which were propelled by gas, were extremely inaccurate, but their hideous shrieking sound in flight and tail of smoke and sparks was supposed to have a demoralising effect on the foe.[11]

Colley had shown during the First Asante (Ashanti) War that he excelled at administrative arrangements, which was just as well since in 1880 he again faced numerous challenges. He established a general depot at Fort Napier with remount depots there and at Newcastle. Bringing up supplies was no easy matter, as he informed Hugh Childers, the Secretary of State for War and a reformist administrator much in Gladstone's confidence.[12] Colley explained

11 *BPP* (C. 2866), no. 37 and encs: Commodore F.W. Richards to the Secretary of the Admiralty, 10 January 1881. For Gatling guns and rockets, see Von Moltke, 'Wapentuig', pp. 20–21; Laband, *Historical Dictionary*, pp. 102, 241. The Navy preferred the rocket tube which was more suitable for shipboard service over the V-shaped trough on a stand employed by land forces.

12 Carr, William, revised by Matthew, H.C.C., 'Childers, Hugh Eardley (1827–1896)', *Oxford Dictionary of National Biography* (Oxford University Press, 2004; online ed., January

that he was trying to avoid the great expenses and all " … the heavy losses, the numerous claims, and the constant labour and friction which a heavy transport train gives rise to" by contracting with private individuals for the carriage of all stores as far as Newcastle. Much would depend, though, on the efficiency and honesty of the contractors. Colley also had to arrange with Commodore Richards the tricky business of landing troops and supplies at Durban because the sandbar across the harbour in the bay meant all had to be brought ashore in lighters. Medical preparations also had to be made, and Colley established a base hospital of 100 beds in huts at Newcastle, three field hospitals of 25 beds each to accompany the troops as they advanced, with more beds and medical equipment to follow later.[13]

Newcastle in northern Natal with Fort Amiel on the heights overlooking the village surrounded by the tents of the camp of the Natal Field Force. (*Illustrated London News*, 16 April 1881)

Colley remained in Pietermaritzburg for the time being to oversee these arrangements. Meanwhile, he ordered forward the guns from Fort Napier to Newcastle, along with all the infantry and mounted troops he had collected. On 30 December Colonel Bonar Millett Deane, Colley's DAG (who had seen considerable service in India, but who had never exercised a field command), took command in Newcastle of the assembled troops whom Colley designated the Natal Field Force (NFF).[14]

Despite all his energetic efforts, Colley knew that the forces at his disposal were still insufficient for a major offensive, and he confided to his sister on New Year's Day, 1881 that he and his staff were " … sad and anxious."[15] Indeed, as soon as he had learned of the Bronkhorstspruit disaster on Christmas Eve he started pestering the War Office for the quick despatch of a cavalry regiment.[16]

The Duke of Cambridge and Childers urgently held a conference at the War Office with Kimberley on Christmas Day itself, and their military advisers convinced the Colonial Secretary of the necessity of sending Colley reinforcements immediately. On 28 December the War Office advised Colley that it was despatching a regiment of cavalry—which on overseas service was nominally made up of 27 officers and 607 men organised in four squadrons of two troops each—along with a complete, mounted field battery of six

2008) <http://www.oxforddnb.com.libproxy.wlu.ca/view/article/5296> (accessed 20 August 2015). Childers' reformist programmes elicited much opposition in naval and military circles and resulted in his frequent breakdowns in health while attempting to implement them.

13   *BPP* (C. 2866), enc. 3 in no. 29: Colley to Childers, 10 January 1881.

14   TNA: WO 32/7803, enc. 3 in no. 079/3765: Col. B.M. Deane to AAG, Pietermaritzburg, 3 January 1881.

15   Colley to his sister, 1 January 1881, quoted in Butler, *Pomeroy-Colley*, pp. 276–277.

16   TNA: WO 32/7798, no. 079/3516, Colley to Childers, telegram, 24 December 1880.

guns.[17] The War Office indicated that, in addition, it was prepared to send a further cavalry regiment and field battery, as well as an infantry regiment, all of which were about to embark from Bombay for England on the expiry of their Indian service. Their arrival could not be expected soon, however. Passage for troop ships from India to Durban took about five weeks, and between three and four weeks from England to Cape Town, when further time was required to sail the remaining 730 miles along the coast to Durban. Mobilisation for embarkation could add months to this timetable. A further difficulty was that these cavalry and artillery units would be unmounted, and Colley feared that the already considerable drain on horses in Natal would make it impossible to mount them unless the Cape was of some assistance in supplying horses.[18] But the Cape was reluctant to help, even to despatch military stores to assist Colley. General Smyth, with his typical caution, insisted it could not be done without creating " … dangerous deficiencies" for the Cape garrison should it have to take the field in Basutoland where the Gun War was being fought by Cape colonial units.[19]

Considering his problems in assembling sufficient troops, it must be questioned why Colley did not raise African levies for logistical and combat support. After all, the British and other colonial powers did so regularly in their African campaigns. It is true that the heavily outnumbered white settlers distrusted the loyalty of African levies, but sheer military necessity had always overridden these apprehensions. In the Ninth Cape Frontier War of 1877–1878, for example, Mfengu levies played the same prominent part in operations they had in all British campaigns against the amaXhosa and on the Cape eastern frontier since 1834; and in the Transkei Rebellion of 1880 (which was currently being suppressed) they were joined by Mpondo and Bhaca auxiliaries to make up the overwhelming majority of the forces deployed.[20] During the Anglo-Zulu War of 1879, no less than 7,000 of the 17,000 British and colonial troops involved were African, besides a further 8,000 black levies raised to guard the borders of Natal.[21] As for the Transvaal itself, in the Second Anglo-Pedi War of 1879 the 1,400 British infantry of Wolseley's Transvaal Field Force were outnumbered eight to one by some 11,000 African levies, auxiliaries, and Swazi allies.[22] Colley's difficulty in late 1880 was that these African forces had been engaged against solely African foes, and in terms of the racial conventions of the time it was simply

---

17 Laband, *Historical Dictionary*, p. 163

18 TNA: WO 32/7798, no. 079/3516: Kimberley to Childers, telegram, 25 December 1880; Childers to Colley, telegram, 26 December; no. 079/3522: Childers to Colley, telegram, 28 December 1880; Colley to Childers, telegram, 28 December 1880; no. 079/3531: R.G.W. Herbert (Under-Secretary of Colonies) to R. Thompson (Under-Secretary of War), 28 December 1880. See Beckett, *Victorians at War*, pp. 98–99.

19 WCPA: DD 8/81: Sir G.C. Strahan, Administrator of the Cape, to Smyth, 9 January 1881; Smyth to Robinson, 12 January 1881.

20 Stapleton, Tim, "'Valuable, Gallant and Faithful Assistants": The Fingo (or Mfengu) as Colonial Military Allies during the Cape-Xhosa Wars, 1835–1881, in Miller (ed.), Stephen M., *Soldiers and Settlers in Africa, 1850–1918* (Leiden and Boston: Brill, 2009), pp. 15–47.

21 Laband, John, and Thompson, Paul, 'African Levies in Natal and Zululand, 1836–1906', in Miller, *Soldiers and Settlers*, pp. 52–60.

22 Laband, *Zulu Warriors*, pp. 268–269.

unthinkable to unleash them against the Boers who were, after all, white settlers. To do so would be to rally every Afrikaner across South Africa behind the Transvaal Boers, and to alarm and alienate English-speaking colonists too.

Beset by all these constraints and difficulties, Colley informed Childers that, in order to keep the Transvaal Rebellion contained, he had no alternative but to restore order with the forces he had available, assisted by reinforcements once they eventually arrived.[23] Indeed, the Bronkhorstspruit debacle had entirely changed the complexion of the uprising. From Pietermaritzburg Colley issued a general order to the troops on 28 December informing them of the disaster and expressing his faith in their " … courage, spirit and discipline" to vindicate British honour. Concerned that anger at Boer 'treachery' might tempt them to abandon normal military constraints, he exhorted them not to permit their outrage to " … degenerate into a feeling of revenge." And with a complacency that was to prove fatal, he concluded: "It is scarcely necessary to remind soldiers of the incalculable advantages which discipline, organization, and trained skill give them over more numerous but undisciplined forces."[24]

While Colley was urgently assembling the NFF and moving it towards the Transvaal border, Commandant General Joubert was on the watch. He had earlier anticipated a British thrust from Natal, and was convinced it would be by way of Laing's Nek, the shortest wagon road from Natal into the Transvaal.[25] Just south of the Transvaal border, the execrable road north out of Newcastle came up against a semi-circle of hills, six miles in length, rising up from the undulating grassy plain.[26] There was no way around them to the east because there the ground falls away below a low, rocky hill (later known to the British as Brownlow's Kop) to the deep valley of the Buffalo River where it swirls through a rugged gorge. It was possible to edge past the line of hills to the west where they rear up in a final flourish to a great flat-topped mass with steep sides and deep wooded ravines called Majuba Mountain (*amajuba* means "doves" in isiZulu). But that meant a considerable detour over difficult terrain with barely a track between Majuba and Inkwelo, another flat-topped mountain rising in the plain to its south. That left the wagon road as Colley's only viable alternative. It skirted the lower spurs of Majuba that commanded it from the west and went over a pass—or *nek*—that pushed through the centre of the barricade of hills at Laing's Nek (named after Henry Laing whose farm lay below). Between the *nek* and Majuba to its west are an impassable series of ridges, shoulders, and deeply furrowed ravines. Commanding the road to the east of the *nek* is a flat-topped feature about 1,000 yards in length and 600 feet above the plain which the British called Table Mountain, and the Boers Engelbrecht Kop.

23 *BPP* (C. 2783), enc. 2 in no. 49: Colley to Childers, 26 December 1880.
24 Lt. Col. A.H. Wavell, AAG, to the troops, 28 December 1880, quoted in Norris-Newman, Charles, *With the Boers in the Transvaal and Orange Free State in 1880–1*, 2nd ed. (London: Abbott, Jones, 1882), pp. 129–130.
25 NARP: JC 25, no. 2389: P.J. Joubert to J.J.G. van der Schyff, 13 December 1880.
26 For a contemporary account of the route between Newcastle and Pretoria and a description of its inhabitants along the way, see Trollope, Anthony, *South Africa*, reprint of the 1878 ed. (Cape Town: A.A. Balkema, 1973), pp. 250–268.

Between it and Brownlow's Kop is another round, rocky hill. In all, this range of hills was a position of great natural strength for defence, lending itself to effective flanking fire across bare, steep slopes.[27]

During the last week of December mounted Boers began patrolling their border with Natal, and reported on Colley's preparations.[28] Joubert acted with determination. Leaving operations against the British garrisons within the Transvaal to acting Commandant General H.P. Malan, on 27 December Joubert led a commando of 800 riders out of Heidelberg, the provisional Boer capital, and advanced towards the vicinity of the strategic pass at Laing's Nek from where he intended to direct operations. On 2 January 1881 the commando established a wagon laager in Transvaal territory at the Meeks' white-washed store three miles beyond where the road levels out after the steep climb to Laing's Nek.[29] From this base Boer mounted patrols kept an eye on British movements, and were shadowed in turn by British scouts. Joubert did not anticipate that Colley would advance until his concentration at Newcastle was complete.[30]

For his own part, Joubert feared that his commando was too small for the part it was expected to play. During the next few weeks it was reinforced by only a trickle of men from various parts of the Transvaal because not all eligible *burgers* had responded to his call to mobilise, and others had already deserted. Moreover, some making their way to Laing's Nek had stopped off instead to assist *burgers* in their investment of the British posts at Standerton and Wakkerstroom.[31] As a consequence, by the end of January there were probably no more than 1,000 *burgers* in that field of operations. And not only was Joubert's commando weak in numbers, it also lacked sufficient ammunition for any prolonged engagement. Each man carried about 75 rounds of his own, but there was no reserve ammunition and heavy rains after 24 January damaged their stocks. Kruger was proving slow in despatching more ammunition from Heidelberg, and none was being supplied by the neutral OVS.[32]

On the Natal side of Laing's Nek, 622 officers and men of the NFF had assembled in Newcastle by 2 January 1881. Grossly inflated intelligence led the British to believe that they were facing 5,000 Boers. But confident in their professionalism, the British officers shrugged off the disadvantage of being apparently outnumbered by eight to one, and planned to advance on 10 January. The column's forward base where its supplies would be assembled was to be Fort Amiel at Newcastle, which a detachment of the 80th Regiment (Staffordshire Volunteers) had constructed in 1878 on the high ground north of the Ncandu River overlooking the village. Its stone wall

---

27 TNA: WO/7818: Wood to Childers, 30 March 1881.

28 NARP: BV 16, pp. 26–27: Van der Schyff to Joubert, 31 December 1880.

29 Norris-Newman, *With the Boers*, p. 187. The Boers later used the store as a hospital.

30 NARP: BV 16, p. 30: Joubert to Kruger and M.W. Pretorius, 7 January 1881; NARP: JC 26, no. 2452: Jooernaal Geschreven door de Heer A. Faure vanaf de Zesde January 1881 oor die Oorlog tusschen de Boeren en Ingelsche.

31 NARP: BV 11, pp. 106–107: Joubert to Kruger, 17 January 1881; p. 157: Joubert to Kruger, 24 January 1881; pp. 177–178: Joubert to Kruger, 26 January 1881; NARP: JC 26, no. 2424: Kruger to Joubert, 4 February 1881.

32 NARP: BV 11, pp. 177–181: Joubert to Kruger, 26 January 1881; pp. 182–3: Joubert to Kruger, 26 January 1881.

and ditch already enclosed officers' quarters, barracks, a hospital, and stores, but on 4 January the NFF began to enlarge and strengthened it.[33] A month's supply of provisions was loaded on wagons that formed part of the sides of the fort, and batteries were constructed for the guns. A laager of wagons was formed in the hollow below the fort for the oxen, mules and horses. Major William Ogilvy of the 3/60th Rifles was given command of the garrison. A telegraph line was laid from the fort to join the main line to headquarters in Pietermaritzburg 180 miles away. Since the line might well be cut by Boer patrols, Colley also established a chain of heliographs which took about three hours to transmit a message between the two places. Cloudy weather could render the heliograph useless for days at a stretch during Natal's rainy summer, but that had to be weighed against sending a dispatch rider who would take three to four days to make the journey.

On 6 January when NMP patrols reported that Joubert's commando intended to attack Newcastle, the tented military camp next to the river was drawn in towards the protection of the fort.[34] The NFF was put on full alert, and two further companies of the 3/60th Rifles on the road to Newcastle (a total of 126 all ranks)—who had merrily been singing 'My Grandfather's Clock' to the accompaniment of two whistles and a makeshift drum played on with two sticks[35]—were ordered to push on over the last 20 mile without halting for the night. For the next few days British scouts continued to encounter small Boer patrols within only a few miles of Newcastle, but Boer activity diminished. As it was clear no Boer attack was in fact imminent, and as the weather continued very hot, bathing parades were ordered for the troops.[36]

On 11 January Colley and his personal staff, escorted by Commandant Mansel and the NMP, rode into Fort Amiel, where Colley established his new headquarters. On 14 January a detachment of 58 mounted infantry under Major William Brownlow trotted into camp.[37] The Remount Committee and the Transport Department were kept busy finding the horses, mules, oxen and wagons required for the impending advance, and in corralling and parking them. Heavy rain on 16 and 17 January caused the rivers to rise several feet and delayed the arrival of the latest detachment from Pietermaritzburg until 18 January. On that day Lieutenant Colonel Cromer Ashburnham of the 3/60th Rifles marched in with another 364 officer and men, including 50 very necessary mounted infantry. The NFF had now come close to doubling its

---

33 The fort, which had functioned as a rear depot and hospital during the Anglo-Zulu War, continued in use by the British during the Anglo-Boer War of 1899–1902. Since restored to the way it looked in *circa* 1902, it now houses a museum. See Laband, Thompson with Henderson, *Buffalo Border*, pp. 88–89; Laband and Thompson, *Anglo-Zulu War*, pp. 144–145.

34 *BPP* (C. 2740), no. 77: Colley to Childers, 5 January 1880.

35 Reminiscences of Lt. Percival Marling, quoted in Emery, *Marching over Africa*, pp. 102–103.

36 TNA: WO 32/7806, no. 079/3903: Colley to Childers, 19 January 1880.

37 Maj. Brownlow had not embarked in November 1880 with the KDG on HMS *Orontes* for India because he was in command of the regimental depot in Pietermaritzburg, and was still awaiting transport when the war broke out. See Cox, Elizabeth, 'The First King's Dragoon Guards in South Africa, 1879–1881', *Military History Journal*, 6: 5 (June 1985) < samilitaryhistory.org/journal.html > (accessed 2 September 2015).

strength since 21 December, and was altogether a more formidable force than it had been. But the Boers also seemed to be consolidating, and conflicting reports continued to come in of their movements and concentrations. What did seem certain is that by 18 January the Boers had occupied Laing's Nek in some strength, thus barring the road to the Transvaal, and had established three wagon laagers on its northern reverse slopes.

Colley erroneously believed the augmented NFF still to be outnumbered by the Boers on Laing's Nek. Why then did he not wait for the large reinforcements promised from overseas to come up before he attempted to force the Boer position? He answered this question himself in his letter of 17 January to Wolseley, his mentor and patron, in which he admitted to his concern that public opinion in Britain—so vital for military reputations and promotions—would censure him for being too slow in moving forward. As for it being rash to attack the Boers without reinforcements, Colley explained that it was nevertheless essential to do so because of the Bronkhorstspruit disaster. The vindication of British honour came into it, but the real imperative was the relief of the invested garrisons. Colley believed most posts could hold out for several months, but he was persuaded that Potchefstroom with its inadequate supplies would fall to the Boers unless relieved before the middle of February. This consideration justified attempting to break through at Laing's Nek. If he succeeded in doing so, Colley planned to push forward to Standerton and to dig in there until reinforced or, strengthened by the Standerton garrison, to advance towards Heidelberg and try to bring the Boers to a decisive battle. This was certainly not without risk, especially without sufficient mounted support. Alternatively, if he were repulsed at Laing's Nek, he calculated that he could always hold on at Mount Prospect—a wide ridge south of Laing's Nek which the Boers called Kokshoogte—until reinforced. Either way, Colley admitted to Wolseley that his men were growing anxious under a veneer of cheery confidence, and that his devoted staff, " … shake their heads gloomily" at the prospect of an immediate advance.[38] However, Colley was not to be dissuaded from the course he had decided on. Two days after writing to Wolseley, he offered the identical justification to Kimberley and Childers for a general advance.[39]

Already, on the moonlight night of 18 January Major J. Ruscombe Poole, RA, Colley's DAAG, had left the Newcastle camp with an escort of 50 NMP and reconnoitred some distance up Laing's Nek.[40] He reported the road clear. More welcome reinforcements were coming up, including some much-needed drafts for the under-strength companies that had disembarked in Durban on 26 December.[41] The Naval Brigade of 128 officers and men, which had landed in Durban on 5 January under Commander Francis Romilly, marched into camp on the evening of 19 January.[42] They were dressed in

---

38 Colley to Wolseley, 17 January 1881, quoted in Butler, *Pomeroy-Colley*, pp. 282–284.

39 *BPP* (C. 2866), no. 49: Colley to Kimberley, 19 January 1881; no. 58: Colley to Childers, 19 January 1881.

40 Colley had recalled Ruscombe Poole from the Castle in Cape Town where he had been serving since September 1879 as the custodian of the deposed Zulu king, Cetshwayo kaMpande.

41 *BPP* (C. 2740), enc. in no. 75: Colley to Childers, telegram, 31 December 1880.

42 *BPP* (C. 2866), enc. 1 in no. 20: Colley to Childers, 10 January 1881.

an assortment of styles of blue uniform, which officers sometimes varied with a white jacket and white canvas leggings or trousers. Many favoured the broad-brimmed straw sennet over their usual headgear.[43] With them were more mounted infantry and other details, making a total of 329 all ranks. The afternoon of Sunday 23 January was hot and dry after days of rain, and the general advance from Newcastle was to commence the next day. Colley reviewed the NFF and then addressed the men formed up in a square to hear to his necessary words of encouragement.

Also on the eve of his advance, Colley wrote Commandant-General Joubert a letter quite stunning in its arrogance and condescension, and unintentionally provocative in its tone. Nothing could better express the gulf of incomprehension that divided the two sides, nor expose more graphically the ingrained hauteur of the imperial stance. Colley began by assuring Joubert that he was still, " … anxious to avoid unnecessary bloodshed" (which was true enough) and called on him to dismiss his men. If he did so, Colley undertook to consider their grievances—a promise reiterated by various British officials, administrators and officers since annexation in 1877, and destined to be scorned by any right-thinking Boer. Having offered these inadequate blandishments, Colley bluntly went on to warn Joubert "how hopeless" it was for the Boers to rebel against Britain's unlimited imperial might, even if this reality was not appreciated by the men he commanded who were "ignorant" and knew and understood "little of anything outside their own country."[44] In confirmation of just how blind he was to the deeply insulting content of his letter, Colley assured Kimberley on 10 February that he had always avoided " … all language or acts which would tend to embitter the relations" between the Boer leaders and the British government![45]

Secure in his imperial presumption, Colley led the NFF out of Newcastle at 5:00 a.m. on 24 January. The column, after its steady trickle of reinforcements (if only the British had realised it), was now more than a match numerically for the Boers holding Laing's Nek. It was made up of a total of 1,462 officers and men—of whom the Mounted Squadron and NMP constituted an inadequate 191—and artillery comprising four 9-pdrs, two 7-pdrs , two Gatling guns and three rocket-tubes. The infantry and Naval Brigade carried 70 rounds per man of Martini-Henry ammunition in their pouches, and the Mounted Squadron 60. To avoid being caught out like Anstruther at Bronkhorstspruit, Colley's exemplary order of march had the transport of 82 ox-wagons, 23 mule-wagons, three American wagons, seven Scotch carts, eight water carts, the field forge and 10 ambulances drawn by 1,338 oxen, 369 mules and 77 horses in the centre with flanking infantry, and artillery and more infantry to front and rear. The mounted men scouted in front and rear.

The column did not get far that day on account of the rain-sodden ground and steep hills—six weeks later the mud on parts of the road were reported

---

43 Sennet (or sinnet) is plaited straw, grass or palm leaf used to make sun hats. Sailors wore them with uniform in the tropics, often with long ribbons hanging down from the hatband.

44 NARP: JC 26, no. 2462: Colley to Joubert, 23 January 1881.

45 *BPP* (C. 2866), no. 74: Colley to Kimberley, 10 February 1881.

Mount Prospect Camp sketched by Capt. R.C. Birkett: (7) small defensive redoubts; (8) wagon laager; (9) camp of 3/60th Rifles; (10) camp of 58th Regiment; (11) camp of the RA and the Naval Brigade; (12) field hospital; (13) camp of 92nd Regiment and 15th Hussars. (*Graphic*, 27 February 1881)

still to be "fully two feet deep."[46] That night and the following the column laagered for protection. Distant Boer patrols monitored their advance. Finally, on Wednesday, 26 January, the column reached a spur below Mount Prospect about five miles from Laing's Nek. Following the textbook instructions for the creation of a secure entrenched camp, Colley ordered the wagons to form a wagon laager.[47] Three entrenchments were prepared at almost opposite angles of the laager to be occupied as posts by the garrison left in charge of the wagons and animals when the bulk of the column attempted to force Laing's Nek the following day. In the early afternoon, soon after the laager was formed, a violent thunderstorm broke over Mount Prospect Camp and heavy rain fell throughout the night.

Throughout 27 January Joubert and his commanders on Laing's Nek followed the laborious British progress through their telescopes, and were prepared to face the intended British attack the next day.[48] But continuous rain and thick, heavy mist caused Colley to postpone his intended advance. The Boers nevertheless remained in position on the heights throughout the

---

46 TNA: WO 32/7833, no. 079/4743: Report by Lt. T. Brotherton, RE, 19 April 1881. For an extremely detailed report, intended for the eyes of Cambridge and Childers, on the deplorable state of communications in the Natal theatre, see TNA: WO 32/7830, no. 079/4999: Brig. Gen. J.W. Baker, Inspector General of the Lines of Communication and Base to the QMG, Horse Guards, 31 May 1881.

47 Great Britain, War Office, *Text Book of Fortification and Military Engineering, for Use at the Royal Military Academy, Woolwich*, 2nd ed. (London: Her Majesty's Stationary Office, 1884), Part I, p. 122. This 1884 edition is essentially the same as the first one of 1878 which would have guided officers in 1880–1881.

48 NARP: BV 11, pp. 182–183: Joubert to Kruger, 26 January 1881; NARP: JC 26, no. 2452: Jooernaal Geschreven door te Heer A. Faure.

day and through the coming night in case the British should make a sudden advance.

While the Boer and British forces confronted each other and a pitched battle seemed imminent, efforts were being made to contain the conflict. To the discomfiture of the British authorities, general sentiment undoubtedly favoured the rebel cause. Throughout the Cape Colony and OVS meetings were held and resolutions passed calling on the British not to enforce their will lest they fatally alienate Afrikaner opinion. In the Netherlands, which felt a deep cultural and ethnic affinity with the Boers, 7,000 people signed an appeal for a peaceful settlement which was presented to the British parliament. In Natal, which had strong trade and business links with the Transvaal, there were vigorous calls for neutrality in both official and commercial circles despite the fact that most Natal settlers were English-speaking. Subscriptions were got up in the Cape and OVS to start a Red Cross society for helping the Boer wounded, and large quantities of provisions, arms and ammunition were sent to the Transvaal through the OVS despite its official neutrality. In this increasingly polarised atmosphere the one voice of statesmanship was that of President Johannes H. Brand of the OVS who believed wholeheartedly in the benefits for South Africa as a whole of Boer–British cooperation. On 25 January he telegraphed Lord Kimberley suggesting mediation. At the Cape the recently arrived new governor, Sir Hercules Robinson, caught gratefully at this initiative. Nevertheless, a promising flow of telegrams, aimed at preventing further bloodshed, was interrupted on 28 January with news that the British and Boers had fought a battle at Laing's Nek.[49]

---

49 Norris-Newman, *With the Boers*, pp. 131–133, 142–145. Brand's and Robinson's telegrams are quoted on pp. 144–145.

7

Laing's Nek and Ingogo

Anticipating that Colley would advance by way of the wagon road over Laing's Nek, Joubert placed his two strongest contingents across the *nek* itself and to the west of the road. A smaller detachment under Commandant Gert Engelbrecht held the rocky hill (Brownlow's Kop) on the far left of the Boer position with 50 men, while Commandant Greyling was positioned on Table Mountain closer to the *nek*. Commandant Basson held the ground between them with 33 men.[1] Joubert put the total number of Boer defenders at 600.[2]

On the evening of 27 January Colley called his senior officers together and informed them of his plan.[3] His intention was first to distract the Boers by opening fire on their positions from one of Majuba's broad spurs, about 2,300 yards away, with his four 9-pdrs, two 7-pdrs and three 24-pdr rockets. The artillery would be supported in threatening the *nek* by the 66 NMP, the 88 men of the Naval Brigade and the 334 men of the 3/60th Rifles. Meanwhile, the 494 men of 58th Regiment would advance up the spur at the eastern end of Table Mountain—which Colley considered the key to the whole Boer position—supported by the Mounted Squadron of 119 men going up the hills to the right to turn the Boers' left flank. Having seized the mountain, the infantry would roll up the Boer defences. Such was Colley's intention, but the day's fighting dictated otherwise.

---

1   Grobler, J.E.H., 'Die Britse Terugslag by Laingsnek', in *Die Eerste Vryheidsoorlog* , p. 149.
2   NARP: BV 11, p. 205: Joubert to Kruger, 30 January 1881.
3   For the first-hand reports of the battle upon which the following account is primarily based, see TNA: WO 32/7810, no. 079/4016: Colley to Childers, 1 February 1881; Butterfield, *War and Peace*, pp. 192–8: Journal of the Natal Field Force, Friday, 28 January 1881; *BPP* (C. 2837), no. 2: Colley to Childers, telegram, 28 January 1881; Colley to Childers, telegram, 29 January 1881; *BPP* (C. 2866), no. 69: Colley to Kimberley, 1 February 1881; enc. in no. 73: Commander F. Romilly to Commodore F.W. Richards, 29 January 1881; Colley to Wolseley, 30 January 1881, quoted in Butler, *Pomeroy-Colley*, pp. 285–289; Carter, *Boer War*, pp. 161–172. T.F. Carter, the correspondent for the *Times of Natal*, had been delayed by the appalling roads and had only reached Newcastle, 24 miles away, on the day of the battle (p. 159). But he was able to interview the British participants on the days immediately following. Also see Norris-Newman, *With the Boers*, pp. 146–153, 177–178; Lady Bellairs, *Transvaal War*, pp. 373–376; Ransford, Oliver N., *The Battle of Majuba Hill: The First Boer War* (London: Thomas Y. Crowell, 1967), pp. 43–51; Lehmann, *Boer War*, pp. 132–159; Grobler, 'Laingsnek', pp. 149–156; Laband, *Transvaal Rebellion*, pp. 146–160.

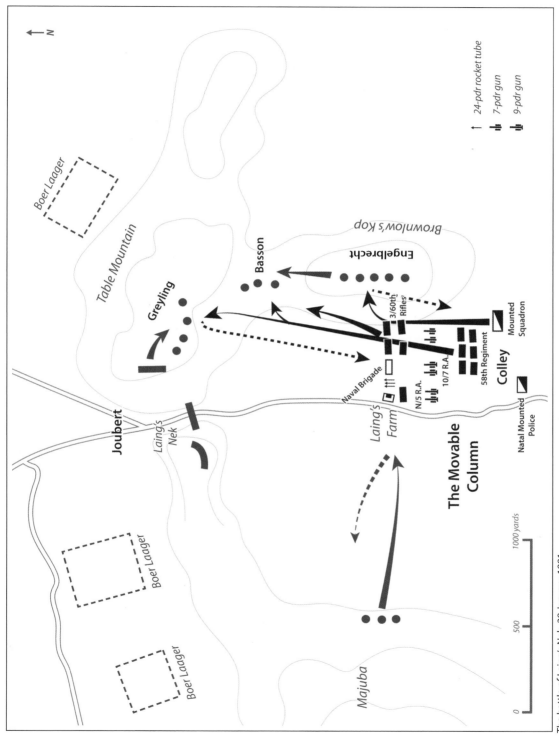

← N

24-pdr rocket tube
7-pdr gun
9-pdr gun

Boer Laager

Table Mountain

Greyling

Basson

Brownlow's Kop

Engelbrecht

3/60th Rifles

Mounted Squadron

58th Regiment

10/7 R.A.

Colley

Naval Brigade

N/5 R.A.

Laing's Farm

Natal Mounted Police

Joubert

Laing's Nek

The Movable Column

Boer Laager

Boer Laager

Majuba

1000 yards

500

0

The battle of Laing's Nek, 28 January 1881

Colley's Movable Column (as it was officially named), numbering 1,211 officers and men, marched out of camp at about 6:15 a.m. with the NMP as an advance-guard. The infantry carried 70 rounds a man. At 9:25 a.m. the artillery and rockets opened fire on the Boer positions across the *nek* and on the reverse slopes, where many men and their horses were collected. Although, as Joubert later admitted, the Boers had " … at first a dread of artillery fire" (and were especially taken aback by the erratic rockets), they quickly realised it was relatively ineffectual and took cover behind rocks and natural folds in the ground.[4]

At 9:40 a.m. Colley ordered the 58th Regiment forward and detached five of his staff officers (who remained mounted) to accompany the attack—a most unusual procedure because the 'proper province' of staff officers was to supervise the attack and not usurp the role of regimental officers.[5] Colonel Deane, who nominally commanded the NFF, immediately took personal command. Covered by rapid artillery fire directed at Table Mountain, and supported far away on its right flank by the Mounted Squadron under Major Brownlow, the 58th Regiment started its advance over the difficult terrain in a tightly packed column four abreast. Quickly becoming exhausted by the hot summer weather as they moved up the broad spur which falls away very steeply from the eastern end of Table Mountain, they came under flanking fire on their right from Engelbrecht's well-concealed skirmishers 900 yards away on Brownlow's Kop. Brownlow, at the head of Mounted Squadron, acted in the impetuous style of the cavalry officer that he was. So, instead of dismounting his men and directing them up the slope in skirmishing order as was appropriate for mounted infantry, he instead led his men in a charge straight up the steepest part of the hill.[6] Basson's horsemen positioned to Engelbrecht's right between Brownlow's Kop and Table Mountain hurriedly reinforced the latter, dismounting (as mounted infantry should) to fire at close range. Many of the Mounted Squadron, who had only recently been mustered as mounted infantry, possessed inadequate riding skills and most of their horses were ill-trained. They were quickly demoralised by the Boer fire. Instead of charging home they halted, turned and blundered down the hill again as fast as they could go.[7]

With their right flank exposed to the now unimpeded Boer fire, the only option for the 58th Regiment was to break into an exhausting, stumbling, crouching half-run to make the summit of Table Mountain. The Boers holding it, although being steadily reinforced, still probably did not number more than between 70 and 80 in number. The British clearly saw several armed *agterryers* among them and were shocked that Africans were fighting in the Boer lines against white men.[8]

At about 10:40 a.m. Colonel Deane, who was leading his men still mounted, reached the ridge where the spur finally joined Table Mountain. He found

4   TNA: WO 32/7818, no. 079/4532: Wood to Childers, 30 March 1881.
5   Bellairs, *Transvaal War*, p. 376.
6   Norris-Newman, *With the Boers*, p. 147.
7   See the accounts of this attack given by Sgt. Madden and Pte. Venables, both British prisoners-of-war in the Boer camp, quoted in Norris-Newman, *With the Boers*, pp. 151–152.
8   Carter, *Boer War*, p. 165.

himself facing a further hillside as smooth and devoid of cover as the glacis before a fort, with the Boers snugly ensconced 160 yards away behind rocks and roughly erected stone breastworks. Deane's men arrived panting and unprepared in a confused mass at the foot of the lethal slope still in the close formation of column of companies (though now strung out over 120 yards) with their left flank completely exposed to the Boer marksmen on Table Mountain. Their packed formation was oddly anachronistic because British troops in South Africa had long since learned to fight in loose skirmishing order. Besides, the official *Field Exercise* of 1877 with which Deane ought to have been familiar, stipulated that a battalion should advance in depth with two companies deployed as skirmishers, two further companies in line some distance behind in support, and the remaining companies in line behind them. The object was to dominate the enemy with firepower while the main body was brought into the extended line as it closed to within 200 yards of the enemy for the final assault at bayonet point. While in extended order the line was permitted to lie down, or single soldiers could use their individual judgement in choosing cover. Section commanders remained to the rear of their men to keep tight control over the commencement of firing, the choice of targets and adjustment of sights. If the bayonet charge stalled, supports to the rear would assist in laying down a heavy fire to cover the retreat.[9]

Deane did urgently attempt to extend his men out of column into line in the approved fashion, but they were too exhausted by the climb and beset by heavy Boer fire to deploy effectively. So although his men were not in position, it seemed to Deane—who was tasting action for the first time in his career —that to charge remained the only option.[10] He gave the order to fix bayonets, and although many men the 58th Regiment were so fatigued that they could barely stand, let alone lift their rifles, they responded gallantly. As stipulated in the regulations they advanced cheering with the Regimental and Queen's Colours carried unfurled by two junior officers, the last time (as it turned out) that a British regiment would carry them into battle.

The Boers responded with a carefully aimed barrage that, as at Bronkhorstspruit, deliberately targeted the British officers and NCOs. As Lance-Sergeant Morris later put it, "the Boers were dead nuts on them."[11] Deane was shot dead through the head, and of the five officers on Colley's staff who had joined the attack, only Major Edward 'Lucky' Essex survived. With the officers of the 58th Regiment all dead or wounded, the command devolved on him. The 58th Regiment's bayonet charge came as close in places as 30 to 40 yards of the Boers' positions, but the Boers, who were especially averse to costly hand-to-hand fighting, resorted to the "hose-pipe" method of intense but less carefully aimed suppressing fire that was so daunting for attacking troops. Unable to maintain their momentum any further, the British troops took what little cover they could find. Boer reinforcements were being

9   Great Britian, *Field Exercise*, pp. 93–4, 96, 210–41.

10   Deane's wife had tried to "keep him in a glass case," but seeing him increasingly unhappy at his lack of active military service, had lobbied in support of his appointment to South Africa. After Laing's Nek she was treated with enormous respect because of his gallant death on the field of battle. See Beckett, *Victorians at War*, p. 26.

11   L.-Sgt. W. J. Morris to his mother, the *Northampton Mercury*, 19 March 1881, quoted in Emery, *Marching over Africa*, p. 104.

Colley's forces covering the retirement of the 58th Regiment after its failure to capture Table Mountain from the Boers at the battle of Laing's Nek on 28 January 1881. (*Illustrated London News*, 26 March 1881)

fed into the front line all through the action, and soon after 11:00 a.m., Major Essex accepted that his demoralised men could not be called on to attempt another charge. He therefore began a disciplined withdrawal supported by covering artillery and rocket fire and by the musketry of two companies of the 3/60th Rifles which Colley had moved to their right at 11:10 a.m. in order to pin down the Boer pursuers. The Colours were saved after heavy casualties to the officers and sergeants of the escorting colour party.[12]

While the 58th Regiment were retiring down the spur a detachment of mounted Boers Joubert had stationed the previous evening in a deep gorge west of the road launched a flank attack on the left of the British line. Despite being surprised, the remaining uncommitted men of the 3/60th Rifles and the sailors of the Naval Brigade drove them off.

The 58th Regiment, once it regained the foot of the spur and was almost out of the reach of enemy fire, reformed and marched back to its original position, taking proud care to maintain its order and soldierly bearing as best it could. The two supporting companies of the 3/60th Rifles then advanced and opened fire on the Boers who soon withdrew beyond range. Many of Joubert's men believed he was being too indecisive and too prudent when he failed to seize the opportunity and order the pursuit of the retreating British. But the commandant-general sensibly decided against abandoning his strong defensive position and risking his men against the British in the open, especially against artillery fire.[13]

As for the British, they were glad of the respite since after their thorough repulse they were in no condition to renew the attack. Colley pulled back very slowly but in good order towards Mount Prospect Camp, which was reached at about 4:00 p.m. There was no disguising that the Movable Column had suffered a stinging and humiliating reverse and Colley fully expected to be "gibbeted" by his critics. He deeply regretted his casualties, especially the loss of so many of his loyal and closely-bonded staff.[14] It was small consolation that Lieutenant Alan R. Hill of the 58th Regiment and Private John Doogan

---

12 Colours no longer had any place on a battlefield dominated by accurate long-range rifle fire. Wolseley believed that to order young officers to carry the Colours into battle was nothing short of murder, and in 1882 it was ordered that the practice must cease. See Knight, *British Soldier*, pp. 191–193.

13 NARP: BV 11, p. 194: Joubert to Kruger, 28 January 1881; Meintjes, *Joubert*, pp. 78–79.

14 Colley to Wolseley, 30 January 1881, quoted in Butler, *Pomeroy-Colley*, pp. 285–286, 289–90.

of the KDG were subsequently both awarded the Victoria Cross for rescuing the wounded under fire.[15]

Indeed, British losses were unacceptably heavy, particularly among the officers and NCOs. The 58th Regiment had borne the brunt. According to the returns kept by Major Essex, the regiment lost three officers and 71 other ranks killed and two officers and 99 men wounded, or a shattering 35 percent of its total strength. The Mounted Squadron lost four killed and thirteen wounded, and the Naval Brigade two killed and one wounded. Throughout the force seven officers were killed and three wounded. Colley's staff was virtually wiped out.[16] In all, 16 per cent of Colley's effective force were killed, wounded or captured, a casualty rate indicative of a thorough-going defeat.

What made these casualty figures seem even worse was that, according to Joubert's official tally, only 16 Boers had been killed or died of their wounds and another 27 wounded (mainly as a result of artillery fire).[17] Yet to inflict these minimal casualties the British had expended an inordinate amount of ammunition: an average of just over 17 rounds a man—almost double the 10 Colonel Callwell reckoned normally shot away in a typical 'small war' battle—along with close to double the number of shrapnel and common artillery shells.[18] It was all too obvious that British tactics had been found dismally wanting.

Something else struck Colley forcibly about his failure to force Laing's Nek. The Boers, he reported ruefully, had fought " … with great courage and determination" and during the close range fighting from 20 to 200 yards " … had shown no fear" of the British troops. And to add to British discomfort, not only were the Boers tougher and braver soldiers than they had given them credit for being, but they were also more gallant than cultural stereotyping had anticipated in permitting the care and removal of the British wounded.[19]

Forty men of the 58th Regiment and 20 of the Naval Brigade were detailed to bury the dead, and the medical personnel went forward to tend the wounded. It took until 8:00 p.m. to clear the field of the wounded that were carried back to Mount Prospect by 40 African bearers, where they lay groaning and crying out in the overwhelmed field hospital.[20] Unlike the egalitarian Boers, who recognised no social distinctions in death, it was

---

15 Six VCs in all were awarded during the Transvaal campaign. Three were won by members of the beleaguered garrisons, two at Laing's Nek and one at Majuba.

16 Butterfield, *War and Peace*, p. 198: Journal of the Natal Field Force, 28 January 1881. See also TNA: WO 32/7810, no. 079/4016: Colley to Childers, 1 February 1881. In the recapitulation to this report made a few days later, Colley gives the final tally as seven officers and 76 men killed and two officers and 109 men wounded with two men taken prisoner. However, although he includes two support personnel killed and two wounded, he leaves out the mounted casualties except those in the KDG (who were part of the Mounted Squadron) who had two men killed and three wounded. Commander Romilly estimated that the British lost 83 killed and 100 wounded, slightly lower than Colley's final count. See *BPP* (C. 2866), enc. in no. 73: Romilly to Richards, 29 January 1881.

17 NARP: BV 11, p. 204: Joubert to Kruger, 30 January 1881.

18 Callwell, *Small Wars*, p. 439.

19 *BPP* (C. 2866), enc. in no. 70: Colley to Childers, 1 February 1881.

20 Sgt. Henry Coombes, Army Hospital Corps, in the *Sheffield Daily Telegraph*, 5 April 1881, quoted in Emery, *Marching over Africa*, p. 106.

British practice to bury other ranks in mass graves on the battlefield, and remove officers for individual burial near the headquarters camp.[21]

The evening of the battle a badly rattled Colley, accepting as best he could " … the verdict of failure," addressed his demoralised officers and men.[22] He assured them that the entire blame for the day's repulse rested entirely upon him, not them, and that in their actions they had " … not lost one atom of the prestige of England." Colley concluded with the extraordinarily lame assurance that " … we certainly shall take possession of that hill eventually."[23] Although his men appreciated his organisational ability and personal courage, Colley's self-abnegation was hardly calculated to restore their confidence in his leadership in the field. As Lieutenant Colonel Cromer Ashburnham of the 3/60th Rifles was reported to have snorted dismissively, "You don't win a battle by making speeches or writing despatches."[24] In Britain, Colley's repulse (the press could not bring itself to describe it as a 'defeat') was not well received either, especially since it had been administered by what public opinion still contemptuously regarded as " … undisciplined bands of yeomen."[25]

Yet, despite his humiliation at Laing's Nek, Colley's own ingrained confidence in his superior tactical skills—though shaken—took only a couple of days to reassert itself. Exposing an inflexible inability to learn from experience, surprising in a man of his undoubted intellect, he assured Wolseley with inappropriate cocksureness that if he were to attack Laing's Nek again with the same number of men he would do it " … in exactly the same manner that I originally intended."[26] In stark contrast, Joubert humbly wrote on the evening of the battle from the Meeks' farm in simple, devout relief to the Assistant Commandant General, P.A. Cronjé. The British, he informed him, "[w]ith the help of God … have been repulsed with heavy losses … Looking up to God that he may further bless us."[27]

Colley assumed personal command of the NFF following Colonel Deane death at Laing's Nek. Despite the decided check his forces had suffered, Colley knew he must not withdraw. To do so would be to admit to a serious defeat and to bring about truly adverse political repercussions both in South Africa and Britain. The beleaguered garrisons in the Transvaal would be disheartened, the Boers would be encouraged to take the offensive, and waverers would be brought onto their side.[28] However, he knew that his situation at Mount Prospect was a vulnerable one. The camp was at the terminus of a long and fragile line of communications which brought up all the NFF's food, ammunition, correspondence and medical supplies, and which even the

21 Chadwick, G.A., 'War Graves Registers, Monuments, Headstones and Crosses with Special Reference to the War of 1880–1881', *Scientia Militaria: South African Journal of Military Studies*, 1: 11 (1981), pp. 31, 35.
22 Colley to Lady Colley, 28 January 1881, quoted in Butler, *Pomeroy-Colley*, p. 291.
23 Carter, *Narrative*, p. 168.
24 Lt .Percival Marling's later comment, quoted in Emery, *Marching over Africa*, p. 106.
25 *Illustrated London News* (*ILN*), 29 January 1881. See Lehmann, *Boer War*, p. 159 for the indignant response in Britain.
26 Colley to Wolseley, 30 January 1881, quoted in Butler, *Pomeroy-Colley*, p. 289.
27 Joubert to Cronje, 28 January 1881, quoted in Carter, *Boer War*, p. 172.
28 Butler, *Pomeroy-Colley*, pp. 293–294.

most amateur enemy could be counted on to attempt to sever.[29] Nevertheless, Colley refused to be daunted. On 29 January he pluckily assured Childers that the effects of his recent check were "not serious" and that his men were "in excellent spirits and eager to attack again."[30]

To strengthen his position against a possible Boer attack from Laing's Nek, Colley constructed an entrenchment on a hill about 1,600 yards east of the camp where he stationed a company of infantry and the division of 7-pdrs. On 1 February, which was the first day without rain since the battle, Colley relocated the camp which had become unsanitary in the wet weather, and the next day built two circular redoubts, each with a diameter of 60 yards, to strengthen its defences.[31]

If Colley was whistling in the dark to keep his spirits up, Joubert for his part was gloomy despite his successful repulse of the NFF at Laing's Nek. While Joubert could see that the morale of his men engaged in strengthening their defences across Laing's Nek was excellent, the commandant general also knew that they were suffering from exposure in the wet weather.[32] He was also concerned that Colley would attack again. So he wrote urgently to Kruger (whose considerable military experience gained fighting Africans he valued) begging him to come to the front with other advisers, and urgently requested reinforcement from Piet Cronjé at Potchefstroom.[33]

While he awaited Kruger's response, Joubert sent mounted patrols deep into Natal as far as the Biggarsberg, a great bush-covered spur of the Drakensberg Mountains over 30 miles south of Newcastle. Ranging freely, they kept him thoroughly informed of every British move. At the beginning of February Joubert learned from his scouts that large British reinforcements, which had landed in Durban in late January, had reached Pietermaritzburg and were now on their way to Mount Prospect. At a council of war Joubert and his officers resolved that every effort must be made to prevent these troops reaching Colley. Accordingly, at 6:00 p.m. on 5 February Field Commandant General Nicolaas Smit (dourly basking in the reputation he had confirmed at Bronkhorstspruit of being the ablest of the Boer military commanders) led out a patrol of 205 men to intercept the reinforcements.[34]

On 8 February Colley received a telegraph from Fort Amiel informing him that it would be unwise to send the anticipated wagon convoy of supplies forward to Mount Prospect because of increased Boer activity in the vicinity.[35] Colley decided he must act at once to remove this growing threat along his lines of communication and supply by making a demonstration in force along the road to Newcastle.

29 For operations by the NFF between the engagements at Laing's Nek and Ingogo, see Butterfield, *War and Peace*, pp. 198–201: Journal of the Natal Field Force, 29 January–7 February 1881.
30 *BPP* (C. 2837), no. 6: Colley to Childers, 30 January 1881
31 TNA: WO 32/7810, no. 079/4016: Colley to Childers, 1 February 1881.
32 Grobler, 'Laingsnek', p. 157. See Norris-Newman, *With the Boers*, p. 170.
33 NARP: BV 1, p. 195: Joubert to Kruger, 28 January 1881; pp. 204–205: Joubert to Kruger, 30 January 1881; p. 263: Joubert to Kruger, 3 February 188; *De Staatscourant Gedurenden den Vrijheidsoorlog van 1881*, p. 17: Joubert to P.A. Cronje, 28 January 1881.
34 Meintjes, *Joubert*, p. 79.
35 Carter, *Boer War*, p. 196.

At first light on 8 February some ambulance wagons and mail carts set out from Mount Prospect for Newcastle.[36] Colley planned to give them a good start and then to follow with a strong escort to see them safely over the most hazardous points of the route before escorting back the stalled convoy from Newcastle. But instead of remaining in camp to direct and coordinate operations and delegating the command of the escort to his next senior officer, Colley himself took command.[37] At 8:30 a.m. he led out six staff officers including a chaplain and civilian interpreter, five companies and the Headquarters (11 officers and 295 men) of the 3/60th Rifles under Colonel Ashburnham, four men of the 2/21st Fusiliers to act as stretcher bearers, and two medical personnel. With them went the Natal garrison's division of two 7-pdr mountain guns and a division of two 9-pdr field guns of N/5 Brigade, RA under Captain Greer, RA , along with another officer and 28 artillerymen to work them. A detachment of three officers and 40 men of the Mounted Squadron under Major Brownlow were detailed to patrol the road ahead. It might well be thought that this mission to escort in a convoy would have been better suited to mounted troops than to infantry, but Colley had few available. He had sent the NMP back to Newcastle to patrol against Boer raiders, and the mounted infantry had suffered heavily at Laing's Nek.

As it was, Colley believed that his column was too strong for the Boers to dare attack it. He consequently gave no orders to issue rations or for a water cart to accompany the column since he expected to be back at Mount Prospect by 3:30 p.m. Once again, the British were under-estimating Boer military resolve and initiative.

About two-and-a-half miles south of Mount Prospect the wagon road crossed the Harte (Imbezane) River by a rocky drift just before it flows into the Ingogo River. A hundred yards further on was another drift across the Ingogo. That morning of 28 February the water at the drifts was only knee-height. Past the double drifts the road climbed gently to a rocky plateau about a mile-and-a-half away, known as Schuinshoogte. Colley detached the two 7-pdrs and one company of the 3/60th Rifles to take up position on a lower spur of the high ground overlooking the two drifts from the north to command the approaches should Boers attempt to dispute his return, and ordered up a company of the 58th Regiment from the camp to reinforce them.

Alerted that Colley was on the move, Smit, whose commando was bivouacked to the west of Schuinshoogte in the foothills of the Drakensberg where it was waiting to intercept the British reinforcements expected

---

36 For first-hand accounts of the battle of Ingogo (Schuinshoogte) upon which the following description are based see, unless otherwise indicated: *BPP* (C. 2837), no. 22: Colley to Childers, 9 February 1881; TNA: WO 32/7813, no. 079/4184: Colley to Childers, 12 February 1881; Butterfield, *War and Peace*, pp. 201–206: Journal of the Natal Field Force, Tuesday, 8 February and Wednesday, 9 February 1881; Butler, *Pomeroy-Colley*, pp. 297–315; Carter, *Boer War,* pp. 197–226. Carter accompanied Colley's column across the Ingogo and was present at the battle and during the retirement that night. See also Norris-Newman, *With the Boers*, pp. 157–164, 344–349; Bellairs , *Transvaal War*, pp. 377–379; Ransford, *Majuba*, pp. 51–60; Lehmann, *Boer War*, pp. 160–183; Grobler, J.E.H. 'Schuinshoogte', in *Eerste Vryheidsoorlog*, pp. 163–175; Laband, *Transvaal Rebellion*, pp. 146–160.

37 Bellairs, *Transvaal War*, p. 379.

Headquarters
7-pdr gun
Hospital
1 Mounted Squadron
2 Half Companies, 3/60th Rifles

1000 yards
500
0

to Mount Prospect Camp

Boer Supports

Smit

Boer Supports

Colley

to Newcastle

The battle of Ingogo (Schuinshoogte), 8 February 1881

The battle of Ingogo, or Schuinshoogte, on 8 February 1881 sketched by Capt. R.C. Birkett. (*Graphic*, 8 February 1881)

to be marching north from Newcastle, immediately roused his men. They hurried eastwards towards Schuinshoogte where Smit intended to attack the British while strung out on the march, just as he had done so successfully at Bronkhorstspruit. Smit's force accordingly took up position in a skirmishing line with several bodies in support on a low ridge about 1,000 yards from the road.

Mounted vedettes duly warned Colley of their presence, and he pushed forward with an advanced guard to occupy the edge of the ridge where the road ascended Schuinshoogte. The highest point of the position was a plateau, roughly triangular in shape, covered in short grass with a perimeter of rough outcrops of rock. As the British artillery came up onto the heights of the plateau, Smit ordered his force down from the ridge to take up position at the foot of the plateau where they dismounted and scattered for cover, setting up a heavy and accurate fire on the two British 9-pdr guns and skirmishers who were beginning to come into action. Butler later wrote that with this intrepid movement the Boers seized the initiative and sealed the fortunes of the day.[38]

When the four British infantry companies came up onto the plateau Colley extended them in skirmishing order around part of the rocky perimeter on both sides of the guns facing the Boers, the right flank parallel to the road, and returned fire. But the Boers did not disperse under this weight of fire as Colley had presumed they would. Instead, they took advantage of the folds in the ground below the plateau and of the ideal cover afforded by the six-foot-tall tambookie-grass (which is commonly used for thatch), and by scatterings of large rocks to work closer towards the British. In danger of being outflanked, Colley extended his men still further in a rough circle around the plateau. The guns were repositioned so that one fired from the south of the perimeter, and the other from the north. But targeting was made difficult by the dispersed deployment adopted by the Boers; while the absence of protective shields on the gun-carriages left crews and teams vulnerable to Boer musketry.[39]

By 12:15 p.m. firing was heavy all around Schuinshoogte. The 3/60th Rifles lay prone, taking what advantage they could of the rocky cover while the surrounding Boer fire raked them from the front and rear. Being against the skyline on the plateau the British made excellent, passive targets for the accurate Boer fire. The British found it almost impossible to raise their heads above the rocks to return fire, and British helmets later picked up by burial parties had at least two bullet holes in them, and one as many as six. Boer fire picked off half the artillerymen serving the guns and forced Colley to withdraw them from the exposed perimeter. Thirty-nine of the 76 British horses fell to Boer fire and most of the rest were wounded with the result that the Mounted Infantry had to abort the sortie Colley ordered. By nightfall Boer numbers had grown by another 100 or so to about 300. Their rapid and sustained firepower persuaded Colley that he was facing at least 1,000 Boers

---

38 Butler, *Pomeroy-Colley*, p. 300.
39 Hall, 'Field Artillery'; Hall, 'Artillery'; Von Moltke, 'Wapentuig', pp. 18–20.

and not a force slightly smaller than his own. Callwell would subsequently reflect in his *Small Wars* that Ingogo was a classic example of disastrous 'passive defence', whereas an 'active defence' was essential for success in 'small wars'.[40]

Colley, as he wrote afterwards to his wife, Edith, found he could not break off the engagement with his small force for want of cavalry, and had no option but to hold the plateau until night, when he hoped to draw off.[41] Throughout the engagement he coolly exposed himself to enemy fire and was in a position to witness with approval the steadiness of the "comparatively young" soldiers of the 3/60th Rifles who, he reported to Childers, "fired steadily, husbanding their ammunition" and held or changed their ground in good order.[42] Of course, this commendation was not entirely disinterested, and was a blow struck for short-service battalions in the simmering dispute with Cambridge and his supporters over the wisdom of Cardwell's reforms.

At one stage soldiers, frustrated at being pinned down for hours, suggested they attempt a bayonet charge against the Boers who were assumed to have no stomach for cold steel. But tactical doctrine laid down that a charge was never to be attempted until the enemy had been thoroughly mauled by fire and was on the verge of breaking. So Colley would not give the order, especially since he had seen the devastating effects of Boer fire against the charging 58th Regiment at Laing's Nek.

Somewhere about 3:30 p.m. there was a lull in the battle, and Colley seized the moment to send off two despatch riders to Mount Prospect Camp with orders for two companies of the 58th Regiment to reinforce the company of the 3/60th Rifles and company of the 58th Regiment already stationed overlooking the two drifts with their two 7-pdrs. When they came up to the two companies overlooking the drifts, the three reinforcing companies used their own initiative to move down towards the drifts and to occupy a fresh position on a ridge overlooking them to the west of the road. Their advance was timely, for during the later afternoon a considerable body of Boers made a move on the double drift with the intention of cutting off Colley's retreat, but the British there were able to drive them off.

Meanwhile, the situation on the plateau was awful. Both sides were suffering from exhaustion brought on by lack of water and food, by the heat of the sultry afternoon which had been resounding with heavy thunder, and by the terrible strain of skirmishing from behind minimal cover—although the Boers were much better than the British in making effective use of the terrain for shelter, and improvising little breastworks of packed stones with loopholes for firing through.[43] Then, as is normal in the summer rainfall area of the foothills of the Drakensberg, a torrential afternoon thunderstorm broke soon after 5:00 p.m. and the men were able to slake their thirst in the downpour. However, the temperature dropped drastically in the pelting rain and many of the wounded succumbed to the sudden wet and chill. At about

40 Callwell, *Small Wars*, pp. 200–202.
41 Colley to Lady Colley, 9–19 February 1881, quoted in Butler, *Pomeroy-Colley*, p. 313.
42 TNA: WO 32/7813, no. 079/4184: Colley to Childers, 12 February 1881.
43 NARP: JC 26, no. 2455: N.J. Smit to Joubert, 9 February 1881; *De Staatscourant*, 9 February 1881, p. 34: Het gevecht bij Schuinshoogte (Door een Engelsh ooggetuige, 8 February 1881).

The Ingogo battlefield photographed several months after the engagement with the skeletons of horses and abandoned equipment littering the ground. (PAR, C. 3049)

6:00 p.m. the light at last began to fade. This was the moment when Colley hoped to withdraw, and Smit tried to urge his men to make a final assault before the British made the attempt. But many of Smit's men contended that the state of the rivers, swollen by the waters that rapidly rise in the nearby mountains during a storm, made it impossible for the British to cross them, and refused to sacrifice themselves in further pointless fighting when their foes were already caught in a trap.[44]

The exchange of fire on Schuinshoogte finally ceased by 7:30 p.m. Colley's sodden men on the plateau were without food or shelter, and very short of ammunition. There were too few troops available to come to their relief, and Mount Prospect Camp was itself now weakly defended and vulnerable to attack. Colley well understood that the only alternative to a shameful capitulation was to undertake the hazardous night retreat he had been contemplating. At about 9:30 p.m., just when heavy rain began to fall again, Colley began his preparations. The few remaining unwounded horses were attached to the two guns and to one of the ammunition limbers. Surplus ammunition was destroyed or buried. Colley ordered those men too seriously wounded to be moved to be left on the field where (as he must have suspected they would) many died of exposure during the cold, rainy night. Presuming that the British could not risk retreating in the dark and rain and would still be stranded on Schuinshoogte in the morning, Smit set no guards. He ordered his cold, rain-soaked men to find what shelter they could and to

---

44 *De Staatscourant*, 23 February 1881, p. 29: Joubert to H.P. Malan, 11 February 1881; Smit's account to an English officer, quoted in Butler, *Pomeroy-Colley*, p. 307

prepare to resume the battle at first light. It was a critical miscalculation that robbed him of an overwhelming victory.

Colley began his march in intense darkness at about 11:00 p.m. with the troops formed in a hollow square in extended order—a protective formation very difficult to maintain even in the most ideal of circumstances. For fear of non-existent Boer patrols the British approached the rivers across the hills rather than by the road, and reached their banks undetected. The three companies positioned there earlier on the ridge to the west of the road had withdrawn with the fall of darkness to concentrate on the ridge overlooking the drifts from the north with the two companies still stationed there. At the drifts the swollen waters had risen to the height of men's armpits and they had to link arms to cross safely. Even so, six of the 3/60th Rifles were drowned. Once across both drifts the men had to help the exhausted horses drag the guns and wagon up the long uphill road until they finally reached Mount Prospect at about 4:00 a.m. on the foggy morning of 9 February.

Prepared to renew the fight, Smit sent urgently to Joubert for more ammunition, but was astounded at daylight to find nothing but the dead and wounded on the battlefield.[45] The Boers humanely allowed British ambulance wagons to load up the surviving wounded, and permitted a burial party of 40 men of the 3/60th Regiment to help bury the dead. Once again, British casualties had been very heavy indeed. The 3/60th Rifles had lost two officers and 56 men killed and three officers and 60 wounded—a quite crushing casualty rate of 40 per cent. The Artillery had fared no better. It lost one officer and two men killed and an officer and 11 men wounded—a casualty rate of 50 per cent. The ineffective Mounted Squadron had suffered only three killed and two wounded, but had lost almost all its horses. Once again Colley's staff had been badly hit. Captain MacGregor, his Assistant Military Secretary, was dead, along with his Dutch and Zulu interpreter, Marthinus Stuart, the Resident Magistrate of the Ixopo Division in southern Natal. Colley was left to lament that he had lost "every personal friend" he had messed with or with whom he and his wife, had "become intimate."[46]

Boer losses are unclear, but seem to have numbered eight killed and nine wounded, two mortally. This meant the British expended 514 rounds of small arms ammunition and 6 shells for each Boer casualty they inflicted. In all, at 40 rounds per man their expenditure of small arms ammunition quadrupled the average in a typical 'small war' battle and doubled the expenditure at Laing's Nek. The artillery once again fired more than double the number of shells typical of a 'small war' engagement.[47]

Despite their evident success, Commandant Smit and the Boers were dismayed at the opportunity they had let slip. As for Colley, his hazardous night retreat might have been successfully executed, but he could not disguise

---

45 NARP: JC 26, no. 2455: N.J. Smit to Joubert, 9 February 1881.
46 Colley to Lady Colley, 9 February 1881; and Colley to his sister, 16 February 1881, quoted in Butler, *Pomeroy-Colley*, pp. 308–309, 311.
47 Butterfield, *War and Peace*, pp. 204–5: Journal of the Natal Field Force, Tuesday, 8 February 1881; TNA: WO 32/7813, no. 079/4184: Report by Capt. E. Essex, 14 February 1881: Natal Field Force, List of Casualties on 8 February 1881; *De Staatscourant*, 16 February 1881, p. 27: note by P.A. Cronjé, 15 February 1881; 11 May 1881, p. 62: Gewond in den slag op Schuinshoogte.

that Ingogo, as the British called the battle, had been a second humiliating and costly defeat. Almost a quarter of the NFF was now dead or wounded. Colley was left deeply demoralised, and feebly admitted to his sister, Lily, that all he wished for now was a quick end to " … this hateful war" in which he had singularly failed to distinguish himself as a field commander.[48] And, difficult as it was for a British officer to admit, the Boer irregulars had distinctly outclassed his professional soldiers.[49] On 16 February Colley informed Childers that his troops were not nearly as well trained as the Boers in musketry, skirmishing, equitation, and the use of cover, and that his artillery did not at all compensate for his crucial lack of good mounted troops. As a consequence of these multiple deficiencies his unfortunate troops (despite a superficial cheeriness) were acquiring a fatal " … sense of inferiority and want of confidence in themselves."[50] With morale in the NFF reduced so dangerously low after their two serious defeats, it seemed that Colley had no option but to remain strictly on the defensive while awaiting the reinforcements promised him.

---

48 Colley to Lily, 16 February 1881, quoted in Butler, *Pomeroy-Colley*, p. 312.
49 Butler, *Pomeroy-Colley*, pp. 313, 316–317.
50 Colley to Childers, 16 February 1881, quoted in Butler, *Pomeroy-Colley*, pp. 317–318.

8

Calculating the Chances

At Mount Prospect Camp Colley had to deal with the consequences of his latest reverse.[1] The government instructed him to treat the Boers according to the recognised rules of civilised warfare and to respect ambulances and Red Cross personnel in accordance with the Geneva Convention of 22 August 1864.[2] He therefore arranged with Joubert for the care and removal of each side's wounded from the Ingogo battlefield.[3] As for the dead, the British treated the bodies of the five officers who had fallen with special consideration. The officers had been hurriedly buried with the other ranks and horses in three large pits before Colley withdrew from Schuinshoogte. On 12 February Colley despatched a party of the 3/60th Rifles under flag of truce to exhume them for reburial. It was a day of pouring rain and vultures were scavenging the battlefield. Many of the soldiers opening the pits were violently sick.[4] The rotting corpses were re-interred with military honours in a third row of graves in the cemetery near the camp where the officers killed at Laing's Nek already lay.[5] To keep flagging spirits up Colley ordered athletic sports in the camp on 16 February. The mule race was apparently " … great fun" and the men were " … thoroughly amused."[6]

Colley had few doubts as to the vulnerability of his situation, and was aware that Boer parties were raiding deep into Natal to his rear and cutting the telegraph wires.[7] Everyone at Mount Prospect was cheered to learn, therefore, that the considerable reinforcements—which Field Commandant General Smit had ridden out on 5 February to intercept—were at last marching upcountry. They comprised the 15th (King's) Hussars, the 2/60th

---

1   For the operations of the NFF between the battles of Ingogo and Majuba, see Butterfield, *War and Peace*, pp. 205–213: Journal of the Natal Field Force, 9 February–26 February 1881.

2   *BPP* (2866), enc. in no. 28: Earl Granville to Count de Bylandt, 7 February 1881; no. 38: Herbert to Thompson, 12 February 1881. Red Cross societies were formed in Cape Town, Bloemfontein and Durban to work in association with similar societies in Britain and the Netherlands engaged in helping both Boer and British wounded. See Norris-Newman, *With the Boers*, pp. 164–165.

3   PAR: WC III/4/2: Colley to Joubert, 9 February 1881

4   Lt. Percival Marling, quoted in Emery, *Marching over Africa*, p. 110.

5   Carter, *Boer War*, p. 226.

6   TNA: WO 32/7817: Journal of Naval Brigade, 16 February 1881.

7   Norris-Newman, *With the Boers*, p. 165.

Regiment (King's Royal Rifle Corps) and F/3 Brigade, RA—all of which had sailed from India on H.M.S. *Euphrates* and disembarked on 25 January in Durban—as well as the 92nd Regiment (Gordon Highlanders), that had likewise sailed from India on H.M.S. *Crocodile* and had landed on 30 January. The 83rd Regiment (County of Dublin), which had sailed on the *Crocodile* with the 92nd Highlanders, remained just south of Pietermaritzburg in the Lilliefontein camp near the Richmond Road station. The 97th (Earl of Ulster's) Regiment from Halifax and Gibraltar, which had arrived in Durban on 4 February on H.M.S. *Tamar*, also remained at the coast. A wing of the 6th (Inniskilling) Dragoons and Barrow's Mounted Infantry, that had landed shortly thereafter from H.M.S. *Hankow*, were proceeding to the front. The mounted infantry were on re-mounts brought around by sea from the Cape. The transports *Ararat*, *Palmyra* and *Queen* were still on their way with the remainder of the Inniskilling Dragoons, and drafts for the 97th Regiment and Royal Artillery.[8]

In command of these reinforcements was the popular, energetic, and very deaf, Sir Evelyn Wood, who was also so notoriously vain that it was said he wore his many decorations to bed.[9] He had begun his career in the Royal Navy in 1852 before joining the army in 1855. He was a gallant soldier, serving with distinction in the Crimean War before earning the Victoria Cross in 1859 when fighting in the last stages of the Indian Mutiny. He was also an intellectual soldier, passing very successfully through Staff College in 1862–1864. Service in the First Asante (Ashanti) War of 1873–1874 had brought him Wolseley's patronage. He had cooperated well with the Boers of the Utrecht District when he had been in command of No. 4 Column during the Anglo-Zulu War, and he had been almost unique in emerging from that unfortunate war with his reputation enhanced.[10]

Although Wood was associated with Wolseley's 'Ashanti Ring' and was a keen proponent of army reform, as a canny political soldier he knew how to keep on the right side of the Duke of Cambridge. Consequently, Cambridge had felt able to approach him as early as 4 January 1881 with the intention of sending him out to South Africa to buttress Colley, in whose operational abilities the Duke (not without reason) had limited faith. Wood consented to serve under Colley as his second-in-command—though in fact one senior to him in the Army List—only on condition that he retained his current rank and pay. His rank of Brigadier General on the Staff of the Army in South Africa thus secured.[11] Wood did not set sail until Queen Victoria, with whom he was a great personal favourite, had graciously received him, and he only arrived in Durban on 9 February.[12]

---

8   Norris-Newman, *With the Boers*, pp. 154–155, 163–164.

9   Lehmann, *First Boer War*, p. 226.

10   Manning, Stephen, 'Evelyn Wood', in Corvi (ed.), Steven J., and Beckett (ed.), Ian F.W., *Victoria's Generals* (Barnsley, South Yorks: Pen & Sword Military, 2009), pp. 30–37; Beckett, Ian F.W., 'Wood, Sir (Henry) Evelyn (1838–1919)', *Oxford Dictionary of National Biography* (Oxford University Press, 2004; online ed., January 2008) <http://www.oxforddnb.com.libproxy.wlu.ca/view/article/37000 > (accessed 20 August 2015).

11   PAR: WC III/1/2: Childers to Wood, 13 January 1881; Manning, Stephen, *Evelyn Wood: Pillar of Empire* (Barnsley, South Yorks: Pen & Sword Military, 2007), p. 143.

12   Wood, Evelyn, *From Midshipman to Field Marshal* , 2nd ed. (London:Methuen, 1906), vol. II, pp. 107–109. On Queen Victoria's insistence, Wood had accompanied the Empress

Colley wrote to Wood proposing that he form a second column with its base at Newcastle and cooperate with Colley when he advanced from Mount Prospect by making a flanking movement east around the Boer positions. The two columns would then unite and march on Pretoria.[13]

Colley rode to Newcastle on 17 February to confer with Wood who instantly gave evidence of his energy. In an initiative that bolstered morale he dashingly set out at midnight on 18 February from Newcastle through enemy territory with a squadron of the 15th Hussars and two companies of the 92nd Highlanders to reconnoitre the prospective route of his intended flanking movement.[14]

Convinced that the British were planning a new advance, Joubert despatched a strong mounted force of several hundred men under Smit to occupy the Biggarsberg pass through which Wood's reinforcements must march on their way to Newcastle. But realizing the daunting size of Wood's column, he recalled Smit, who was back in the Boer laager by 18 February.[15] The Boers thereupon set about constructing entrenchments either side of

Brig. Gen. Evelyn Wood, VC (seated left) consulting with Lt. Col. Redvers Buller during the Anglo-Zulu War of 1879 surrounded by the staff of the Flying Column. Both promoted and the recipients of honours, they worked together again in 1881 during the final stages of the Transvaal Rebellion when Col. Buller, VC, CMG served as Chief of Staff to Maj. Gen. Sir Evelyn Wood, VC, GCMG. (Author's collection)

Eugénie to Zululand in 1880 to visit the grave of her son, the Prince Imperial of France, who had been killed in action during the Anglo-Zulu War. See Laband, John, 'An Empress in Zululand', *Natalia*, 30 (December 2000), pp. 45–57.

13   Colley to Wood, 4 February 1881, quoted in Butler, *Pomeroy-Colley*, pp. 294–296.

14   Norris-Newman, *With the Boers*, p. 199.

15   *BPP* (C. 2837), no. 31: Colley to Childers, 15 February 1881; Holt, *Mounted Police*, p. 106; Meintjes, *Joubert*, p. 80. .

Laing's Nek, clearly confident they could hold their position against any attack.[16]

Meanwhile, in London the government was patently divided over what policy to pursue regarding the Transvaal. The more conservative Whig faction—who included Kimberley at the Colonial Office—was for militant coercion. Its members were prepared to consider the urgings of General Smyth at the Cape who was by now alarmed by Colley's series of defeats, and believed that a second column operating out of Cape Town should be sent north through the OVS to assist the NFF.[17] But in the cabinet Kimberley's faction was opposed by another which included Gladstone himself and Childers at the War Office. This grouping was instinctively against pursuing a military solution and favoured a policy of conciliation.

Uncertainty at Downing Street was reflected in the set of "Instructions" Kimberley issued Sir Hercules Robinson on 30 December 1880 to guide him as High Commissioner at the Cape. On the one hand, it seemed that the cabinet's intention was indeed to apply coercion and hold onto the Transvaal in the interests of South African confederation; yet point 9 in the selfsame document muddied the waters by promising the " … Dutch of the Transvaal … [a] generous peace" once " … the authority of the Crown had been vindicated," and assured them of " … such full control of their local affairs as may be consistent with the general interests of Her Majesty's dominions in South Africa."[18]

Part of the reason for the government's uncertain response to the Transvaal crisis was that its attention was constantly being diverted by the intractable and violent Irish Land War much closer to home. Nor did it help that there was a lack of public concern that might otherwise have guided it. Opinion was formed in later nineteenth century Britain by the newspaper media, and war correspondents and special artists had become a standard presence with British armies fighting their 'small wars' of empire.[19] However, the British press was slow to turn its attention to the Transvaal campaign because of uneasy doubts about the propriety of fighting the Boers at all, and was then muted on account of embarrassment at repeated military defeats.[20] The Transvaal campaign was in any case brief, so that by the time 'specials' such as Sir J.Luther Vaughan of *The Times* did begin to arrive in any numbers an armistice was already in place.[21] Press criticism of Colley's generalship only became widespread in mid-February after the Ingogo fiasco. This was the moment for organs of the Conservative opposition like the *Army and Navy Gazette* or *Daily Telegraph* to excoriate Liberal policy in South Africa,

---

16 TNA: WO 32/7817: Journal of Naval Brigade, 22 February 1881.

17 TNA: WO 32/7811, no. 079/4018: Smyth to Robinson, 7 February 1881.

18 *BPP* (C. 2754): Kimberley to Robinson, 'Instructions Addressed to Governor H. Robinson, G.C.M.G.', 30 December 1880. See especially points 5, 8–23.

19 For a discussion on British war correspondents and special artists in the 1870s and 1880s, see Laband, John, and Knight, Ian, *The War Correspondents: The Anglo-Zulu War* (Stroud, Glocs: Sutton Publishing, 1996), pp. v–xx.

20 Emery, *Marching over Africa*, pp. 100–102.

21 Norris-Newman, *With the Boers*, pp. 195–196.

denounce short service (again) and revel in the humiliation of the brightest star in Wolseley's 'Ring'.[22]

By the end of January the bellicose faction in the cabinet and its supporters among the permanent officials of the Colonial Office was in retreat, and Gladstone's opposing conciliatory faction had prevailed. Their victory was consequent on a number of factors. Colley, for all his assurances, was not currently winning the war in the Transvaal, although once all the reinforcements being sent him had arrived it was presumed he must prevail. However, the cabinet was shaken by the alarmed tone of despatches from the Cape concerning hardening support among Afrikaners throughout South Africa for their blood-brothers in the Transvaal, and by mounting reports of their burgeoning anti-British sentiment.[23] It now seemed that the inevitably prolonged military operations must irrevocably damage relations between Afrikaners and British settlers, even to the point of conflict. Another element of cabinet concern was that Africans in the Transvaal and elsewhere in the sub-continent might take advantage of the conflict between the white races.[24] Nothing, as Kimberley later expressed it, could be "more lamentably disastrous to the interests of white colonists" than "a war of races throughout South Africa."[25] The difficulty, though, following mounting humiliations inflicted on British arms, was how to find a creditable way out of the disastrous war that was not an affront to British national honour and prestige.[26]

Happily for Gladstone's government, the intervention of President Brand of the OVS made this objective attainable. As early as 10 January Brand had offered Kimberley his services as mediator to broker a settlement for the Transvaal before his own neutral republic was drawn into the war.[27] He was concerned that increasing numbers of men from the OVS were already going to the aid of their blood-brothers in the Transvaal, and that a commando of volunteers under Cornelius de Villiers had joined the Boer defenders at Laing's Nek.[28]

Bolstered by Brand's offer to mediate, the government proceeded to disengage itself from the Transvaal. At the cabinet meeting of 29 January—held in the midst of the crisis precipitated by Gladstone's determined effort to ram his government's Coercion Act aimed at curbing the activities of the Irish Land League through a reluctant parliament—Kimberley presented his arguments in favour of negotiation.[29] The faction favouring them carried the day and Kimberley was authorised to initiate peace feelers with the rebel leaders. For their part, the Transvaal Triumvirate were also keen to negotiate.

---

22 Lehmann, *Boer War*, pp. 181–183.
23 Adlam, Lt. A.M., 'Die Pers as Bron oor die Geskiedenis van die Eesrste Vryheidsoorlog', *Scientia Militaria: South African Journal of Military Studies*, 1: 11 (1981), pp. 62–68.
24 Laband, *Transvaal Rebellion*, pp. 186–187.
25 *BPP* (C. 2866), no. 64: Kimberley to Sir F. Roberts, 4 March 1881.
26 Butler, *Pomeroy-Colley*, pp. 319–320, 324–325, 335–336.
27 On 24 February 1881 a large majority of the *volksraad* in Bloemfontein voted to maintain the republic's neutrality despite the impassioned opposition of a minority who wanted to declare war on Britain.
28 Norris-Newman, *With the Boers*, pp. 178–179.
29 Ensor, R.C.K., *England 1870–1914* (Oxford: Clarendon Press, 1968), pp. 72–73. The Coercion Bill was introduced on 24 January 1881 and was subjected to a gruelling filibuster from 31 January until 2 February.

They were fearful of the weight of reinforcements being built up against them, and wished to use their temporary military advantage to secure a political settlement before they were inevitably overwhelmed.[30]

Colley had been kept relatively in the dark concerning his government's pursuit of peace, but on 8 February Kimberley telegraphed him advising that the British government was willing to treat with the Boers if they would submit and " … cease from armed opposition."[31] Colley was disconcerted by the course his government's directives were taking and began strenuously to demur.[32] But he was not making policy. A significant step towards eventual retrocession was taken when Kruger, who had learned through Brand of Kimberley's conditions of 8 February, arrived at Laing's Nek to inspect the Boer positions. On 12 February he wrote Colley that his government was willing " … to submit to a Royal Commission of Enquiry, who we know will place us in our just rights." He further undertook to permit all British troops " … to retire with all honour" when withdrawn. However, warned Kruger, should " … the annexation be persevered in … [then] … subject to the will of God" the Boers were prepared to fight to the last man and the responsibility for all the attendant miseries would be on Colley's shoulders.[33]

In London, the cabinet met again on 15 February. Kimberley and Gladstone persuaded their colleagues that the rising Boer unrest in South Africa was akin to the troubles sweeping Ireland, and that to avoid being embroiled in a second, comparable rebellion, the Transvaal must be let go.[34] When Colley met Wood in Newcastle on 17 February, he was handed Kimberley's telegram of 16 February which followed hard on the cabinet decision the day before. Kimberley announced that he was ready to accept Kruger's terms of 12 February and to call a Royal Commission. He authorised Colley to suspend hostilities if the Boers agreed to end their armed opposition.[35]

At this point Colley baulked. Many believed this was on account of the urging of his wife Edith, Lady Colley, the daughter of Major-General H. Meade 'Tiger' Hamilton, whom Colley had married in 1878 at the age of 45, much to the surprise of vice-regal society in Simla. Lady Colley was no Victorian shrinking violet and played a very active role in Colley's public life. Wood wrote to the Queen that he believed her burning ambition for her husband " … obliterates apparently every thought of the personal danger which he has undergone."[36] This ungenerous judgement is contradicted by two of Lady Colley's letters to her husband on 15 and 24 February. In them she regretted that nothing she could do would keep him from performing his soldierly duty. She touchingly declared that she would never again, " … care a rush for any such rubbish as work or success" if she could but see him safe

---

30 Schreuder, *Gladstone and Kruger*, pp. 100–117.
31 Kimberley to Colley, 8 February 1881, quoted in Butler, *Pomeroy-Colley*, p. 329.
32 Butler, *Pomeroy-Colley*, pp. 322–329.
33 Kruger and Bok to Colley, 12 February 1881, quoted in Butler, *Pomeroy-Colley*, pp. 330–331.
34 Schreuder, *Gladstone and Kruger*, pp. 118–122.
35 *BPP* (C. 2837), no. 34: Kimberley to Colley, telegram, 16 February 1881. Kimberley also telegraphed Wood and Brand to ensure that his message got through to the Boers and was not smothered by Colley.
36 Wood to Queen Victoria, 27 February 1881, quoted in Beckett, *Victorians at War*, p. 27.

home again, and that, " … nothing in this world is worth anything to me in comparison with that."[37] No letter from his wife goading Colley into action has survived, although malicious rumour had it that one such was later found on his body on Majuba. Even so, it is clear that Colley was resolved to retrieve his blemished reputation and foil the government's misguided peace plans through a decisive engagement. He wrote to his wife on 18 February that while he " … would rather resign" than support the government's peace initiative, he nevertheless would soon have " … broken the back of military resistance," and that his "words may carry more weight than they would just now."[38]

Colley's frustration boiled over when he received Kimberley's unambiguous telegram of 19 February. It forbade him to " … march to the relief of garrisons or occupy Lang's Nek" and ordering him instead to fix a "reasonable time" within which the Boers must respond to Kimberley's peace proposal.[39] Colley vented his spleen against his political masters when he wrote on 21 February to Wolseley, his patron:

> I am now getting together a force with which I think I could command success, but the Home Government seems so anxious to terminate the contest, that I am daily expecting to find ourselves negotiating with the 'Triumvirate' as the acknowledged rulers of a victorious people; in which case my failure at Lang's Nek will have inflicted a deep and permanent injury on the British name and power in South Africa which it is not pleasant to contemplate.[40]

On the same day, and in the same fractious frame of mind, Colley wrote to Kruger as instructed informing him that if the Boers ceased their "armed opposition" the British government was prepared to appoint a Commission "with large powers" to "develop" Kimberley's proposal of 8 February. Colley ended: "I am to add that upon this proposal being accepted within forty-eight hours, I have authority to agree to a suspension of hostilities on our part."[41] This limited deadline of 48 hours was Colley's unauthorised intervention and would have fatal consequences.

While very grudgingly opening peace negotiations with Kruger as instructed, Colley was sorely tempted by the steady build-up of reinforcements in Newcastle to believe that he would very soon be strong enough to break through at Laing's Nek and relieve the beleaguered garrisons in Pretoria, Potchefstroom, Lydenburg, Rustenburg, Standerton, Wakkerstroom, and Marabastad that were hanging grimly on in generally deteriorating circumstances.[42] With further operations clearly in view, on 21 February he addressed the newly arrived reinforcements in Newcastle. The 15th Hussars and Gordon Highlanders had come straight from India where they had fought with distinction in the Second Afghan War of 1878–1880.

---

37 Lady Colley to Colley, 15 and 24 February 1881, quoted in Butler, *Pomeroy-Colley*, pp. 347–348.
38 Colley to Lady Colley, 18 February 1881, quoted in Butler, *Pomeroy-Colley*, p. 339.
39 *BPP* (C. 2837), no. 50: Kimberley to Colley, telegram, 19 February 1881.
40 Colley to Wolseley, 21 February 1881, quoted in Butler, *Pomeroy-Colley*, p. 343.
41 Colley to Kruger, 21 February 1881, quoted in Butler, *Pomeroy-Colley*, p. 344.
42 See Laband, *Transvaal Rebellion*, pp. 179–182.

Reinforcements for the Natal Field Force being hauled across a stream on a pont, as depicted by Charles E. Fripp, special artist for the *Graphic*. (Collection of Ian Castle)

They were consequently accustomed to irregular warfare in difficult terrain against a determined foe, but Colley made a point of warning them against underestimating the Boers who fought and shot so well.[43]

Colley dubbed the troops concentrating at Newcastle the 'Indian Column' on account of so many of them being India veterans. The Indian Column was made up of two squadrons of the 15th Hussars (103 all ranks), six companies of the 92nd Highlanders (518 all ranks), the Naval Brigade of 58 officers and men from H.M.S. *Dido* (who had landed in Durban on 7 February) with their two 9-pdr guns, and various other details, making up a total of 727 officer and men, 105 horses, 81 wagons and 4 carts. On the morning of 23 February he led them into Mount Prospect Camp and the 15th Hussars and 92nd Highlanders camped on the hill to the east of the existing camp.

To the eyes of the troop already in camp the 15th Hussars looked very odd in their big India-issue helmets and khaki jackets, as did the bronzed and shaven Gordon Highlanders in their very light khaki tunics which they wore with their kilts, and with khaki covers for their white helmets.[44] The widespread use of mud-coloured uniforms had begun in India in the 1840s, although the use of khaki (from Urdu *khak*, or 'dust') by British regiments serving in India was not adopted until the Indian Mutiny. In South Africa the 74th (Highland) Regiment had worn khaki battledress in 1851–1852 during the Eighth Cape Frontier War, but the experiment was not repeated. Indeed, the adoption of khaki throughout the army was slow and often reluctant, and it was only in 1897 that it was finally adopted as service wear on all overseas postings.[45]

With the departure of the India Column for Mount Prospect, Wood returned to Pietermaritzburg from Newcastle, officially to accelerate the advance of other reinforcements—such as the 97th Regiment which had been ordered up from Ladysmith, and the mounted infantry, drawn from the 83rd Regiment and the Inniskilling Dragoons—though there is more than a hint that Colley wanted his famous subordinate out of the way while he planned his next, unauthorised, move.[46] Wood must have strongly suspected what Colley had in mind; otherwise there is no point to the exchange Melton

43 Norris-Newman, *With the Boers*, p. 199.

44 TNA: WO 32/7817: Journal of Naval Brigade, 22 February 1881. The officers of the 92nd Highlanders were all wearing the Sam Browne belt, recently introduced in India and not worn before in South Africa.

45 Mollo, John, *Military Fashion: A Comparative History of the Uniforms of the Great Armies from the 17th Century to the First World War* (New York: G.P. Putnam's Sons, 1972), pp. 210–216.

46 Norris-Newman, *With the Boers*, p. 199; Cromb,(ed.), James, *The Majuba Disaster: A Story of Highland Heroism, Told by Officers of the 92nd Regiment* (Dundee: John Leng, 1891; reprinted Pietermaritzburg: Africana Book Collectors, 1988), p. 40.

Sir Hercules Robinson, GCMG, H.M. High Commissioner for South Africa and Governor of the Cape, 1881–1889. (National Library of South Africa, Cape Town Campus, PHB 1774)

Prior, the celebrated special artist for the *Illustrated London*, recorded in his memoirs. They were published much later in 1912, so it is difficult to know what credence to give them, but Prior was positive that Colley gave his word of honour that he would not move out of camp until Wood returned from Pietermaritzburg.[47] Certainly, Major the Hon. J. Scott Napier was quite precise that " … it was almost universally known and believed in camp that General Wood had desired that no offensive movement was to be undertaken by his second in command [sic: Colley was in fact his superior officer] till his return."[48]

It was only on 24 February that Commandant Smit on Laing's Nek received Colley's letter of 21 February offering Kruger terms. Edouard Bok, the Triumvirate's State Secretary, acknowledged receipt of the letter on 25 February. He informed Colley that, since Kruger had already returned to Heidelberg, he had despatched the letter there by horseman, and that an answer could not be expected in less than four days. On 26 February Lieutenant Colonel Herbert Stewart, 3rd (Prince of Wales's) Dragoon Guards, Colley's new chief of staff and military secretary, learned from Smit that Kruger had gone on to Rustenburg to handle a potential uprising by the local Tswana people, so any reply to the letter must be further delayed.[49] Forty-eight hours had now passed, and Colley could conveniently convince himself that, " … by the rules of war and of honour he was free to move."[50] The Boers, on the other hand, could be confident in their reasonable belief that they had done their best to demonstrate their good faith and had presented legitimate reasons for a delayed response.

In London, meanwhile, Kimberley's determination to find a way out of the war was reinforced on 19 February by a telegram he received from Sir Hercules Robinson at the Cape. Robinson presented a chilling picture of the intensification of hatred between the two white races in South Africa, and raised the unpalatable prospect of having to maintain indefinitely a large force of occupation in the intransigent Transvaal. That was all Kimberly required to convince the cabinet that peace was absolutely and immediately imperative.[51] The same strong peace current was flowing in the OVS where there were also fears of an imminent race war. In Bloemfontein the *volksraad* resolved on 24 February by 36 votes to 3 to maintain the republic's neutrality and to work for an "amicable arrangement" for the peace of South Africa based on British concessions to the "just demands" of her "sister state," the ZAR.[52]

Ignoring these accelerating peace initiatives and in defiance of his own government—which he kept in the dark regarding his intentions—Colley pig-headedly proceeded with his preparations for a renewed offensive. Very early on the morning of 24 February Colley and his staff, escorted by the 15th Hussars and the Mounted Squadron, crossed the Buffalo River at Van

---

47 Manning, *Evelyn Wood*, p. 145.
48 Cromb,(ed.), James, *Majuba*, p. 41.
49 Schreuder, *Gladstone and Kruger*, p. 132.
50 Butler, *Pomeroy-Colley*, p. 360.
51 Schreuder, *Gladstone and Kruger*, pp. 127–129.
52 *BPP* (C. 2837), no. 58: Brand to the Orange Free State Consul, London, 24 February 1881.

der Merwe's Drift east of Mount Prospect and proceeded to a hill below Phogwane Mountain. There they obtained a full view of the Boers' position. They saw that the Boers were throwing up fresh entrenchments either side of Laing's Nek and also on the lower slopes of Majuba. These defences would make any frontal attack on the *nek* even more hazardous than previously.[53]

Colley had known his chief of staff, Lieutenant Colonel Stewart, since the Zulu campaign of 1879, if not before in India. The amiable, charming and efficient Herbert Stewart had served in the Second Anglo-Pedi War as well as in Zululand when Wolseley had recognised his talents and assigned him to his staff.[54] Colley respected his judgment as a favoured member of Wolseley's 'Ring', and pondered alternative strategic options with him. Stewart later affirmed that it seemed a good idea to seize Majuba which commanded the right of the Boer position, and that since it was only guarded by a day-time picquet, it was quite feasible to do so in a night attack. No documentation survives to explain precisely what Colley's strategic intentions were in occupying Majuba, but Stewart believed he intended to seize the summit, build redoubts there to secure the position, man them for at least three days, and keep his line of approach to the mountain open with two entrenched posts on its flanks supported by artillery fire from Mount Prospect Camp. Within a day or so the fresh reinforcements marching from Newcastle would be able to join him, when they and the troops on Mount Prospect would be in a position to turn the flank of the Boers on Laing's Nek. Either that, or the sight of the British occupation of Majuba would make the Boers believe that their position had been turned and so induce them to withdraw, opening the road to the Transvaal without further fighting.[55]

Subsequently, critics have questioned Colley's state of mind at this juncture, citing his exhaustion and anguished determination to retrieve his shredded military reputation as reasons for contemplating an absurd *coup de main*, one for which he would gain all the credit since Wood was still away.[56] Yet it is also certain that Colley and his staff did not embark on the venture without careful preparation. They spent the next few days following their reconnaissance of 24 February gaining what intelligence they could about Majuba. They also attempted to mislead the Boers by staging a diversion on the opposite flank when, on the morning of 25 February, a company of the 92nd Highlanders with a Gatling gun secured a farmhouse on the banks of the Buffalo River reportedly used as a base by Boer patrols.[57] The next morning, 26 February, the Mounted Squadron left camp at 1: 30 a.m. with a convoy of empty wagons for Newcastle, their routine departure disguising

53 Laband, *Transvaal Rebellion*, p. 192.

54 Beckett, Ian F.W., 'Stewart, Sir Herbert (1843–1885)', *Oxford Dictionary of National Biography* (Oxford University Press, 2004; online ed. January 2008) http://www. oxforddnb.com.libproxy.wlu.ca/view/article/ 26474 (accessed 20 August 2015). After Colley's death Stewart became Wolseley's firm favourite and was killed in 1885 serving under him in the Gordon Relief Expedition.

55 TNA: WO 32/7827, enc. 2 in no. 079/4617: Lt-Col H. Stewart to Wood, 4 April 1881; Butler, *Pomeroy-Colley*, pp. 352, 361–362, 364.

56 Ransford, *Majuba*, pp. 66, 71–72; Saks, David, 'Tragic Failure: The Last Campaign of Maj-Gen George Pomeroy Colley', *Military History Journal*, 13:6 (December 2006) <samilitaryhistory.org/journal.html > (accessed 27 August 2015).

57 TNA: WO 32/7817: Journal of Naval Brigade, 25 February 1881.

covert preparations for an assault on Majuba that coming night. Colley was readying himself to stake the campaign and his reputation on a single throw. In a still moment before fall-in Colley wrote a last, prescient and fatalistic letter to his wife:

> I am going out tonight to try and seize the Majuba Hill … and leave this behind, in case I should not return, to tell you how very dearly I love you, and what a happiness you have been to me … It is a strange world of chances; one can only do what seems right to one in matters of morals, and do what seems best in matters of judgment, as a card-player calculates the chances, and the wrong card may turn up and everything turn out to be done for the worst instead of the best.[58]

---

58 Colley to Lady Colley, 26 February 1881, quoted in Butler, *Pomeroy-Colley*, pp. 367–368.

9

Majuba

If Majuba were to be seized without Boer opposition, surprise was essential. Colley divulged his intentions to no one besides Colonel Stewart and another recently arrived staff officer, Major Thomas Fraser, RE. The drawback was that the officers to be left behind at Mount Prospect Camp under Lieutenant Colonel William Bond of the 58th Regiment had no idea of the destination or object of the expedition. To maintain secrecy until the last moment, it was only after lights out had been routinely sounded at 8:30 p.m. on 26 February that staff officers issued orders for two companies of the 58th Regiment, two companies of the 3/60th Rifles, three companies of the 92nd Highlanders and a company-strength Naval Brigade drawn from the *Boadicea* and *Dido*, as well as small detachments from other units and the Army Medical Department, to be ready to march at 11:00 p.m. in that order. Colley ordered that his brother-in-law and member of his staff, Lieutenant Bruce Hamilton, who was lying ill in his tent, should not be wakened. "I don't mean to take him tonight," he explained. "There seems a kind of fatality about my staff. If anything were to happen to him it would kill his sister."[1]

It has been a matter of conjecture ever since why Colley chose to lead out a mixed force when a single regiment, with its developed *corps d'esprit,* was likely to have proved more cohesive and reliable. The consensus is that Colley intended to provide representatives of the 58th Regiment and the 3/60th Rifles with an opportunity to redeem their poor showings at Laing's Nek and Ingogo. Furthermore, as a prominent member of Wolseley's 'Ring' committed to upholding recent army reforms, it most likely would have occurred to Colley that a successful action would demonstrate that new short-service regiments such as these two could perform just as well as the old long-service ones favoured by the Duke of Cambridge and his conservative circle.[2]

At the appointed hour Colley led out his mixed force of 27 officers and 568 men, three newspaper correspondents, and an unrecorded number of African guides and servants who carried three days' rations for the troops. Each soldier was ordered to carry the regulation 70 rounds of ammunition, a greatcoat, waterproof sheet, and a full water bottle. Four picks and six

---

1   Quoted in Butler, *Pomeroy-Colley*, p. 369.
2   Butler, *Pomeroy-Colley*, p. 370; Ransford, *Majuba Hill*, p. 78; Lehmann, *Boer War*, p. 236.

shovels for entrenching were issued to each company. The men were not told of their destination. No artillery or Gatling guns accompanied the task force because Colley considered the mountain too steep and there was in any case no proper tackle available to strap the guns onto draft animals. Even so, lack of artillery would prove crucial in the coming battle, and speaks to Colley's curiously nebulous plan of campaign.[3]

From the outset, the going was not easy for Colley's force. It was a moonless night and no lights were carried. Strict silence was observed, but there were in any case no Boers on Majuba to hear the troops stumbling along. The daytime picquet regularly posted on Majuba had indeed withdrawn in order to be present at the Sunday divine service to be held early the next morning at the Boer laagers.[4] The spirits of the men were reported high, although there is evidence too of grumbling and an expressed lack of faith in Colley's generalship—not altogether surprising with his dismal record of two defeats in row.

The column moved out west from Mount Prospect, crossed the Laing's Nek road, and climbed the lower eastern slopes of Inkwelo Mountain. After an hour's march it straggled onto a plateau halfway up the mountain, where it proved necessary to re-form. The column then turned north-west and followed a track traversing the mountain which came out on another plateau on the northern slopes of Inkwelo. Here Colley detached two companies of the 3/60th Rifles to secure his line of march, cryptically giving Captains C. Smith and R. Henley no orders other than to entrench and hold their position. From this plateau Colley marched northwards along the wide ridge

3 Unless otherwise indicated, the following account of the battle of Majuba is based upon TNA: WO 32/7817, enc. in no. 079/4389 [also printed in *BPP* (C. 2950), enc. 2 in no. 27]: Maj. Fraser to the GOC Natal, 5 March 1881; *BPP* (C. 2950), enc. in no. 31: Commodore F.W. Richards to the Secretary of the Admiralty, 14 March 1881; Report by Sub.-Lt. A.L. Scott, 1 March 1881; Report by Surgeon E.H. Mahon, 4 March 1881; TNA: WO 32/7827, enc. 1 in no. 079/4617: Memorandum by Wood, 20 April 1881; enc. 2: Lt. Col. H. Stewart to Wood, 4 April 1881; enc. 5: Lt. H.A. Macdonald to Chief of the Staff, 13 April 1881; enc. 6: Maj H.C. Hay to the Chief of the Staff, 2 March 1881; enc. 7: Capt. E.H. Thurlow to Officer Commanding 3/60th Rifles, 28 February 1881; enc. 8: Capt. F.M.E. Vibart, RA to the Chief of the Staff, 28 February 1881; enc. 9: Capt. C.H. Smith to the Chief of the Staff, 28 February 1881; enc. 11: Lt. H. Morgan to the Chief of the Staff, 28 February 1881; enc. 12: Report by Capt. G. Sullivan, 27 February 1881; see enclosures 14–18 for clarifications of the above statements; see enclosures 19–27 for courts of enquiry held at Fort Amiel on 3 April 1881 to enquire into the circumstances under which officers and men became prisoners of war; Butterfield, *War and Peace*, pp. 213–215: Journal of the Natal Field Force, 26 –27 February 1881; *De Staatscourant*, 16 March 1881: 'Het Gevecht bij Amajuba, door een ooggetuig, 5 March 1881'; *ILN*, 23 April 1881: account by J.A. Cameron, special correspondent of the *Standard*; Butler, *Pomeroy-Colley*, pp. 368–406; Carter, *Boer War*, pp. 253–303; Bellairs, *Transvaal War*, pp. 379–383; Norris-Newman, *With the Boers*, pp. 201–6, 350–1; Cromb, *Majuba* , pp. 5–44; Bond, Brian, 'The Disaster of Majuba Hill 1881', *History Today* (July 1965), pp. 491–5; Ransford, *Majuba*, pp. 72–123; Lehmann, *Boer War*, pp. 236–260; Bakkes, C.M., 'Die Slag van Majuba, 27 Februarie 1881,' in *Eerste Vryheidsoorlog*, pp. 179–197; Grobler, J.E.H., 'Die Eerste Vryheidsoorlog, 1880–1881: 'n Militêre-Historiese Benadering' (unpublished PhD thesis, University of Pretoria, 1981), chapter 11; Duxbury, *David and Goliath*, pp. 31–44; Castle, Ian, *Majuba 1881: The Hill of Destiny* (London: Osprey Military, 1996), pp. 60–85; Laband, *Transvaal Rebellion*, pp. 198–212; Laband, John, 'Beaten by the Boers', *Ancestors*, 42 (February 2006), pp. 56–60.

4 Otto, Brig. W., 'Die Slag van Majuba 27 Februarie 1881', *Scientia Militaria: South African Journal of Military Studies*, 1: 11 (1981), p. 2.

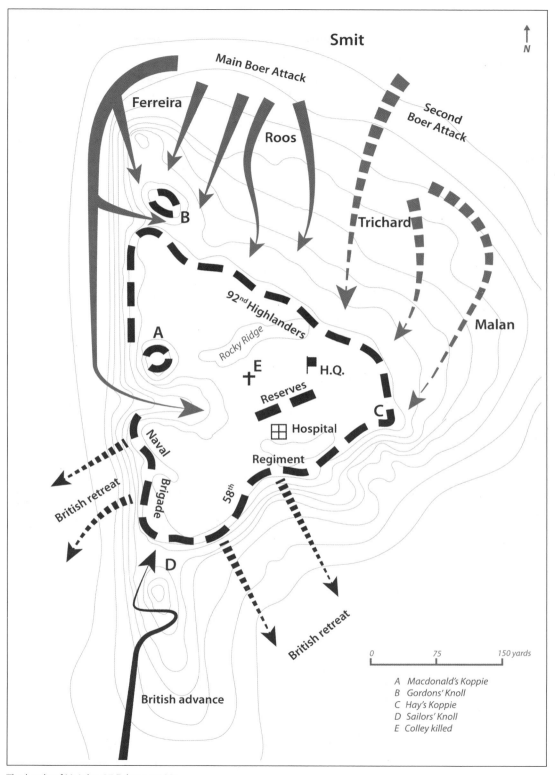

The battle of Majuba, 27 February 1881

The British forces under Colley's command scrambling up Majuba in the early hours of 27 February 1881. *(Illustrated London News, 23 April 1881)*

which connects Inkwelo to Majuba. At about midnight the column halted for about an hour at the far end of the ridge to allow part of the rear of the column, which had lost its way in the dark and difficult terrain, to be brought in.

Colley then detached a company of the 92nd Highlanders at this location under Captain P. Robertson with orders to take charge of the officers' horses and the reserve ammunition. On his orders a further three officers and 77 men of the 3/60th Rifles with 10 mules carrying 16 boxes of ammunition moved up from Mount Prospect Camp at 12:30 a.m. to reinforce them. By 6:00 a.m. Robertson's augmented force had completed a small earthwork redoubt and shelter trench.

In the early hours of 27 February Colley's reduced column began the ascent of Majuba itself. For grip and ease of movement Colley changed his boots for tennis shoes with flat vulcanised rubber soles and soft uppers of canvas and leather.[5] The men found the going ever more difficult up the steep gradient and had to scramble up the final slope on hands and knees. To make matters worse, guides occasionally lost the path that gained the south-western summit and it became necessary to halt every 100 yards to keep the column more-or-less together. Colley feared the Boers might have detected the blundering column and sent scouts on ahead, but to his relief they reported the mountaintop deserted. Surprise had been achieved. The first troops breasted the summit at 3:40 a.m. in the dark, "straggling up by twos and threes."[6] The rear of the labouring column was not finally up much before 5:30 a.m., just as dawn began to break. All order and formation had been lost in the arduous climb, and the men milled about looking for their units while staff officers tried to get them into position. Winded stragglers were pushed into the nearest gap in the perimeter regardless of which unit they belonged to. Much was later made of the difficulty of the gruelling ascent in explaining the debilitated condition of the troops on the day of the battle. Yet their degree of fatigue is debatable. Colley himself, whom Butler described as a man of "extremely active habits," was reported by Stewart to have been "as fresh and bright as possible" when he reached the summit.[7] Besides, as Sir J. Luther Vaughan, *The Times* special correspondent and a veteran of the North-West Frontier of India, pointed out, Majuba was nothing as formidable a mountain as many previously encountered by the 92nd Highlanders during the recent Second Anglo-Afghan War.[8] One can only surmise that many of the troops—and their officers—were out of condition for lack of sufficient exercise while holding Mount Prospect Camp.

The summit of Majuba where the troops found themselves is roughly triangular in shape. It has a rocky perimeter of about three quarters of a mile which slopes inwards to form a basin, in some places nearly 40 feet below the outer line of boulders. It is bisected from east to west by a low

---

5   See Turner, Thomas. 'Lawn Tennis Shoes for Men and Women, c. 1870 –c. 1900' <www. academia.edu/3542656 > (accessed 3 December 2015). The uppers of tennis shoes for men in this period were often intricately detailed and highly decorated.

6   *The Times*, 4 March 1881: report, 3 March 1881.

7   Butler, *Pomeroy-Colley*, p. 384.

8   Sir J.L. Vaughan, *My Service in the Indian Army—and After* (London: Archibald Constable, 1904), p. 248.

A jingoistic representation of the pugnacious Lt. Hector ("Fighting Mac") Macdonald of the 92nd Highlanders vigorously resisting capture on Majuba with his bare fists. (Collection of Ian Castle)

rocky ridge which in the darkness Colley mistakenly believed to mark the northern perimeter of the summit. On the western side of the mountaintop the rocky ridge about shoulder-high runs to the foot of a rounded rocky outcrop, or *koppie*, later known as Macdonald's Knoll (or Koppie) after Lieutenant Hector Macdonald. Macdonald, a craggy, square-faced Scottish crofter's son with a bulldog jaw, had enlisted in the 92nd Highlanders and distinguished himself in the Second Afghan War when he earned the nickname 'Fighting Mac' and was very exceptionally commissioned from the ranks in January 1880.[9] To the east the ridge terminates in another, less well defined feature somewhat to its rear later called Hay's Koppie after Major H.C. Hay, also of the 92nd Highlanders.

Colley was satisfied with the apparent strength of the position, but his confidence was misplaced. With the detachment of the two companies of the 3/60th Rifles and the company of the 92nd Highlanders to secure his lines of communication, he had only 19 officers and 383 men left to hold the position, or about half a battalion. Although the troops had been jumbled up somewhat when chivvied into position, in effect the two companies of the 92nd Highlanders (141 officers and men) held the perimeter along the rocky ridge from Macdonald's Koppie to Hay's Koppie. The two companies of the 58th Regiment (171 officers and men) continued the line on their right along the south-eastern perimeter to the south-western point where the force had reached the summit. The 65 officers and men of the Naval Brigade then completed the line along the western side of the mountain up to a steep grass gully which extends downs the mountainside below Macdonald's Koppie. The men were placed in extended skirmishing order with 15-pace intervals between files and reserves in support. A further mixed reserve, drawn from all the units, was formed up in the hollow behind the rocky ridge close by Colley's headquarters beside the hospital and commissariat. Water was found at only three feet—although its availability is disputed by some witnesses—and Colley was assured that his men could maintain their position on top of Majuba for as long as required. With their objective attained and apparently secured, the mood of the men became relaxed and optimistic.

The first faint glimmers of morning light dispelled British complacency. The rocky ridge held by the 92nd Highlanders was revealed not to be the true northern perimeter of the summit. In fact, the ground slopes gently away from the ridge before dropping abruptly to a wide, flat grassy terrace. On its far side the ground once more slopes sharply downwards. To rectify this

9   Stearn, Roger T., 'Macdonald, Sir Hector Archibald (1853–1903)', *Oxford Dictionary of National Biography* (Oxford University Press, 2004; online ed., January 2011) <http://www.oxforddnb.com.libproxy.wlu.ca/view/article/34702 > (accessed 20 August 2015).

faulty disposition, at about 4:30 a.m. Colley ordered the 92nd Highlanders to move forward from the ridge and occupy the true brow of the mountain. A handful of the Gordon Highlanders took up an exposed position on an isolated, featureless knoll which juts out from the north-western angle of the mountain like a bastion from a curtain wall. Gordons' Knoll, as it later became known in their honour, would prove the key to Majuba. If lost to the Boers the northern perimeter would be exposed to enfilading fire and be made untenable. However, at this stage the tactical significance of Gordons' Knoll was not properly appreciated.

Extending the British defensive perimeter north to Majuba's brow had the effect of dispersing the already widely spaced Highlanders still further, yet Colley seems unaccountably not to have been concerned by this development. His original intention had been to fortify his position by constructing small square redoubts—one on Macdonald's Koppie, another on Hay's Koppie and a third on the knoll overlooking the path to the summit, dubbed 'Sailor's Knoll' after the Naval Brigade—and the hurried northwards attenuation of his line upset his plan. However, he then failed to order alternative perimeter entrenchments. Smug over-confidence in the successful occupation of the mountaintop must have played its part, but so too did Colley's habitual concern for the welfare of the men he commanded. In his estimation the troops were still too fatigued from their climb to begin work immediately. Perhaps more than anything else this soft-hearted decision has been considered fatal to Colley's situation. Yet it is not as if he was unaware of the necessity to construct defences; nor were his men were without entrenching tools. As the *Field Exercise* puts it with great clarity:

> Taking into consideration the long range, extreme accuracy and great rapidity of fire of the rifled guns and small arms now in use, it may be desirable to shelter the troops as much as possible from unnecessary exposure … It is self-evident that troops behind cover must have a considerable advantage over an enemy advancing, unprotected, against them.[10]

It was well understood that a very slight earthen parapet one-and-a half feet high was sufficient to protect men from rifle bullets, and that for a kneeling man the trench behind the parapet had only to be one-and-a half feet deep and two-and-a half feet wide. A soldier was expected to complete five feet of such a trench and parapet in only 30 minutes when it made for the best form of defence whenever time of preparation was short.[11] Understanding this well, some of Colley's junior officers took the initiative despite Colley's inaction and encouraged the men under their immediate command to improvise defences and pile rocks and stones in front of their positions, rather as the Boers had done at Ingogo. The Naval Brigade also went its own way and doggedly erected some strong stone breastworks.

It seems it was Colley's intention, once his men were firmly established on Majuba, to hand over command to Commander Francis Romilly of the Naval Brigade (whose face was very noticeably scarred by smallpox) and

---

10   Great Britain, *Field Exercise*, p. 382.
11   Great Britain, *Field Exercise*, pp. 382-340; Great Britain, *Fortification*, p. 51.

to return to Mount Prospect Camp—where reinforcements were expected imminently—to take command of joint operations against Laing's Nek. Yet the viability of this plan depended on holding Majuba to threaten the Boer flank. However, the British position on Majuba was very far from secure. It was bad enough that it was only thinly held and lacked defensive redoubts and comprehensive perimeter entrenchments. But to make matters worse, the nature of the north and north-eastern slopes of the mountain turned them into dead ground for the defenders, making it possible for assailants to advance two-thirds of the way up the mountain without being seen. Moreover, ravines and eroded *dongas* (gullies) which ran down the mountain and were choked by thick bush provided them with excellent cover. Possibly the worst dereliction committed by Colley and his staff was their failure to order a proper reconnaissance to ascertain the extent to which the mountain slopes were dead ground. Consequently, their troops were not on heightened lookout for Boers taking advantage of the favourable terrain to approach their positions undetected.

Unconscious, therefore, of the precariousness of their situation, and pumped up by their successful seizure of Majuba and the commanding position it gave them over the Boer positions, the British advertised their presence at first light. When at 5:45 a.m. a few shots were enthusiastically fired off by his men Colley was not perturbed and made no reprimand. After all, the Boers were supposed to know the British were there. Highlanders standing on the skyline shook their fists and yelled at the four Boer laagers far below where, on that Sunday morning, some Boers were being mustered to take up their positions on the *nek* while the rest were preparing for divine service. Certainly, the Boers did not expect to have to fight on the Sabbath, and were scandalised as well as astounded at the unexpected and unwelcome sight of the British on the mountain above them.[12] Many, including Commandant General Joubert himself, were gripped by initial panic. Some saddled up and inspanned their wagons to escape the anticipated bombardment by the guns they supposed the British must surely have dragged up to the summit of Majuba. Others rushed to man the defences across the *nek* against an anticipated coordinated British advance from Mount Prospect. Such expectations made tactical common sense, but no shells fell because Colley had no artillery, and there was no sign of activity in the British camp.

Joubert recovered his nerve and, spurred on by his indomitable wife, Hendrina, who had accompanied him to war,[13] rode through the laagers calling for volunteers to drive the British off Spitskop, as the Boers called Majuba. While about 100 volunteers began gathering at his headquarters, Joubert called a council of war. According to some, pointless recriminations flew between Nicolaas Smit and Frans Joubert over whose responsibility it had been to station a night-time picquet on Majuba to give due warning of a British attack, and it seems that on Saturday night a picquet had indeed been ordered up the mountain but had lost its way and had encamped half-

---

12 NARP: BV 13, p. 454: Joubert to Kruger, 27 February 1881; Cromb, *Majuba*, p. 31; Visser, Kaptein G.E., 'Die Eerste Vryheidsoorlog : Enkele Aspekte met die Britse Siening van die Boere en die Verskille tussen Boer en Brit', *Scientia Militaria: South African Journal of Military Studies*, 1: 11 (1981), p. 74.

13 Meintjes, *Joubert*, p. 82.

way up. But all agreed that now the British were unfortunately in possession of the mountain and had succeeded in turning their flank, that they must be promptly evicted. So before Joubert rode off to encourage the *burgers* holding the Laing's Nek defences against the British attack they were sure must follow, he tersely ordered Smit, the hero of Bronkhorstspruit and Ingogo, to " … bring the enemy down from the mountain."[14] Smit accordingly led the mounted volunteers, among whom morale was high, to the lower slopes of Majuba. More men would gradually follow as the Boers in the laagers immediately behind Laing's Nek realised that there was to be no British attack on the *nek* that day. That development was crucial, and as Major Hay would reflect several years later,

> … the only way to have saved the disaster on Majuba was by an attack to have been made from Mount Prospect as soon as it was found the position was so faulty. The Boers must have then either relinquished the attack on Majuba or lost Lang's Nek. But seeing no move made from the Mount Prospect Camp, they sent every available man to attack Majuba. As Majuba was in signalling communication with Mount Prospect, all orders for the attack could have been communicated by General Colley.[15]

Smit coordinated Boer strategy and confirmed his reputation, as Butler generously expressed it, " … as one of the ablest leaders of mounted infantry that have appeared in modern war."[16] In support of the men about to scale Majuba he organised a second group of about 150 horsemen to ride around the western side of the mountain to prevent any British reinforcements reaching Colley and to cut off a British withdrawal. The boot was now firmly on the other foot and Colley, rather than intimidating the Boers into a precipitate withdrawal from Laing's Nek through his bold stroke in seizing Majuba, found his little force besieged and in imminent danger of being isolated and overrun.

The initial group of Boers riding up to the base of Majuba dismounted under cover and Smit formed them into two assault groups under Assistant Field Cornet Stephanus J. Roos from Pretoria and Commandant Joachim J. Ferreira from Utrecht. With Roos on the left and Ferreira 100 yards away on his right, the two parties began to clamber up the lower slopes of the mountain. They went unchallenged because not only were they in dead ground, but Colley had unaccountably failed to set any picquets or to send out any patrols to monitor Boer movements. So, largely out of sight of the British on the summit, Roos's and Ferreira's men worked expertly up the mountain taking every advantage of the natural cover provided by the rocky outcrops, bushy gullies and sparse scrub on the open slopes (the dense growth of trees and bushes that cloak the mountainside today were not present then). A second group of Boers joined the assault under Field Cornet D.J.K. Malan and Field Cornet Stephanus Trichard and advanced on Roos's left.

14 Nöthling, 'Commanders', p. 80.
15 Crombe, *Majuba*, pp. 28–29.
16 Butler, *Pomeroy-Colley*, p. 390.

The British in retreat from Majuba on 27 February 1881 sketched by Melton Prior from the hill above Mount Prospect Camp: (1) Boers rounding Majuba to cut off the retreating British; (2) Boers in possession of the summit of Majuba; (3) Boers in dongas on the side of the mountain; (4) British retreating down the side of Majuba under heavy fire; (5) shellfire from Mount Prospect Camp; (6) ledge of rocks; (7) Hussar picquets and some officers of the 60th Rifles observing the battle; (8) the 15th Hussars retreating; (9) small waterfalls. (*Illustrated London News,* 23 April 1881)

Throughout the morning more volunteers continued to trickle up the mountain to join the three assault parties and eventually swelled them to about 450 men. Smit deployed a cordon of the older and less physically active Boers at the foot of the mountain who from about 6:00 a.m. opened a heavy fire covering the skirmishers working up the slopes in two supporting lines. The rear line provided covering fire for the advance line until it had come to a halt behind suitable cover; it then moved up to join the advance line and the process was repeated. As at Ingogo, the weight of incessant Boer covering fire deterred the British from exposing themselves along the skyline to fire down at the Boer assault groups. [17]

At first, when they realized they were under attack, the British on the summit felt no alarm since they mistakenly believed their position to be unassailable. The reserve in the hollow behind the rocky ridge breakfasted, and many fell asleep, tired out by the difficult climb and sleepless night. Colley still did not divulge his intentions to his officers, but at 8:00 a.m. he signalled Mount Prospect by flag (the signalmen were stationed on the brow

---

17 Pitout, D.N., 'Die Slag van Amajuba, 27 Februarie 1881' (unpublished M.A. thesis, University of Pretoria, 1980), p. 6.

of Majuba facing the camp) directing them to telegraph Childers at the War Office that he had occupied Majuba " … immediately overlooking Boer position," and that the Boers were firing from below. Since Childers believed operations had ceased while negotiations progressed, this news would come as a distinct and unwelcome surprise. Three-quarters of an hour later Colley again signalled the camp. This time he ordered forward the 2/60th Rifles and three troops of the 15th Hussars stationed at Newcastle, urging them to arrive at Mount Prospect Camp by the next morning, and also ordered up the scattered detachments of the NMP. It is not known for certain how Colley envisioned using these reinforcements, but it must be presumed they were intended to strengthen a direct assault on Laing's Nek combined with a flanking movement from Majuba. For the present, Colley continued to believe his occupation of Majuba to be secure, and his next two signals dealt mundanely with bringing up fresh rations. That of 9:30 a.m. cockily ended: "All very comfortable. Boers wasting ammunition. One man wounded in foot."[18]

Only an hour later, however, Colley was becoming concerned by the increasing rate of Boer fire. A little after 10:30 a.m., he very belatedly began to consider the construction of defences. While Colley was standing on the exposed south-western point of the summit held by the Naval Brigade discussing the matter with his staff, a Boer marksman 900 yards below shot Commander Romilly through the body. He collapsed mortally wounded at Colley's side gamely declaring, "I am all right."[19] All evidence points to the bullet having been an explosive, or expanding Dum-Dum one, the only recorded case of these "barbarous missiles" being fired by the Boers.[20] Colley was deeply dismayed by the loss of his second-in-command, and his demeanour became markedly gloomy and constrained. Even so, the situation for the defenders still seemed favourable. They underestimated the size of the Boer assault groups because so few of the *burgers* were visible to them; and they were heartened when at about 11:00 a.m. they spotted a few Boer wagons driving off from the laagers. Colley could consequently reassure himself that all was well, and immediately signalled Mount Prospect Camp to inform Childers that "Boers still firing heavily on hill, but have broken up laager and begin to move away."[21] Unfortunately for the British, Colley had entirely misread the unfolding situation,

The most northerly sector of the British defensive perimeter was occupied by some 18 men of the 92nd Highlanders under Lieutenant Ian Hamilton, a veteran of the Second Anglo-Afghan War and a protégé of Sir Frederick Roberts. Of skeletal appearance, Hamilton was tough, intelligent, charming, and indifferent to personal danger.[22] He had stationed about five of his men

18   All four of these messages are quoted in Butler, *Pomeroy-Colley*, pp. 386–387.
19   Quoted in Lehman, *Majuba*, p. 243.
20   *BPP* (c. 2950), enc, in no. 31: Commodore Richards to the Secretary of the Admiralty, 14 March 1881. Romilly was evacuated from Majuba and died in Mount Prospect Camp on 2 March 1881.
21   At the same time Colley signalled Commodore Richards concerning Romilly's dangerous wound. Both signals quoted in Butler, *Pomeroy-Colley*, pp. 391–392.
22   Cassar, George H., 'Hamilton, Sir Ian Standish Monteith (1853–1947)', *Oxford Dictionary of National Biography* (Oxford University Press, 2004; online ed., January 2011) <http://www.oxforddnb.com.libproxy.wlu.ca/view/article/33668 > (accessed 20 August 2015)

on the isolated Gordons' Knoll that commanded the northern perimeter and along the spur that connected it to the summit. The Boers commanders grasped that it was tactically imperative to gain possession of the knoll. An assault group under Ferreira concentrated under the protection of the edge of the rocky-sided terrace directly below, but to storm the knoll required a 20-yard dash across the flat, grassy terrace, fully exposed to British fire. Success hinged on the extent to which the Boers had made themselves the masters of fire and movement techniques, and they proved to be experts. Roos's men extended to the left of Ferreira's along the edge of the terrace and opened a heavy fire on the Highlanders, pinning them down under cover. With British fire suppressed, small groups of Boers took it in turn to rush unscathed across the terrace and take shelter in the dead ground immediately under the rocky face of the knoll itself.

Hamilton, who was an efficient and experienced officer, well understood the threat this posed to his position. Risking Boer fire he reported in person to Colley, whom he found in the hollow behind the rocky ridge where the reserve was comfortably eating, sleeping or smoking. No serious Boer threat was apparent in this safe haven, and Colley politely but dismissively sent Hamilton back to his post. However, when Hamilton saw that the number of Boers sheltering below the terrace in support of the assault group directly under the knoll had grown considerably, he once again braved Boer musketry to request Colley for reinforcements to help suppress their covering fire. Despite the urgency of the young officer before him, Colley remained sceptical of his report and finally agreed to spare him only five men and an officer of the 58th Regiment.

The increasing volume of Boer fire convinced Hamilton that, although he could barely see them, at least 400 Boers must be concentrated directly below his position. This was a great over-estimation of their strength which was about half that number, but Hamilton was not wrong in believing that the Boers must be on the verge of storming his position. Shortly after midday—and for the third time—he made his hazardous dash back to headquarters to beg Colley for assistance. But the general, exhausted no less with the mental strain than with physical exertion, was asleep. Protectively, Stewart would not waken him. There was nothing else for Hamilton but to make an unheeded report to Major Hay, his senior officer, before returning to his imperilled post weighed down by the certain knowledge that his superior officers had signally failed him.

Once Ferreira had collected between 60 and 80 men directly below Gordons' Knoll, they suddenly emerged from their cover somewhere between 12:30 p.m. and 12:45 p.m. and opened fire on the Highlanders. Three of the defenders on the knoll were killed and the two survivors fled to the British perimeter. Ferreira's men took possession of Gordons' Knoll and opened a heavy flanking fire on the thinly extended Highlanders from only 70 yards away. With the British along their northern perimeter pinned down by this covering fire and unwilling to lean over the brow of the mountain to shoot, Roos led his men in a dash across the open terrace to the dead ground some 100 yards directly below them.

The outbreak of unprecedentedly heavy firing at the knoll literally caught Colley and his staff napping. All was confusion and disarray at headquarters where the reserve was ordered out to reinforce the threatened northern perimeter. But the men, unprepared, semi-awake and half dressed, and with their units all jumbled together, only reluctantly breasted the security of the rocky ridge to the north of them. Once over it they flung themselves down in the grass and opened a heavy but ineffectually random fire on the knoll which nevertheless caused the Boers to fall back for cover behind its crest. A lull in the firing ensued as both sides regrouped. An intense outburst of firing then broke the uneasy spell as the *burgers* on the knoll covered Roos and about 50 of his men who were scrambling up the steep approach to just below the brow of the hill to within only yards of the British perimeter. Roos encouraged his men by misleadingly telling them that the British were already in flight, and they climbed over the brow to join in the firefight.

This proved too much for the British reserve which had already suffered about 16 casualties. They stampeded back towards the shelter of the rocky ridge, and were joined in their flight by the enfiladed Highlanders from the northern perimeter. The fugitives did not stop when they reached the rocky ridge but carried on running in panicked disarray, making for the southern-western side of the summit and the path back to Mount Prospect. Their officers succeeded in rallying most of them, and brought them back to the rocky ridge where they apprehensively clustered towards the higher ground of Macdonald's Koppie at its western end. That would not do, and officers strove to budge the mob back into their own units and to extend them along the full length of the ridge. Colley, who was undoubtedly courageous, kept a cool head and did much to calm his men as he paced slowly up and down. But in his memoirs of 1927 Hamilton remembered that he did so " … looking on the ground … [and that] … he said nothing and appeared to be thinking of things far away."[23] This observation might well be hindsight, but it is clear that Colley was stunned by the abrupt turn of events and was in a state verging on shock.

The British were given a brief respite in which to regroup while the Boers reduced their firing as they consolidated their own new positions on the mountaintop preparatory to renewing the attack. The British now occupied the perimeter they had initially held during the previous night before pushing forward to occupy the brow of the mountain. And while it was certainly a major setback to have allowed the Boers onto the summit, their situation was not yet disastrous. Macdonald's Koppie was analogous to Gordons' Knoll in that it commanded the new northern perimeter along the rocky ridge. The men posted on it could provide effective covering fire for the soldiers behind it, and also dominated the ground between the ridge and the brow of the mountain. For their part, the troops on Hay's Koppie on the eastern side of the mountain were positioned to provide protective flanking fire to the rear of the rocky ridge for the headquarters and hospital in the bowl. The men along the more southerly sectors of the perimeter had not yet seen action and their morale should have remained unshaken.

---

23   Ian Hamilton's memoir, 'A Subaltern at Majuba', quoted in Saks, 'Colley'.

Yet morale in combat is a volatile thing. Primary group motivation is considered essential in battle, yet on Majuba the British troops were widely spaced along the perimeter and sometimes separated from their units. This meant they did not have the support and encouragement of their familiar comrades. Troops often fail in combat because of poor leadership, and on Majuba they were often isolated from their officers' words of encouragement and had no real sense of what they were expected to achieve, or what the enemy were up to.[24] Certainly, it would have been obvious to regimental officers such as Hamilton, if not to their men as well, that their commanders were in disarray and possessed no considered plan of action. In the ranks the over-confidence of the morning was being rapidly overtaken by perplexity and anxiety.

Meanwhile, on the northern side of the mountain, some Boers were working their way forward to within 40 yards of the rocky ridge in best fire and movement style, taking advantage of every fold in the ground while those in support pinned the British down with a heavy covering fire. The troops on Macdonald's Koppie proved disappointingly ineffective in enfilading the Boers on the open ground north of the ridge because they in turn were pinned down by Boer fire from Gordons' Knoll. Their flank was in any case about to be turned because a party of Ferreira's men was manoeuvering around the western slopes of the mountain below them with the intention of clambering up the gully south of Macdonald's Kop. At the same time, on the eastern side of Majuba, Malan's men, who were working their round behind the rocky ridge, opened fire at the men of the 58th Regiment holding Hay's Koppie who were already taking casualties from high fire from the Boers attacking the ridge.

While the Boers were closing in on the British in a classic pincer movement as they had at Bronkhorstspruit, the British officers succeeded in restoring some order among their troops behind the ridge, and the command was given to fix bayonets. Yet, even though some officers were all for it, Colley never gave the order for the standard volley followed by a bayonet charge. It is one of the abiding debates about the battle whether or not it would have succeeded. Given the faltering morale of the men, and the fact that the Boers were scattered, under cover and out of sight, it is most unlikely. As Hay recollected, Colley was right in refusing to allow the men to charge because "There was nothing to charge. There was not a Boer to be seen."[25] Meanwhile, British casualties were slowly mounting and their return fire against the Boers was singularly ineffective. The Boers later claimed that many of the captured British firearms were sighted at 400 yards—far too high for the increasingly close-range fire-fight. It was for officers to order their men to change their sights, and their inability to make them do so speaks for the increasing breakdown of cohesion.

The Naval Brigade positioned along the south-west perimeter reported to headquarters that Ferreira's men were now swiftly moving up the large gully below Macdonald's Kop and that the British along the rocky ridge were in danger of being enfiladed. Colley responded by ordering his men nearest to

---

24 See Lynn, *Battle*, pp. 241, 251–254.
25 Cromb, *Majuba*, pp. 20–21.

The panicked flight of British troops down the rock-strewn slopes of Majuba under fire from the Boers who had seized the crest of the mountain. (*Illustrated London News*, 23 April 1881)

Melton Prior's pencil sketch of March 1881, based on information from eye-witnesses, of Colley on Majuba attempting to rally his men a minute before he was shot. The sketch was substantially reworked and engraved for the *Illustrated London News* of 14 May 1881 with the gruesome depiction of casualties omitted, along with the unacceptable portrayal of soldiers running away with their officers vainly trying to stop them. (Collection of Ian Knight)

the gully behind the rocky ridge—a medley of the 92nd Highlanders, 58th Regiment and some sailors—to extend their line about twenty yards to their left to block the gap. But faltering morale affected discipline and the men proved unwilling to leave the cover of the rocky ridge or to follow officers who were not their own. Stewart and Major Fraser of the staff joined the regimental officers in exhorting them, and a few small groups finally pulled themselves forwards on their stomachs under blistering Boer fire. Their reluctant effort was negated because troops along the untested southern perimeter, unnerved by the sounds of firing and the obvious confusion among other troops to the north of them, weakened the outer defences by starting to slip away from their exposed posts and, ignoring the attempts of their officers to stop them, to make for the apparent greater security of the rocky ridge.

Amidst these growing signs of breakdown Major Hay reported to Colley that Malan's men were threatening Hay's Koppie which, if lost, would expose the rear of the rocky ridge to Boer fire. Colley, who now had his .45 Holland and Holland revolver drawn, ordered the 92nd Highlanders to hold Hay's Koppie at all costs, and directed his men behind the rocky ridge to extend further to the right in support.

Before they could respond—if indeed they were disposed to obey—the left of the British position suddenly collapsed. Soldiers at the head of the gulley facing Ferreira's men broke and rushed with cries of terror towards the southern side of the mountain and the path back to Mount Prospect. With their flank turned, and facing what Major Hay and Major Macgregor agree was a "crushing" and "overwhelming" fire from a largely invisible enemy[26]—Major Fraser, the most senior officer neither killed nor captured in the battle, wrote in a private letter of 2 March 1881 that " … we could see nothing but muzzles and smoke"[27]—the men behind the ridge faltered in their firing. Small groups of them began to break away and make for the rear despite threats from their officers to shoot them. General panic then set in, and " … with a wild, despairing cry" the whole line along the ridge collapsed as the men sprinted "helter-skelter" to the rear.[28]

Colley was seen standing at the centre of the line close to the hospital, about 15 yards from the ridge, with his revolver held above his head, yelling at the men to make a stand at the higher ground that commanded the way down the southern side of the mountain. But the day was lost and Colley was heard to groan, "Oh, my men, do not run."[29] The triumphant Boers seized the abandoned rocky ridge and Hay's Koppie, and opened a devastating fire on the fleeing British. The hospital was left exposed with the collapse of the British line. Surgeon Arthur J. Landon, who had passed through the Army Medical School at Netley only two years before, was shot dead as he tended the wounded.[30] While trying to indicate the presence of the hospital to the Boers by waving a white bandage above his head, Lance Corporal Joseph J. Farmer of the Army Hospital Corps was shot through the right wrist. Yelling that he had "another arm," he picked up the bandage with his left hand and continued to wave it until his left elbow was smashed.[31] Queen Victoria herself later decorated him at Osborne with the Victoria Cross for his determined courage.[32]

With the ridge and two koppies lost the British made no further attempt at a stand. They simply threw themselves over the edge of the southern side of the mountain in a desperate *sauve qui peut*, bounding and tumbling down the steep, boulder-strewn slopes, many dropping their rifles as they went.[33] In the contemptuous opinion of Arthur Aylward, the controversial Fenian correspondent of the *Daily Telegraph* who was imbedded with the

L. Cpl. Joseph John Farmer of the Army Hospital Corps first served in the Anglo-Zulu War. He was photographed for the *Windsor Magazine* before joining the Natal Field Force. At the battle of Majuba he earned the Victoria Cross for his valiant conduct. Soon obliged to retire from the army on account of his wounds, he became a house-painter. (Collection of Ian Knight)

---

26 Cromb, *Majuba*, pp. 22–23.

27 Emery, Frank, 'Soldiers' Letters from the First Anglo-Boer War, 1880–81, *Natalia*, 11 (1981), p. 25.

28 *The Times*, 4 March 1881: report, 3 March 1881.

29 Quoted in Butler, *Pomeroy-Colley*, pp. 403–404.

30 *The Times*, 8 February 1881; *ILN*, 19 March 1881.

31 *BPP* (C. 2950), enc. 1 in no. 27: Wood to Childers, 9 March 1881.

32 *ILN*, 13 August 1881.

33 *The Times*, 1 March 1881: report, 28 February 1881.

Boers, the troops were " … hurled down the mountain side more like sheep" than anything else he could compare them to.[34] Lieutenant Macdonald concentrated a group of about twenty men on Macdonald's Koppie, presuming that the rest of the force would rally to the south of him. But when he saw that no stand was being attempted and that his men were taking heavy casualties, he ordered them to retire as well. All were killed or wounded except for Macdonald and one other man. Their surrender—but not before Macdonald had kicked one of his captors who was trying to grab his sporran as a trophy in the stomach—ended organised resistance on the mountaintop. It had taken only thirty minutes from the Boer assault on Gordons' Kop to sweep the British from the summit of Majuba.

Colley was fatally shot through the head, the bullet entering through the helmet above the right eye and exiting behind the left ear. However, the circumstances surrounding his last moment are unclear.[35] Accounts have him dying as he tried to rally his men; as he was retiring slowly with his face to the enemy; or as he walked towards the Boers in an attempt to surrender with a white handkerchief tied to his sword. One report has him shot at very short range by a twelve-year-old boy; and others say that he was shot at longer range by a group consisting of Ferreira, Roos and Gideon Erasmus. Rumours also abounded that his wound was self-inflicted. Wood later obtained the helmet Colley had been wearing, and sent it to Lady Colley as a relic. In his covering letter Wood opined that the damaged helmet showed without question that Colley had died "with his face to the foe."[36] Colley's widow (to whom he had left a disappointing bequest of less than £5,000) entertained no doubts about the matter.[37] She tartly responded that the precise position of Colley's head when he was shot was an accident of no interest to her because she had " … never heard him charged with any fault in regard of personal courage except having it in excess."[38]

The victorious Boers who had stormed Majuba seized the abandoned British ammunition and firearms and looted the dead and wounded before opening a heavy fire from the southern side of the mountain on the fleeing British.[39] Later that day the Boers rounded up many fugitives from their hiding-places behind bushes and rocks from which they had hoped to make their way back to camp under cover of darkness.

At about 1:45 p.m. the approximately two-company-strong force comprised of 92nd Highlanders and men of the 3/60th Regiment under Captain Robertson, which Colley had posted on the ridge between Majuba and Inkwelo, made ready to defend their little redoubt to cover the troops scrambling down the mountain. However, they began to come under attack from the mounted Boers whom Smit had despatched around the western flank of Majuba at the onset of the battle, and from a fresh group on foot under Commandant J. Uys who hurried up from the *nek* to the north-east.

---

34 *Daily Telegraph*, 15 April 1881.
35 For discussion on the various accounts, see Butler, *Pomeroy-Colley*, pp. 404–406; Lehman, *Majuba*, pp. 247–248; Duxbury, *David and Goliath*, p. 42.
36 PAR: WC III/3/6: Wood to Lady Colley. 17 September 1881.
37 *ILN*, 17 December 1881.
38 PAR: WC III/2/6: Lady Colley to Wood, 26 October 1881.
39 NARP: BV 13, p. 454: Joubert to Kruger, 27 February 1881

Almost surrounded, Robertson's position became increasingly untenable. Under heliographed orders from Mount Prospect Camp—where the 'assembly' had sounded at about 3:00 p.m. and the garrison had gone into the entrenchments—he withdrew his men with considerable difficulty. A troop of the 15th Hussars came up on their left flank, dismounted and gave them essential covering fire. Losses were nevertheless heavy with an officer and six men killed and 12 wounded, and with an officer and 23 men taken prisoner. Even so, Robertson lost none of the reserve ammunition entrusted to him and succeeded in evacuating all his wounded. The two companies of the 3/60th Rifles which Colley had posted to Robertson's rear on the shoulder of Inkwelo were not engaged. Without making any attempt to support the troops falling back from Majuba they cravenly withdrew to the safety of Camp Mount Prospect—thus confirming Cambridge's doubts about the effectiveness of short-term battalions.

In contrast to the Rifles' poor performance, the garrison under Lieutenant Colonel Bond at Mount Prospect Camp took positive steps to cover the retreat. The two 9-pdr guns of N/5 Brigade, RA, the Naval Brigade's two Gatling guns, and two companies of the 92nd Highlanders were advanced to below the ridge connecting Inkwelo and Majuba. Their fire, in which 30 shells were expended, helped deter the Boers from advancing any further and cutting off the retreating British. The NMP were sent out to carry exhausted fugitives away on their horses. In the camp itself preparations were made for meeting the attack which seemed imminent and the men engaged frenziedly in "fortifying it at every corner."[40] But the Boer did not press on and firing ceased by 3:30 p.m. Some Boer leaders saw the sudden descent of a thick mist, accompanied by a drizzling rain, as God's way of telling them to go thus far and no further. More prosaically, Joubert judged the British defences at Mount Prospect Camp too strong to risk assaulting.[41] Nevertheless, the garrison remained extremely jittery and on high alert until it was finally stood down at 5:30 a.m. the following morning.

Once the survivors from Majuba itself had finally straggled into camp, and the dead had been buried on the summit where, as Captain Forbes MacBean remembered with a shudder, "the grass was a mass of blood and brains, and was red all over,"[42] the scale of the British reverse became clear. Five officers were dead, eight wounded and seven prisoner, a total of 71 percent of those engaged. Eighty-seven men were killed, 123 wounded and 50 taken prisoner with two more missing. This was 46 percent of the rank-and-file engaged. The 92nd Highlanders suffered the worst with a loss of 58 percent of those in action. Casualty figures such as these attended only the most crushing of defeats, and were made to seem even worse when contrasted with the Boer losses which comprised only one man killed and six wounded (one mortally).[43]

---

40 *Natal Witness*, 28 February 1881, quoted in Jordan, Rob, 'The Battle of Majuba: telegrams of 27 February 1881', *Military History Journal*, 5:2 (December 1980) < samilitaryhistory.org/journal.html > (accessed 27 August 2015).

41 NARP: BV 13, p. 473: Joubert to Kruger, 1 March 1881.

42 Cromb, *Majuba*, p. 35.

43 NARP: BV 16, p. 82: List of killed and wounded at the taking of Colley's Mountain on 27 February 1881.

Captain MacBean noted that the British dead were " … all shot above the chest" and that helmets were riddled with bullet holes. Some men had as many as six bullet wounds to the head.[44] Indeed, the battle was a devastating vindication of Boer marksmanship and their fire and movement tactics that brought comparable British marksmanship and discipline into considerable question. Ironically, untrained irregulars had demonstrated a better grasp of modern fighting techniques than their professional opponents. The total collapse of British morale on Majuba was perhaps the most troubling aspect of the whole miserable debacle. It was later attributed by the mortified military authorities to the unwise lack of cohesion and familiar command structure in Colley's mixed task force. But the NMP (who were accustomed to being held in contempt by British professional soldiers) noted with wry colonial amusement that there was " … much heartburning that night amongst the troops, for each regiment accused the other of having been the first to run."[45]

In the Boer camp where British and Boer wounded alike were being tended, Commandant Joachim Ferreira declared: "I do acknowledge that it was not US who defeated them, but the Lord our God. It was utterly impossible for humans alone."[46] Indeed, the Boers, like the Israelites of old, saw their victory over impossible odds as nothing less than God's support in their fight for freedom against oppression.[47] Kruger, in his response to Joubert's report penned on the evening of his God-given victory,[48] declared in an Order of the Day:

> We glory not in human power, it is God the Lord who has helped us—the God of our fathers, to whom for the last five years, we have addressed our prayers and supplications. He has done great things to us, and hearkened to our prayers. And you, noble and valiant brothers, have been in His hands the means of saving us.[49]

---

44 Cromb, *Majuba*, p. 36. For corroboration of this impression, see the Return of Officers and Men of the Naval Brigade Killed and Wounded at Majuba Mountain in *BBP* (C. 2950), enc. in no. 31: Commodore Richards to the Secretary of the Admiralty, 14 March 1881. All the dead were shot in the head or chest, and most of the wounded were shot in the upper body.

45 Holt, *Mounted Police*, p. 109.

46 Meintjes, *Joubert*, pp. 83–84.

47 NARP: JC 26, no. 2457: Kruger to Joubert, 5 March 1881

48 NARP: BV 13, p. 454: Joubert to Kruger, 27 February 1881

49 Order of the Day by Vice-President Kruger: To the Commandant General, Commanders, Officers, and Burghers in the Transvaal Army at the Drakensberg, 7 March 1881, quoted in Carter, *Boer War*, p. 301. For the original, see *De Staatscourant*, 9 March 1881: Dagorder, 7 March 1881.

10

Winding up an Inglorious Campaign

At daylight on the wet and foggy morning of 28 February an unarmed British burying party of three officers and 100 men left for the battlefield where (with some Boers assisting them) they laid the 59 British dead to rest three deep in a communal grave on the mountaintop. They then roughly walled the graves in. Fourteen more bodies were gathered on the mountainside and buried 200 yards below the summit.[1] The Boers would not let them take anything from the bodies of the fallen. They had already partially stripped the corpses, collecting up rifles, belts and other equipment. They reportedly prized most the dead Highlanders' sporrans as trophies to hang up at home; and passed on their kilts for their young daughters to wear.[2] Another party was sent to assist in bringing down the wounded to the camp. A small house on the farm Stonewall at the foot of Majuba about two miles from Mount Prospect Camp, which was known as O'Neill's cottage after its owner, R.C. (Ou Gert) O'Neill, was used as a temporary halting place. The weather improved on 2 March and a convoy of ambulances with 49 British wounded set out from Mount Prospect for Newcastle, where the hospital rapidly became completely overcrowded.

The Boers sent down a list of prisoners, and blankets and medical supplies were forwarded up to them. Colonel Stewart, seven other captured officers and 49 men were sent under armed escort to Heidelberg. According to Stewart, who had expected otherwise, the Boers treated them throughout their captivity with " … exceptional kindness."[3] The valiant Hamilton, whose left wrist had been shattered by a bullet (leaving his fingers permanently shrivelled and unbendable), and who was struck unconscious by a spent bullet, was released by the Boers who thought he was dying. He would later

---

1   NARP: JC 26, no. 2465: Maj. Essex to Joubert, 27 February 1881. For operations of the NFF between the battle of Majuba and 12 March 1881, see Butterfield, *War and Peace*, pp. 216–220: Journal of the Natal Field Force, 28 February–12 March 1881

2   Cromb, *Majuba*, p. 37.

3   PAR: WC III/2/18: Stewart to Wood, 10 March 1881. Stewart was later held at Heidelberg, where Wood sent him "articles of apparel and kit." See NARP: JC 26, no. 2467: Wood to Joubert, 8 March 1881.

Colley's grave at Mount Prospect with the cross his wife, Edith, Lady Colley, had placed there in March 1881. Col. Bonar Deane, who fell at Laing's Nek, lies next to Colley. (Collection of Ian Knight)

receive a hero's welcome in England and was recommended for the Victoria Cross. It was denied him on the bizarre grounds that he was too young.[4] Macdonald, who had shown conspicuous gallantry, gave his parole on being taken prisoner and helped with the wounded. His conduct so impressed Joubert that on his release his prized claymore, which had been presented to him by his fellow officers, was returned to him. Thereafter, Macdonald was rapidly promoted and pursued a prestigious army career which ended in a great scandal and in his suicide over allegations of homosexual relations with boys in Ceylon.[5] The Boers also held Colley's African guides captive and Joubert was uncertain what to do with them since he regarded them as spies.[6] Their fate is unrecorded.

"No word of exultation" was uttered by the suspicious Boers when Vaughan, the special correspondent of *The Times*, finally succeeded in persuading them that it was indeed Colley's body that lay on the summit where the "poor general" had fallen.[7] The Boers carried the corpse from the battlefield to Joubert's laager at Laing's Nek where it lay in a tent watched over by captured Highlanders. It began, as Joubert complained, to smell, and

---

4   Cassar, 'Hamilton'.
5   Stearn, 'Macdonald'; Farewell, *Victorian Soldiers*, pp. 274–301; Hyam, Ronald, *Empire and Sexuality: The British Experience* (Manchester: Manchester University Press, 1991), pp. 33–35.
6   NARP: BV 13, p. 473: Joubert to Kruger, 1 March 1881.
7   *The Times*, 3 March 1881: report, 28 February 1881.

was brought into the British camp early on the rainy morning of 1 March.[8] That afternoon Colley in his coffin made of packing-crates was placed on a gun-carriage covered by the Union Flag and buried in the officers' cemetery at Mount Prospect along with the bodies of the other officers who had died on Majuba. His grave was in the place of honour at the extreme right of the line next to that of Colonel Deane who at perished in the battle of Laing's Nek. During March Sappers Halliday and O'Brien were detailed to put up tombstones.[9]

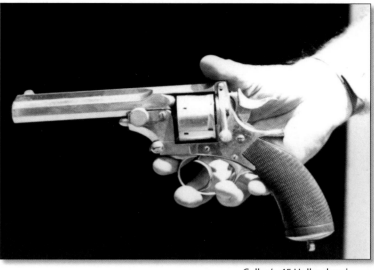

Colley's .45 Holland and Holland revolver taken from his body on Majuba. It remained in the possession of the Joubert family until donated to the museum at Fort Klapperkop, Pretoria. (Photo: Martin Boswell)

Colley's wife and friends petitioned Joubert to return Colley's personal belongings, but he sent back only Colley's patrol jacket without the private letters and other papers believed to have been in its pockets.[10] Wood later obtained his helmet, as we have seen. The rest was looted, and today his revolver (which for a century remained in the possession of Joubert's family) can be seen in the Fort Klapperkop Museum outside Pretoria, while his sword is reported to be in a private collection.

The NFF's comprehensive rout on Majuba had thrown the British entirely onto the defensive. Lieutenant Colonel Bond, who was now the senior officer, ordered the fortifications around Mount Prospect Camp strengthened with the construction of earthwork entrenchments and additional redoubts. Because of the heavy rains the sodwork parapets had to be constantly repaired.[11] The two naval 9-pounder guns were placed in a redoubt on the hill and a detachment of 20 men of the Naval Brigade encamped nearby. The Boers made no attempt, however, to attack the demoralised NFF behind their daunting defences.

Colonel Bond at once telegraphed the news of Colley's defeat and death to Pietermaritzburg, and that very evening Wood had himself sworn in as Acting Governor of Natal and Administrator of the Transvaal in Colley's place. Early on 28 February, the morning after the battle, he left Pietermaritzburg to take command of the troops in the field and to restore badly shaken morale.[12] In the pouring rain he arrived at Mount Prospect on the afternoon of 3 March escorted by a troop of the 15th Hussars and promptly inspected the camp and its defences. He and his staff returned very early the next morning

8   Meintjes, *Commandant-General*, p. 83.
9   TNA: WO 32/7833, no. 079/4743: Report by Lt .Brotherton, 19 April 1881. For the British cemeteries and monuments on Majuba and at Mount Prospect Camp, see Chadwick, 'War Graves', pp. 36–37.
10   NARP: BV 16, p. 89: Bond to Joubert, 1 March 1881; p. 100: Lady Colley to Joubert, n.d.; Joubert to Lady Colley, n.d.
11   TNA: WO 32/7833, no. 079/4743: Report by Lt. Brotherton, 19 April 1881.
12   Manning, 'Evelyn Wood', p. 38; Manning, *Evelyn Wood*, pp. 147–148.

to Newcastle where the 2/60th Rifles and one-and-a-half squadrons of the 15th Hussars were stationed, and where there was only enough food stored in Fort Amiel to last the men for twelve more days. Reinforcements in the form of the 6th (Inniskilling) Dragoons, one-and-a half batteries RA, the 58th Regiment, and the 83rd Regiment were marching for Newcastle, but the distances and the heavy rain which completely flooded the roads meant that they did not reach Newcastle until 25 March—by which stage the Dragoons had not a hundred horses still fit for work.[13]

On 4 March 1881 Kimberley appointed Sir Frederick Roberts to succeed Colley in South Eastern Africa. Roberts had made his reputation in the Second Afghan War while in command of the Kurram and Kabul Field Forces and was celebrated for his relief of Kandahar in September 1880.[14] He was precisely the sort of high-profile commander required to assure the public that the government was now seriously prosecuting the disastrous war in the Transvaal. Childers therefore made it clear to Wood that it was for Roberts to clear up the mess left by Colley, and that although Wood was to remain in command until Roberts arrived, he was to " ... exercise military discretion."[15] The news of Roberts's appointment was received with "little enthusiasm" in South Africa where it was felt Wood should have continued in command.[16]

Roberts and his staff boarded the SS *Balmoral* on 5 March for South Africa, but not before Kimberley had written to him indicating the cabinet's deep ambivalence about the future of the Transvaal. He informed Roberts that while the government would not " ... relax their determination to carry on the military operations with the utmost vigour, they would rejoice should any opportunity present itself for an honourable and satisfactory settlement of the affairs of the Transvaal without further bloodshed."[17] It should not have caused the consternation it did, therefore, when at Madeira on his passage from England Roberts and his staff learned that Wood had arranged a 'ruinous' armistice with the Boers. When they entered Cape Town harbour on the evening of 28 March, a boat came out with people crying 'Peace'. A furiously disappointed Roberts, who deeply resented what he perceived as the government's shabby and fumbling treatment, would not stay in South Africa a moment longer than he had to. He and his staff took the very first ship back to England they could, leaving Cape Town on SS *Trojan* on 30 March. Once at sea Viscount Melgund (the eldest son of the Earl of Minto and Roberts's private secretary) damned Wood in his diary in the most partisan fashion as a " ... talking swaggering man" who had been playing his own game and who had settled with the Boers to gain all the kudos and to

---

13 PAR: WC III/1/3: Memorandum by Sir E. Wood showing the state of affairs at and about Newcastle in the first week, March 1881; Wood, *Midshipman to Field Marshal*, vol. II, p. 111.

14 Mason, Philip, *A Matter of Honour: An Account of the Indian Army, its Officers and Men* (Folkestone, United Kingdom: Peregrine Books, 1976), pp. 345, 381; Haythornthwaite, *Colonial Wars*, pp. 322–324.

15 PAR: WC III/5/2: Childers to Wood, 2 March 1881.

16 *The Times*, 3 March 1881: report, 2 March 1881.

17 *BPP* (C. 2866): no. 64: Kimberley to Sir F. Roberts, 4 March 1881.

thwart any chance Roberts might have had of garnering success.[18]

Paranoia such as this was a feature of the bitter rivalry between the Wolseley and Roberts 'rings'. Members of Roberts's staff might continue over the years to vilify Wood as, " … a shifty chap—too much of a Political Soldier," but the truth of the matter is that in 1881 Roberts's proverbial good luck had not deserted him.[19] While he was able to sail huffily back to England with his reputation unsullied, Wood was lumbered with the odium of pursing the negotiations he privately deplored with the Transvaal rebels.[20] His initial and instinctive response had been stoutly to insist to the government that with the number of troops soon reaching the front—which would eventually give him an available force of a little short of 15,000 men—he could guarantee the entire success of a renewed offensive.[21] Nevertheless, the reality was that in early March the 1,400 men holding Mount Prospect Camp were badly demoralised and poorly supplied, and that the other British forces were still dispersed around Natal.[22] In these circumstances Wood reluctantly came to the unpalatable conclusion that he must suspend hostilities if he could.[23]

President Johannes Brand of the OVS was concerned to bring about peace before the rest of South Africa was dragged into the conflict. Through his determined meditation Wood (now holding the local rank of major general) met Joubert on Sunday, 6 March at O'Neill's cottage, half-way between the British camp and the Boer positions on Laing's Nek. The two commanders agreed to an armistice up to midnight on 14 March which would allow Kruger time to respond to Colley's ill-fated letter of 21 February. In addition, the British were to be permitted to send eight days' supplies to their beleaguered

It was customary to auction off the belongings of soldiers who died on campaign to meet their debts and benefit their next-of-kin. Melton Prior recorded such an occasion in Mount Prospect Camp when the kit of the soldiers killed on Majuba was being sold. In the original pencil drawing (now in the National Army Museum, Chelsea)—of which this is a somewhat clumsy engraving—he noted that the articles on sale included books, jerseys, coats, shirts, soap, tobacco and hold-all's. (*Illustrated London News*, 25 June 1881)

---

18 The National Library of Scotland (TNLS) Minto Papers, MS 12505: Viscount Melgund's diary, 5, 11, 13, 31 March 1881.

19 TNLS: Minto Papers, MS 12830: G. Pretyman to Melgund, 18 January 1892. Pretyman had been Roberts's assistant military secretary 1881.

20 Farwell, *Victorian Soldiers*, p. 178; Wood, *Midshipman to Field Marshal*, vol. II, p. 115.

21 For a list of the troops due in South Africa by April 1881, see *The Times*, 10 March 1881.

22 PAR: WC III/1/3: Memorandum by Sir E. Wood showing the state of affairs at and about Newcastle in the first week, March 1881; TNA: WO 32/7818, no. 079/4455: Wood to Childers, 19 March 1881: State of Troops.

23 PAR: WC III/6/2: Wood to Childers, cypher telegram, 6 March 1881.

The Boer and British negotiators posing outside O'Neill's cottage after signing an armistice on 21 March 1881. Front row, holding his helmet in front of him, is Maj. Gen. Sir Evelyn Wood. Standing to his right (from right to left) are President Johannes Brand of the OVS with his white beard; Paul Kruger, former ZAR vice-president and member of the Boer Triumvirate, who is doffing his hat; Marthinus Wessel Pretorius, former ZAR president and member of the Boer Triumvirate, and *Kmdt. Generaal* J. Petrus Joubert, the third member of the Boer Triumvirate. (WCPA, E3095)

garrisons in the Transvaal. The commencement of the armistice at each fort was to date from the receipt of a convoy of provisions.[24]

Wood received Kruger's reply to Colley's letter on 7 March.[25] Dated 28 February, it expressed Kruger's willingness to agree to a cessation of hostilities and for plenipotentiaries to determine the preliminaries for an honourable peace. On 11 March Colonel Redvers Buller, VC, a hero of the Anglo-Zulu War, a dashing leader of irregular horse and a close associate of Wood's, joined him as his chief of staff to assume responsibility for military affairs while Wood focused on the peace negotiations and civil administration.[26] Like Wood, Buller would have preferred an immediate offensive against the Boers, but had to bow to the instruction of the British government which Wood received on 12 March. These stated the government's willingness to name commissioners if the Boer forces first dispersed, and authorised a commission to consider self-government for the Transvaal under British

---

24 NARP: JC 26, no. 2529: Heads of Conditions of an Armistice Proposed to be Agreed between the British and Boer Forces, 6 March 1881.

25 For Wood's spirited account of the negotiations at O'Neill's cottage, see Wood, *Midshipman to Field Marshal*, vol. II, pp. 118–121.

26 Melville, Colonel Charles .H., *Life of General the Right Hon. Sir Redvers Buller V.C., G.C.B., G.C.M.G.* (London: E. Arnold, 1923), vol. 1, p. 147; Miller, Stephen M., 'Redvers Buller', in Corvi (ed.), Steven J., and Beckett (ed.), Ian F.W., *Victoria's Generals* (Barnsley, South Yorks: Pen & Sword Military, 2009), p. 58; Beckett, Ian F.W., 'Buller, Sir Redvers Henry (1839–1908)', *Oxford Dictionary of National Biography* (Oxford University Press, 2004; online ed., January 2008) <http://www.oxforddnb.com.libproxy.wlu.ca/view/article/32165 > (accessed 20 August 2015).

suzerainty—provided there was protection for African interests, and provided frontier issues and foreign relations were reserved.

With Kruger's arrival with his associates on 16 March negotiations reconvened at O'Neill's cottage. Joubert took a conciliatory line but Kruger bargained very stiffly, and for a few days it looked as if negotiations would break down. President Brand arrived on 20 March as " … a friend of both parties," and thanks to his skilful mediation a provisional agreement (or armistice) was reached on 21 March and its terms ratified on 23 March. The British acknowledged the complete independence of the Transvaal people subject to British suzerain rights. In return, the Boers agreed to disperse in order to await the final settlement of a Royal Commission.[27]

At daylight on 24 March the Boers fulfilled their side of the bargain and quit their position at Laing's Nek. They broke up their laagers, the long train of their ox-wagons threading its way over the undulating plain towards the Transvaal.[28]

Yet Wood did not believe that there should be any immediate reduction of British forces in South Africa lest the Boers not abide by the terms of the agreement. Accordingly, while the Royal Commission was sitting, he concentrated the scattered British detachments in Natal at Newcastle to be available as a striking force to suppress any possible outbreak in the Transvaal, and maintained a reduced garrison at Mount Prospect Camp.[29]

Wood's precautions were not ill-founded, for the Boers were not entirely straight in carrying out the terms of the armistice affecting the British garrisons. At Potchefstroom Cronjé deliberately misled Lieutenant Colonel Richard Winsloe into capitulating on 21 March before supplies arrived for his starving garrison.[30] The Boers attempted a similar stratagem at Lydenburg, but Lieutenant Long hung on until the terms of the armistice were adhered to on 30 March. At Wakkerstroom the siege did not end until 24 March, and the firing only ceased at Standerton a day later. Peace did not come to Rustenburg until 30 March, or to Marabastad until 3 April.[31] Operations around Pretoria ceased on 15 March, and on 29 March civilians were allowed to move back into town.[32] Lanyon finally revoked martial law on 31 March and quietly left Pretoria on 8 April. He had been recalled in semi-disgrace, and would never again be employed in the colonial service.[33]

Hostilities might have ended, but it was difficult to reverse the momentum of cavalry, artillery, and infantry reinforcements Childers

27 *BPP* (C. 2950), enc. 2 in no. 40: Minutes of Proceedings of Meeting, 21 March 1881; enc. 3 in no. 40: Result of a Meeting, 21 March 1881; enc. 6 in no. 40: Wood, Krüger, Pretorius and Joubert to Kimberley, telegram, 21 March 1881; enc. 7 in no. 40: Minutes of the Proceedings at the Meeting of March 23, 1881; enc. 8 in no. 40: Ratification of Provisional Agreement of 21 March 1881, 23 March 1881.

28 *Natal Advertiser*, 26 March 1881: special war correspondent, Mount Prospect, 24 March 1881.

29 WO 32/7818, no. 079/4532: Wood to Childers, 30 March 1881; WO 32/7824, no. 079/4767: Wood to Childers, 8 May 1881. The need for the services of Naval Brigade had gone, however, and it was released.

30 Bennett, *Rain of Lead*, pp. 202–212.

31 Laband, *Transvaal Rebellion*, p. 219.

32 Bellairs, *Transvaal War*, pp. 225–235.

33 Theron-Bushell, 'Lanyon', pp. 285–286, 290–295.

had begun despatching in mid-February to Natal from India, Ceylon, and Bermuda. Consequently, in early April Wood found himself in command of a NFF far too large for its current mission.[34] As for the troops stationed in the Transvaal, Wood concentrated the Rustenburg and Marabastad garrisons in Pretoria, but left all the others temporarily in place except for the severely debilitated Potchefstroom garrison which he withdrew to Natal. But to retrieve the latter's honour and cancel out a capitulation achieved by dishonourable means, on 30 May he ordered a column consisting of the 6th Dragoons, 15th Hussars and the 94th Regiment under the command of Lieutenant Colonel F.G.S. Curtis to reoccupy Potchefstroom and hoist the British flag. Its symbolic mission accomplished, the column was back in Newcastle by 4 July.[35] With its return, operations in the Transvaal came to a definitive close, although Wood remained prepared for renewed hostilities should continuing negotiations break down.[36]

The three Royal Commissioners Kimberley appointed to treat with the Boers were Wood, the High Commissioner, Sir Hercules Robinson, and Sir Henry de Villiers, the Chief Justice of the Cape. After prolonged bargaining with the Boer representatives, the Pretoria Convention was agreed upon. It was signed on 3 August 1881, symbolically in the very same room in Pretoria in which, four years before, Sir Theophilus Shepstone had affixed his signature to the Annexation Proclamation. The *Vierkleur* was hoisted at Pretoria on 8 August 1881 when the transfer of power ceremonially took place.[37] It was not until 18 November 1881, however, that the last detachment of British troops evacuating the Transvaal marched over Laing's Nek into Natal under the command of Colonel Gildea.[38]

Despite his government's eventual extreme satisfaction with his handling of negotiations and his winding down of the war, Wood, overworked and querulous, confided in Buller that he had not been suited to the uncongenial task.[39] The Duke of Cambridge, who certainly did not support the humiliating retrocession of the Transvaal, wrote to commiserate with Wood: "I can well imagine that the duties you have been engaged upon are not agreeable ones to you, and that you are glad they are over."[40] Wood was publicly attacked in the press, although *The Times* conceded that in having to " … wind up an inglorious campaign" with an equally " … inglorious peace" his mission had been an " … anomalous and thankless one."[41] An outraged Queen Victoria was not so forgiving, and was scarcely mollified by Wood's explanation that

34 *BPP* (C. 2837), no. 28: Childers to Colley, 12 February 1881. For the dispositions of the NFF on 10 April 1881, see TNA: WO 32/7818, no. 079/4565: GOC, Natal to the AG to the Forces, 10 April 1881.

35 TNA: WO 32/7828, enc. in no. 079/4965: Maj.-Gen. R. Buller to GOC, Natal and Transvaal, 4 July 1881.

36 PAR: WC III/3/5: Wood to Childers, 4 December 1881.

37 *BPP* (C. 3098), enc. 1 in no, 23: Pretoria Convention, 3 August 1881. See also *BPP* (C. 3114), Appendix no. 1: Convention.

38 *The Times*, 29 December, 1881. The detachments consisted of N/5 Brigade, RA and the Headquarters and six companies of the 21st Fusiliers.

39 PAR: WC III/3/9: Robinson to Wood, 26 September 1881; PAR: WC III/3/2: Wood to Buller, 23 June 1881.

40 WC III/2/9: Cambridge to Wood, 9 August 1881.

41 *The Times*, 18 January 1882.

The Boers jubilantly hoisting the Vierkleur (the flag of the ZAR) in one of their laagers at Laing's Nek on receiving word of the signing of the armistice on 21 March 1881. Note Majuba looming in the background. (*Illustrated London News,* 14 May 1881)

he had been obliged to obey the government's orders.[42] Many in the army were disgusted by his 'abject surrender' and Wolseley could not forgive Wood for not driving the Boers out of Natal before agreeing to a settlement. As a consequence, Wood lost Wolseley's valuable patronage for a number of years and his career stalled accordingly.[43]

The Pretoria Convention was a complex document which conceded the substance of Transvaal independence while appearing to retain ultimate imperial control under the nebulous concept of the Queen's 'suzerainty'. The Boers only accepted this provision with reluctance and distaste. It was not long before Kruger renegotiated the Pretoria Convention and all reference to 'suzerainty' was removed from the London Convention, signed on 27 February 1884. From the British point of view this did not greatly matter because the Pretoria and London Conventions heralded a new approach to dealing with South Africa. The Transvaal Boers had been placated and the Cape and OVS Afrikaners conciliated: the grim possibility of a united Afrikaner front challenging British dominance in South Africa had thereby been defused. The retrocession of the Transvaal also indicated the end of Tory plans for formal confederation. Instead, the idea of informal paramountcy was to be pursued with its aim of courting the Boers and creating stronger and more amiable ties for the future. What this meant was that British colonists, who

---

42 Manning, *Evelyn Wood*, pp. 153–155.
43 Manning, 'Evelyn Wood', pp. 39, 42.

In a symbolic pantomime a crowd of about 2,000 British loyalists buried the Union Flag in Pretoria on 2 August 1881. On the tombstone was inscribed: "In loving memory of the British flag in the Transvaal, who departed this life on the 2nd August 1881, in his fifth year. 'In other climes none knew thee but to love thee.' *Resurgam*." Lt. Col. Gildea rescued the flag and took it back with him to England. (NARP, TAB 16791)

formed the settler minority in South Africa, were to be sacrificed on the altar of improved Anglo-Boer relations.[44]

While the Royal Commission was negotiating the Pretoria Convention, Kimberley had categorically stated that " ... Her Majesty's Government are bound to take care that those who have been faithful to the British cause during the late war shall not suffer any detriment in consequence of their loyalty."[45] Nevertheless, despite this glib assurance, British settlers across South Africa were convinced that Gladstone and his ministers had thrown the Transvaal 'English' (or *uitlanders*) to the Boers and petitioned and protested with outrage.[46]

Nor was there any disguising that during the war the Transvaal 'English' had suffered. Farmers and townspeople—especially storekeepers—who had abandoned their property to take refuge with the British garrisons, or to trek for safety out of the Transvaal altogether, usually had it looted or commandeered. Nor did these depredations ceased with the armistice. As a consequence, many more of the 'English'—along with those Afrikaners who had remained loyal to the British administration—feared that the restored ZAR would be untenable for them, and packed up what they could carry,

---

44 Schreuder, *Gladstone and Kruger*, pp. 212-214, 222-224, 465-469.

45 *BPP* (C. 2892), no. 1: Kimberley to Robinson, 31 March 1881.

46 For the range and scope of protest by English settlers, see Laband, *Transvaal Rebellion*, pp. 224–227.

and left.[47] Sir H. Rider Haggard (who had been a member of Shepstone's staff when he annexed the Transvaal in 1877) saw them pouring through Newcastle in their hundreds: "There were people of all classes, officials, gentlefolk, work-people, and loyal Boers, but they had a connecting link; they had all been loyal, and they were all ruined."[48]

Gladstone deflected many pleas for restitution or compensation, finally remitting them to the Royal Commission for its consideration.[49] In the end, to the disappointment of many, only direct losses as a result of war were recognised in Article 8 of the Pretoria Convention, and not any indirect ones. But at least Article 12 allayed perhaps the greatest concern among the Transvaal 'English' (and loyalist Afrikaners) when it stipulated that they would "suffer no molestation" on account of having supported British forces.[50] Even so, many were left believing—paper guarantees notwithstanding—that a Transvaal no longer under British rule was "a country that could no longer be their home."[51]

47 Laband, *Transvaal Rebellion*, p. 225.
48 Haggard, Sir H. Rider, *The Last Boer War* (London: Kegan Paul, Trench, Trubner, 1899), p. 363.
49 *BPP* (C. 2950), no. 57: Gladstone to White, 1 June 1881.
50 *BPP* (C. 3098), enc. 1 in no. 23: Convention, 3 August 1881: Articles 8 and 12.
51 Haggard, *Last Boer War*, pp. 178–180.

Conclusion

"Britannia needs Instructors"

As it turned out, despite their fears and complaints the Transvaal 'English' emerged relatively unscathed from the Transvaal Rebellion. Those who remained in the restored Boer republic suffered no persecution and eventually received £110,000 for their direct material losses which the Imperial Government defrayed when the Boers defaulted from paying their share.[1] Along with those who continued to invest in the ZAR they were rewarded tenfold when in 1886 the discovery of gold in huge paying quantities on the Witwatersrand heralded boom economic conditions. Still, what they perceived of as their betrayal by Gladstone's administration continued to rankle, and *uitlanders* were never to be reconciled to living in a despised and retrograde Boer republic, and looked to future Tory administrations to safeguard their interests.

As for Africans in the reinstated ZAR, their circumstances deteriorated under Boer rule as many had feared they would. The Native Location Commission, set up in terms of Article 21 of the Pretoria Convention, proceeded under the chairmanship of Vice-President Kruger to delimit locations for all the large African chiefdoms where they would be under closer administrative surveillance.[2]

For Afrikaners, their astonishing military success against Britain's imperial power, capped by their victory at Majuba, encouraged them to flex their muscles in South Africa. The actual military campaign of 1880–1881 may have been confined to the Transvaal itself and to northern Natal but, thanks to the rebellion's provocative nature as an Afrikaner uprising against British colonial rule, it sent out shockwaves throughout the subcontinent. British and Afrikaner communities were galvanised as never before into taking stock of their respective identities and were increasingly divided as a result. The British realised that the majority of the Boers of the OVS, the Cape, and Natal actively sympathised with their blood-brother of the Transvaal. And even if very few actually took up arms in their support, the British government was constrained to terminate the campaign to forestall

---

1   Haggard, *Last Boer War*, p. 178.
2   *BPP* (C. 3098), enc. 1 in no. 23: Convention, 3 August 1881: Article 21; Davenport (ed.), T.R.H., and Hunt (ed.). K S., *The Right to the Land* (Claremont: David Philip, 1974), pp. 31, 40.

The School of Musketry. Boer (to F.-M. H.R.H. the Commander-in-Chief. "I say Dook! You don't happen to want a practical 'Musketry Instructor', do you?" (*Punch*, 7 May 1881)

a Boer uprising across all of southern Africa that would seriously have threatened British political and economic and preponderance. As it was, conceding independence to the Transvaal rebels seriously tarnished the aura of British paramountcy.

Many in the British Army—and among the general public—continued to find it more comforting to attribute their inglorious defeat in the Transvaal campaign to dishonorable and duplicitous Boer strategisms and deceptions rather than to the shortcomings in British military technique exposed in that disastrous 'small war'. The satirical magazine, *Punch*, knew otherwise. In "a Military Ode" to the British infantry, it declared:

> Britannia needs instructors
> To teach her boys to shoot,
> Fixed targets and mere red-tape drill
> Have borne but bitter fruit … [3]

Nevertheless, as *The Times* expressed it, the lesson learned in South Africa was "a severe one," and did seem " … to have produced some impression" on the military authorities.[4] Colonel Gildea, who had studied the Boer way of war during the siege of Pretoria, was reported in October 1881 to be energetically training his men of the Royal Scots Fusiliers at shelter breastworks, and then to be pulling them down in order to instruct them in forming "hasty entrenchments."[5] In other words, as an intelligent and active officer Gildea had taken the military lessons of the recent war to heart. He had seen that even if the necessity for shelter trenches in the new age of accurate, long-range, high velocity and rapid firing rifles was already acknowledged in the British manuals of military practice, British soldiers were not being sufficiently drilled in their effective use.

Likewise, in the aftermath of the Transvaal campaign where the record of British marksmanship had been nothing short of dismal, and where, as *The Times* put it, British soldiers " … were literally over-powered and their courage quelled solely by the superior shooting of the Boers,"[6] the 1881 Report of the Committee on Musketry Instruction in the Army recommended radical improvements in musketry instruction, and suggested that firing be regularly practised at extreme ranges over broken country against moving targets.[7] However, turning soldiers used to minimal practice against fixed targets into real marksmen adept at skirmishing required a much increased expenditure of ammunition which the War Office proved initially reluctant to countenance.[8]

That problem was not insurmountable, and it was recognised that the recommendations for practice in using shelter trenches and for a much greater emphasis on musketry instruction actually amounted to no more

---

3   *Punch*, 7 May 1881.
4   *The Times*, 19 April 1881.
5   PAR: WC III/3/3: Wood to Cambridge, 25 October 1881. By that date the 2/21st Fusiliers had been re-designated the Royal Scots Fusiliers
6   *The Times*, 21 April 1881.
7   TNA: WO 33/37: Report of the Committee on Musketry Instruction in the Army, 1881.
8   *The Times*, 16 March and 21 April 1881; *ILN*, 23 April and 23 July 1881.

than better training in methods already set down in the regulations. The disastrous campaign against mobile Boer irregulars had, it seemed, shown that British shortcomings lay with poor leadership and execution, rather than with faulty military doctrine. It was with this mind-set that the British would go to war again with the Boers in 1899, determined to restore their bruised military honour. At the battle of Elandslaagte on 21 October 1899, Ian Hamilton, a survivor of Colley's ultimate defeat and now holding the temporary rank of major general, would urge on his men with the cry: "Remember Majuba!"[9]

Boer military success against Britain and the imperial power's capitulation encouraged Afrikaners to believe that they had the potential to assert their power more generally in South Africa and to fill the vacuum left by the evaporation of Britain's forward confederation policy.[10]

Yet, paradoxically, the very extent of Boer success in the war of 1880–1881 would lie at the root of their military failure in the conventional stage of the Anglo-Boer War of 1899–1902. In 1899 the Boers realistically assessed that, since time was not on their side, they must achieve such remarkable early military successes that, as in the previous war, the Cape Afrikaners would be encouraged to flock to their cause and the British would again lose heart and negotiate a settlement.[11] When relations with Britain reached breaking-point in 1899 the Boers were encouraged (so Haggard believed) by the British capitulation eighteen years before to presume " … that England, wearying of an unpopular struggle, [would] soon cede to them all they ask."[12]

The Liberals may have insouciantly killed off confederation in 1881, but the game was not entirely over. Imperial agents who had been closely involved in Transvaal affairs—men such as Shepstone, Frere, Wolseley and Lanyon—held the retrocession of the Transvaal to be both a humiliation and a critical blow to Britain's position in southern Africa. Wolseley was concerned that because the British were widely believed in South Africa to have made peace with the Boers because they " … feared to continue the war," that British military power would no longer act as a deterrent in the subcontinent. The result, Wolseley presciently warned, would be serious future wars.[13] Nevertheless, for the time being confederation was thoroughly discredited. The dream of a white-ruled South African dominion as an addition to the Empire's strategic strength had proved a chimera for which a "wretched conflict" had been fought which had brought "neither profit nor honour," and for which the authorities could not bring themselves even to award the usual campaign medal.[14] Yet, in 1899, on the eve of the terrible

9   Judd, Denis, and Surridge, Keith, *The Boer War* (London: John Murray, 2002), p. 110. Hamilton was recommended for the Victoria Cross at Elandslaagte but was denied it as he had been after Majuba, this time on the grounds that it had never been awarded to a general who had personally led his men in battle, and that it was undesirable to establish a precedent. See Cassar, 'Hamilton'.

10   Nasson, Bill, *The South African War 1899–1902* (London: Arnold, 1999), p. 23.

11   Judd and Surridge, *Boer War*, p. 106.

12   Rider Haggard, *Boer War*, p. xix.

13   TNA: WO 32/7835, no. 079/5282: Confidential Memorandum by Wolseley, 31 October 1881.

14   *ILN*, 19 February 1881; Goodfellow, *Confederation*, pp. 202–2033; Bennett, *Rain of Lead*, p. 239.

Second Anglo-Boer War, Haggard saw clearly that Britain was paying the bill for abandoning confederation in 1881, and was again being forced " … to assert its dominion even at the price of war."[15]

The farm on which Majuba stands became in 1981 the property of the Potchefstroom University for Christian National Education and was administered until 2000 by the Voortrekker Museum in Pietermaritzburg. Under their joint administration Majuba long remained a site of fervent pilgrimage and nationalist commemoration for many Afrikaners. Here the victory of *die Volk* over British imperialism could be joyously celebrated, unlike the Second Anglo-Boer War which was remembered with bitter tears.

In post-apartheid South Africa, however, there has been a realignment of museum and university policies and functions so that Majuba and its battlefield is now in the hands of a private foundation, and the state no longer plays any part in keeping the memory of the war of 1880–1881 alive.[16] The monuments and war graves of the Transvaal Rebellion, along with those of other South African wars, have since 1999 been in the charge of the South African Heritage Resources Agency and Burial Sites Unit.[17] One can still visit the military cemeteries at Bronkhorstspruit, Laing's Nek, Ingogo (Schuinshoogte), Mount Prospect, and that on the summit of Majuba; while the graves of those who died in the various sieges are generally to be found in the town cemeteries. Natural deterioration and vandalism are the foes of such memorials, and in recent years these inimical processes have much accelerated for lack of funds for restoration and custodianship, and by an increasing rejection of the colonial past.[18] The new South Africa celebrates the recent heroes of the freedom struggle against apartheid. It does not remember those Afrikaners who, in a strange and distant age, pitted themselves like David against the British Goliath, nor those British soldiers who died in performance of their imperial duty in a forgotten 'small war' so far from home.

---

15 Haggard, *Boer War*, p. xxiii.

16 The Amajuba Commemorative Farm incorporates Majuba Mountain and its battlefield, as well as a small orientation museum and a farm museum. There is a youth centre with accommodation for 80 children and 10 teachers. <www.openafrica/experiences/participant/1833-majuba-commemorative-farm > (accessed 4 April 2017). Bed & breakfast accommodation is available in the vicinity for tourists.

17 War graves and monuments were initially the responsibility of the South African War Graves Board, formed in 1956, which was then absorbed in 1982 into the National Monuments Council before reorganization in 1999 into its present form. <www.sahra.org.za/sahris/about/burial-grounds/graves > (accessed 4 April 2017).

18 Chadwick, 'War Graves', pp. 34 –38 and personal observation by the author while serving on various museum and heritage committees in South Africa.

Bibliography

Manuscript Sources

National Archives Repository, Pretoria (NARP)
A 14: P.J. Joubert Collection (JC): 25, 26
Argief Boeren Voormannen: BV 3, 11, 13, 16, 17, 19
Staatsekretaris ZAR: SS 8834
Pietermaritzburg Archives Repository (PAR)
A598: Sir Evelyn Wood Collection (WC): III/1/2 –3; III/2/5, 9, 13, 18; III/3/2–3,
    5, 9; III/4/2; III/5/2; III/6/2
The National Archives, Kew (TNA)
War Office, 32, Papers Relating to the Transvaal Rebellion: WO 32/7797–7798,
    7803, 7806, 7810–7814, 7816–7818, 7820, 7827–7828, 7833, 7835
WO 33/37: Report of the Committee on Musketry Instruction in the army, 1881
WO 33/39: Report of the Colour Committee, 1883
The National Library of Scotland (TNLS)
Minto Papers, MS 12505, 12830
Western Cape Provincial Archives and Records Service (WCPA)
Department of Defence, Cape Colony: DD 8
Government House, Cape Colony: 30

Official Printed Sources

Blue Book for the Transvaal Province 1879 (Pretoria: Coppen, Deecker, 1879).
British Parliamentary Papers 1878-1879, LII (C. 2220). South Africa,
    Correspondence, 1878-1879.
British Parliamentary Papers 1880, LI (C. 2676). South Africa, Correspondence,
    1879-1880.
British Parliamentary Papers 1881, LXVI (C. 2740), (C. 2783). South Africa,
    Correspondence, 1880-1881.
British Parliamentary Papers 1881, LXVII (C. 2837), (C. 2838), (C. 2866). South
    Africa, Correspondence, 1881.
British Parliamentary Papers 1881, LXVII (C. 2950), (C. 2959). South Africa,
    Correspondence, 1880–1881.
British Parliamentary Papers 1882, XLVII (C. 3098). Correspondence *re*
    Transvaal, 1881–1882.
Callwell, Colonel C.E. *Small Wars: Their Principles and Practice*, 3rd edition
    (London: His Majesty's Stationary Office, 1906).
De Staatscourant Gedurenden den Vrijheidsoorlog van 1881.
Great Britain, War Office. *Field Exercise and Evolution of Infantry*, pocket
    edition (London: Her Majesty's Stationary Office, 1877).

— *Text Book of Fortification and Military Engineering, for Use at the Royal Military Academy, Woolwich,* 2nd edition (London: Her Majesty's Stationary Office, 1884).

— Intelligence Department. *Précis of Information Concerning South Africa. The Transvaal Territory* (London: Harrison and Sons, 1878).

Newspapers and Periodicals

Daily Telegraph, 1881
Illustrated London News, 1881
Natal Advertiser, 1881
Punch, 1881
The Times, 1881

Books

Beckett, Ian F.W. *The Victorians at War* (London: Hambledon, 2003).

— (ed.) *Wolseley and Ashanti. The Asante War Journal and Correspondence of Major General Sir Garnet Wolseley 1873–1874* (Stroud, Glocs.: The History Press for the Army Records Society, 2009).

Bellairs (ed.), Lady. *The Transvaal War 1880–81* (Edinburgh and London: William Blackwood and Sons, 1885).

Bennett, Ian. *A Rain of Lead: The Siege and Surrender of the British at Potchefstroom* (London: Greenhill Books, 2001).

Benyon, John. *Proconsul and Paramountcy in South Africa: The High Commission, British Supremacy and the Sub-Continent 1806–1910* (Pietermaritzburg: University of Natal Press, 1980).

Brice, Christopher. *The Thinking Man`s Soldier. The Life and Career of General Sir Henry Brackenbury 1837–1914* (Solihul, England: Helion, 2012).

Burman, Sandra. *Chiefdom, Politics and Alien Law: Basutoland under Cape Rule, 1881–1884* (New York: Africana Publishing Company, 1981).

Butler, Lt. Gen. Sir William F. *The Life of Sir George Pomeroy-Colley, KCSI, CB, CMG Including Services in Kaffraria—in China—in Ashanti and in Natal* (London: John Murray, 1899).

Butterfield (ed.), Paul .H. *War and Peace in South Africa 1879–1881: The Writings of Philip Anstruther and Edward Essex* (Melville, South Africa: Scripta Africana, 1987).

Carter, Thomas Fortescue. *A Narrative of the Boer War: Its Causes and Results,* new edition (Cape Town: J.C. Juta; London: John Macqueen, 1896).

Castle, Ian. *Majuba 1881: The Hill of Destiny* (London: Osprey Military, 1996).

Clayton, Anthony. *The British Officer: Leading the Army from 1660 to the Present* (Harlow, United Kingdom: Pearson Longman, 2006).

Cope, Richard. *Ploughshare of War: The Origins of the Anglo-Zulu War of 1879* (Pietermaritzburg: University of Natal Press, 1999).

Cromb, (ed.), James. *The Majuba Disaster: A Story of Highland Heroism, Told by Officers of the 92nd Regiment* (Dundee: John Leng, 1891; reprinted Pietermaritzburg: Africana Book Collectors, 1988).

Davenport (ed.), T.R.H., and Hunt (ed.), K.S. *The Right to the Land* (Claremont, South Africa: David Philip, 1974).

Davenport, Rodney, and Saunders, Christopher. *South Africa: A Modern History,* 5th edition (London: Macmillan, 2000).

Davey, A.M. 'The Siege of Pretoria 1880–1881', in *Archives Year Book for South African History*, Nineteenth Year, vol. 1 (Parow, South Africa: The Government Printer, 1956).

Dominy, Graham. *Last Outpost on the Zulu Frontiers: Fort Napier and the British Imperial Garrison* (Urbans, Chicago and Springfield: University of Illinois Press, 2016).

Duxbury, George R. *David and Goliath: The First War of Independence, 1880–1881* (Saxonwold, South Africa: South African National Museum of Military History, 1981).

Eldredge, Elizabeth A. *Power in Colonial Africa: Conflict and Discourse in Lesotho, 1870–1960* (Wisconsin: University of Wisconsin Press, 2007).

Emery, Frank. *Marching over Africa: Letters from Victorian Soldiers* (London: Hodder and Stoughton, 1986).

Ensor, R.C.K., *England 1870–1914* (Oxford: Clarendon Press, 1968).

Etherington, Norman. *The Great Treks: The Transformation of Southern Africa, 1815–1854* (London: Longman Pearson, 2001).

Farwell, Byron. *Eminent Victorian Soldiers: Seekers of Glory* (New York and London: W.W. Norton, 1985).

Garrett Fisher, William E. *The Transvaal and the Boer: A Short History of the South African Republic, with a Chapter on the Orange Free State* (London: Chapman & Hall, 1900).

Goodfellow, C.F. *Great Britain and South Africa Confederation (1879–1881)* (Cape Town: Oxford University Press, 1966).

Haggard, Sir H. Rider. *The Last Boer War* (London: Kegan Paul, Trench, Trubner, 1899).

Haythornthwaite, Philip J. *The Colonial Wars Source Book* (London: Caxton Editions, 2000).

Holt, H.P. *The Mounted Police of Natal* (London: John Murray, 1913).

Hyam, Ronald. *Empire and Sexuality: The British Experience* (Manchester: Manchester University Press, 1991).

Judd, Denis, and Surridge, Keith. *The Boer War* (London: John Murray, 2002).

Knight, Ian. *Go to Your God like a Soldier: The British Soldier Fighting for Empire, 1837–1902* (London: Greenhill Books, 1996).

Kruger, Paul. *The Memoirs of Paul Kruger, Four Times President of the South African Republic, Told by Himself* (London: T. Fisher Unwin, 1902).

Laband, John. *The Atlas of the Later Zulu Wars 1883-1888* (Pietermaritzburg, University of Natal Press, 2001).

— *Historical Dictionary of the Zulu Wars* (Lanham, Md., Toronto and Oxford: The Scarecrow Press, 2009).

— *The Rise and Fall of the Zulu Nation* (London: Arms and Armour Press, 1997).

— *The Transvaal Rebellion: The First Boer War 1880–1881* (Harlow: Longman Pearson, 2005).

— *Zulu Warriors. The Battle for the South African Frontier* (New Haven and London: Yale University Press, 2014).

Laband, John, and Knight, Ian. *The War Correspondents: The Anglo-Zulu War* (Stroud, Glocs: Sutton Publishing, 1996).

Laband, John, and Paul Thompson. *The Illustrated Guide to the Anglo-Zulu War* (Pietermaritzburg: University of Natal Press, 2000).

Laband , John and Thompson, Paul, with Henderson, Sheila. *The Buffalo Border 1879: The Anglo-Zulu War in Northern Natal* (Durban: Department of History, University of Natal, Research Monograph No. 6, 1983).

Labuschange, Pieter. *Ghostriders of the Anglo-Boer War (1899–1902): The Role and Contribution of Agterryers* (Pretoria: University of South Africa, 1999).

Lehmann, Joseph. *The First Boer War* (London: Jonathan Cape, 1972).

Le May, G.H.L. *Afrikaners: An Historical Interpretation* (Oxford: Blackwell, 1995).

Long, Mrs W.H.C. *Peace and War in the Transvaal: An Account of the Defence of Fort Mary, Lydenburg* (London: Low's, 1882).

Lynn, John A. *Battle: A History of Combat and Culture* (Boulder, Col. and Oxford: Westview Press, 2003).

Manning, Stephen. *Evelyn Wood: Pillar of Empire* (Barnsley, South Yorks: Pen & Sword Military, 2007).

Mason, Philip. *A Matter of Honour: An Account of the Indian Army, its Officers and Men* (Folkestone, United Kingdom: Peregrine Books, 1976).

Meintjes, J. *The Commandant-General: The Life and Times of Petrus Jacobus Joubert of the South African Republic 1831–1900* (Cape Town: Tafelberg, 1971).

Melville, Colonel Charles H. *Life of General the Right Hon. Sir Redvers Buller V.C., G.C.B., G.C.M.G.* (London: E. Arnold, 1923).

Mollo, John. *Military Fashion: A Comparative History of the Uniforms of the Great Armies from the 17th Century to the First World War* (New York: G.P. Putnam's Sons, 1972).

Nasson, Bill. *The South African War 1899–1902* (London: Arnold, 1999).

Norris-Newman, Charles. *With the Boers in the Transvaal and Orange Free State in 1880–1*, 2nd edition (London: Abbott, Jones, 1882).

Preston (ed.), Adrian. *The South African Journal of Sir Garnet Wolseley 1879–1880* (Cape Town: A.A. Balkema, 1973).

Ransford, Oliver N. *The Battle of Majuba Hill: The First Boer War* (London: Thomas Y. Crowell, 1967).

Richards, Walter. *Her Majesty's Army: A Descriptive Account of the Various Regiments Now Comprising the Queen's Forces, from their First Establishment to the Present* (London: H. Virtue, n.d. [c.1888]), 2 volumes.

St. Aubyn, Giles. *The Royal* George, *1819–1904. The Life of H.R.H. Prince George Duke of Cambridge* (New York: Alfred A. Knopf, 1964).

Saunders (ed.) Christopher. *Reader's Digest Illustrated History of South Africa: The Real Story*, 3rd edition (Cape Town: The Readers' Digest Association, 1994).

Schreuder, Deryck M. *Gladstone and Kruger. Liberal Government and Colonial 'Home Rule', 1880–1885* (London: Routledge and K. Paul; Toronto: University of Toronto Press, 1969).

— *The Scramble for Southern Africa, 1877–1895* (Cambridge: Cambridge University Press, 1980).

Spiers, Edward .M. *The Army and Society 1815–1914* (London and New York: Longman, 1980).

— *The Late Victorian Army, 1868–1902* (Manchester: Manchester University Press, 1992).

Stapleton, Timothy J. *A Military History of South Africa from the Dutch-Khoi Wars to the End of Apartheid* (Santa Barbara, Calif.: Praeger, 2010).

Storey, William Kelleher. *Guns, Race, and Power in Colonial South Africa* (Cambridge: Cambridge University Press, 2008).

Strachan, Hew. *European Armies and the Conduct of War* (London and New York: Routledge, 1983).

Swart, Sandra. *Riding High: Horses, Humans and History in South Africa* (Johannesburg: Wits University Press, 2010).

Templin, J. Alton. *Ideology on a Frontier: The Theological Foundations of Afrikaner Nationalism, 1652–1910* (Westport, Conn. and London: Greenwood Press, 1984).

Trollope, Anthony, *South Africa*, reprint of the 1878 edition (Cape Town: A.A. Balkema, 1973).

Vaughan, Sir J.L. *My Service in the Indian Army—and After* (London,: Archibald Constable, 1904).

Walker, Eric A. *The Great Trek*, 3rd edition (London: Adam and Charles Black, 1948).

Warwick, Peter. *Black People and the South African War 1899–1902* (Johannesburg: Ravan Press, 1983).

Wood, Evelyn. *From Midshipman to Field Marshal*, 2nd edition (London: Methuen, 1906), volume II.

Worsfold, Basil. *Sir Bartle Frere. A Footnote to the History of the British Empire* (London: Butterworth, 1923).

Articles and Chapters

Adlam, Lt. A.M. 'Die Pers as Bron oor die Geskiedenis van die Eesrste Vryheidsoorlog', *Scientia Militaria: South African Journal of Military Studies*, 1: 11 (1981), pp. 62–68.

Bailes, H. 'Technology and Tactics in the British Army, 1866–1900', in Haycock (ed.), R., and Neilson (ed.), K., *Men, Machines and War* (Waterloo, Ontario: Wilfrid Laurier University Press, 1988).

Bakkes, C.M. 'Die Slag van Majuba, 27 Februarie 1881', in Van Jaarsveld (ed.), F.A., Van Rensburg (ed.), A.P.J., and Stals (ed.), W.A., *Die Eerste Vryheidsoorlog van Verset en Geweld tot Skikking deur Onderhandeling 1877–1884* (Pretoria and Cape Town: Haum, 1980).

Beckett, Ian F.W. 'Buller, Sir Redvers Henry (1839–1908)', *Oxford Dictionary of National Biography* (Oxford University Press, 2004; online edition, January 2008) <http://www.oxforddnb.com.libproxy.wlu.ca/view/article/32165> (accessed 20 August 2015).

— 'Colley, Sir George Pomeroy Pomeroy (1835–1881)', *Oxford Dictionary of National Biography* (Oxford University Press, 2004; online edition, January 2008) <http://www.oxforddnb.com.libproxy.wlu.ca/view/article/5910> (accessed 20 August 2015).

— 'George Colley', in Corvi (ed.), Steven J., and Beckett (ed.), Ian F.W., *Victoria's Generals* (Barnsley, South Yorks: Pen & Sword Military, 2009).

— 'Military High Command in South Africa, 1854–1914', in Boyden (ed.), Peter B., Guy (ed.), Alan J., and Harding (ed.) Marion, *'Ashes and Blood'. The British Army in South Africa 1795–1914* (London: National Army Museum Publication, 2001).

— 'Stewart, Sir Herbert (1843–1885)', *Oxford Dictionary of National Biography* (Oxford University Press, 2004; online edition, January 2008) <http://www.

oxforddnb.com.libproxy.wlu.ca/view/article/26474> (accessed 20 August 2015).

— 'Wolseley, Garnet Joseph, first Viscount Wolseley (1833–1913)', *Oxford Dictionary of National Biography* (Oxford University Press, 2004; online edition, May 2009) <http://www.oxforddnb.com.libproxy.wlu.ca/view/article/33372> (accessed 20 August 2015).

— 'Wood, Sir (Henry) Evelyn (1838–1919)', *Oxford Dictionary of National Biography* (Oxford University Press, 2004; online edition, January 2008) <http://www.oxforddnb.com.libproxy.wlu.ca/view/article/37000> (accessed 20 August 2015).

Benyon, John. 'Frere, Sir (Henry) Bartle Edward, first baronet (1815–1884)', *Oxford Dictionary of National Biography* (Oxford University Press, 2004; online edition, January 2011) <http://www.oxforddnb.com.libproxy.wlu.ca/view/article/10171> (accessed 20 August 2015)

Bond, Brian. 'Cardwell, Edward, first Viscount Cardwell (1813–1886)', *Oxford Dictionary of National Biography* (Oxford University Press, 2004; online edition, January 2008) <http://www.oxforddnb.com.libproxy.wlu.ca/view/article/4620> (accessed 20 August 2015).

— 'The Disaster of Majuba Hill 1881', *History Today* (July 1965), pp. 491–495.

Bou, Jean. 'Modern Cavalry: Mounted Rifles, the Boer War, and the Doctrinal Debates', in Dennis (ed.), Peter, and Grey (ed.), Jeffrey, *The Boer War: Army, Nation and Empire* (Canberra: Army History Unit, Australian Department of Defence, 2000)

Carr, William, revised by Matthew, H.C.C. 'Childers, Hugh Eardley (1827–1896)', *Oxford Dictionary of National Biography* (Oxford University Press, 2004; online edition, January 2008) <http://www.oxforddnb.com.libproxy.wlu.ca/view/article/5296> (accessed 20 August 2015).

Cassar, George H. 'Hamilton, Sir Ian Standish Monteith (1853–1947)', *Oxford Dictionary of National Biography* (Oxford University Press, 2004; online edition, January 2011) <http://www.oxforddnb.com.libproxy.wlu.ca/view/article/33668> (accessed 20 August 2015)

Chadwick, G.A. 'War Graves Registers, Monuments, Headstones and Crosses with Special Reference to the War of 1880–1881', *Scientia Militaria: South African Journal of Military Studies*, 1: 11 (1981), pp. 31–39.

Conradie, D. 'The Vierkleur and the Union Jack in the 1880–1881 War between the Zuid-Afrikaansche Republiek and Britain', *Scientia Militaria: South African Journal of Military Studies*, 1: 11 (1981), pp. 58–61.

Cox, Elizabeth. 'The First King's Dragoon Guards in South Africa, 1879–1881', *Military History Journal*, 6: 5 (June 1985) < samilitaryhistory.org/journal.html> (accessed 2 September 2015).

Davenport, T.R.H. 'Kruger, Stephanus Johannes Paulus [Paul] (1825–1904)', *Oxford Dictionary of National Biography* (Oxford University Press, 2004; online edition, May 2006) <http://www.oxforddnb.com.libproxy.wlu.ca/view/article/41290> (accessed 20 August 2015).

Emery, Frank. 'Soldiers' Letters from the First Anglo-Boer War, 1880–81', *Natalia*, 11 (1981), pp. 16–26.

Friend, D. 'Training Doctrines of the Staatsartillerie of the Zuid-Afrikaansche Republiek', *Military History Journal*, 11: 5 (June 2000) < samilitaryhistory.org/journal.html> (accessed 27 August 2015).

Gordon, Peter, 'Herbert. Henry Howard Molyneux, fourth earl of Carnarvon (1831–1890)', *Oxford Dictionary of National Biography* (Oxford University Press, 2004; online edition, January 2011) <http://www.oxforddnb.com. libproxy.wlu.ca/view/article/33859> (accessed 20 August 2015).

Grobler, J.E.H. 'Die Beleëring van die Britse Garnisoene', in Van Jaarsveld (ed.), F.A., Van Rensburg (ed.), A.P.J., and Stals (ed.), W.A., *Die Eerste Vryheidsoorlog van Verset en Geweld tot Skikking deur Onderhandeling 1877–1884* (Pretoria and Cape Town: Haum, 1980).

—'Die Britse Terugslag by Laingsnek', in Van Jaarsveld (ed.), F.A., Van Rensburg (ed.), A.P.J., and Stals (ed.), W.A., *Die Eerste Vryheidsoorlog van Verset en Geweld tot Skikking deur Onderhandeling 1877–1884* (Pretoria and Cape Town: Haum, 1980).

— 'Paardekraal: Eensydige Herstel van die Onafhanklikheid', in Van Jaarsveld (ed.), F.A., Van Rensburg (ed.), A.P.J., and Stals (ed.), W.A. *Die Eerste Vryheidsoorlog van Verset en Geweld tot Skikking deur Onderhandeling 1877–1884* (Pretoria and Cape Town: Haum, 1980).

— 'Schuinshoogte', in Van Jaarsveld (ed.), F.A., Van Rensburg (ed.), A.P.J., and Stals (ed.), W.A., *Die Eerste Vryheidsoorlog van Verset en Geweld tot Skikking deur Onderhandeling 1877–1884* (Pretoria and Cape Town: Haum, 1980).

— 'Die Sege by Bronkhorstspruit', in Van Jaarsveld (ed.), F.A., Van Rensburg (ed.), A.P.J., and Stals (ed.), W.A., *Die Eerste Vryheidsoorlog van Verset en Geweld tot Skikking deur Onderhandeling 1877–1884* (Pretoria and Cape Town: Haum, 1980).

Hall, Major D.D., 'The Artillery of the First Anglo-Boer War 1880–1881', *Military History Journal*, 5: 2 (December 1980) < samilitaryhistory.org/ journal.html> (accessed 27 August 2015).

— 'Field Artillery of the British Army 1860–1960', *Military History Journal*, 5:1 (December 1980) <samilitaryhistory.org/journal.html> (accessed 25 August 2015).

Heathcote, Tony. 'Academies, Military', in Holmes (ed.), Richard, *The Oxford Companion to Military History* (Oxford: Oxford University Press, 2001).

Heydenrych, D.H. 'The Boer Republics, 1852–1881', in Cameron (ed.), Trewhella, and Spies (ed.,) S.B., *An Illustrated History of South Africa* (Johannesburg: Jonathan Ball, 1986).

Jordan, Rob. 'The Battle of Majuba: Telegrams of 27 February 1881', *Military History Journal*, 5:2 (December 1980) <samilitaryhistory.org/journal.html> (accessed 27 August 2015).

Laband, John. 'Beaten by the Boers', *Ancestors*, 42 (February 2006), pp. 56–60.

— '"The Dangers of Divided Command": British Civil and Military Disputes over the Conduct of the Zululand Campaign of 1879 and 1888', *Journal for the Society of Army Historical Research*, 81: 328 (Winter 2003), pp. 339–335.

— '"The Direction of the Whole of the Forces Available': The Disputed Spheres of the Military and Civil Authorities in the Eastern Cape (1877–1878), Natal (1879) and Zululand (1888)," *Scientia Militaria: South African Journal of Military Studies*, 41: 2 (2013), pp. 60–76.

— 'An Empress in Zululand', *Natalia*, 30 (December 2000), pp. 45–57.

— 'The Slave Soldiers of Africa', *Journal of Military History*, 81: 1(January 2017), pp. 1–38.

— 'War and Peace in South Africa', in Boyden (ed.), Peter B., Guy (ed.), Alan J., and Harding (ed.) Marion, *'Ashes and Blood'. The British Army in South Africa 1795–1914* (London: National Army Museum Publication, 2001).

Laband, John, and Thompson, Paul. 'African Levies in Natal and Zululand, 1836–1906', in Miller (ed.), Stephen M., *Soldiers and Settlers in Africa, 1850–1918* (Leiden and Boston: Brill, 2009).

— 'The Reduction of Zululand, 1878–1904', in Duminy (ed.), Andrew, and Guest (ed.), Bill, *Natal and Zululand from Earliest Times to 1910: A New History* (Pietermaritzburg: University of Natal Press and Shuter & Shooter, 1989).

Lloyd E.M., revised by Lunt, James. 'Smyth [*formerly* Curzon-Howe], Sir Leicester (1829–1891)', *Oxford Dictionary of National Biography* (Oxford University Press, 2004; online edition, May 2009) <http://www.oxforddnb.com.libproxy.wlu.ca/view/article/25955> (accessed 20 August 2015).

Machanik, Felix. 'Firearms and Firepower, First War of Independence, 1880–1881', *South African Military History Journal*, 5: 1 (December 1980) <samilitaryhistory.org/journal.html> (accessed 25 August 2015).

Manning, Stephen. 'Evelyn Wood', in Corvi (ed.), Steven J., and Beckett (ed.), Ian F.W., *Victoria's Generals* (Barnsley, South Yorks: Pen & Sword Military, 2009).

Miller, Stephen M. 'Redvers Buller', in Corvi (ed.), Steven J., and Beckett (ed.), Ian F.W., *Victoria's Generals* (Barnsley, South Yorks: Pen & Sword Military, 2009).

Moreman, T.R. 'Callwell, Sir Charles Edward (1859–1928)', *Oxford Dictionary of National Biography* (Oxford University Press, 2004; online edition, January 2008) http://www.oxforddnb.com.libproxy.wlu.ca/view/article/32251 (accessed 20 August 2015).

Nasson, William, 'Africans at War', in Gooch, John, *The Boer War: Direction, Experience and Image* (London, Portland, Or: Frank Cass, 2000).

Nöthling, Cmdt. C.J., 'Military Commanders of the War (1880–1881)', *Scientia Militaria: South African Journal of Military Studies*, 11: 1 (1981), pp. 76–80.

Otto, Brig. W. 'Die Slag van Majuba 27 Februarie 1881', *Scientia Militaria: South African Journal of Military Studies*, 1: 11 (1981), pp. 1–7.

Powell, John. 'Wodehouse, John, first earl of Kimberley (1826 –1902)', *Oxford Dictionary of National Biography* (Oxford University Press, 2004; online edition, May 2009) <http://www.oxforddnb.com.libproxy.wlu.ca/view/article/36987> (accessed 20 August 2015).

Pugh, Martin. 'Beach, Michael Edward Hicks, first Earl St Aldwyn (1837–1916)', *Oxford Dictionary of National Biography* (Oxford University Press, 2004; online edition, January 2011) <http://www.oxforddnb.com.libproxy.wlu.ca/view/article/33859> (accessed 20 August 2015).

Saks, David. 'Tragic Failure: The Last Campaign of Maj-Gen George Pomeroy Colley', *Military History Journal*, 13:6 (December 2006) <samilitaryhistory.org/journal.html> (accessed 27 August 2015).

Saunders, Christopher. 'The Transkeian Rebellion of 1880: a Case Study of Transkeian Resistance to White Control', *South African Historical Journal*, 8 (1976), pp. 32–39.

Saunders, Christopher, and Smith, Iain R. 'Southern Africa, 1795–1910' in Porter (ed.), Andrew, *The Oxford History of the British Empire*, vol. 3, *The Nineteenth Century* (Oxford: Oxford University Press, 2001).

Scott, Louis. 'Boereweerstand teen Gedwonge Britse Bestuur in Transvaal, 1877–1880', in Van Jaarsveld (ed.), F.A., Van Rensburg (ed.), A.P.J., and Stals (ed.), W.A. *Die Eerste Vryheidsoorlog van Verset en Geweld tot Skikking deur Onderhandeling 1877–1884* (Pretoria and Cape Town: Haum, 1980).

Spiers, Edward M. 'The British Army in South Africa: Military Government and Occupation, 1877–1914', in Boyden (ed.), Peter B., Guy (ed.), Alan J., and Harding (ed.) Marion, *'Ashes and Blood'. The British Army in South Africa 1795–1914* (London: National Army Museum Publication, 2001).

— 'George, Prince, second Duke of Cambridge (1819 –1904)', *Oxford Dictionary of National Biography* (Oxford University Press, 2004; online ed., May 2009) <http://www.oxforddnb.com..libproxy.wlu.ca/view/article/33372> (accessed 20 August 2015).

— 'The Late Victorian Army 1868–1914', in Chandler (ed.), D.G., and Beckett (ed.), I., *The Oxford History of the British Army* (Oxford: Oxford University Press, 2003).

Stapleton, Tim. '"Valuable, Gallant and Faithful Assistants": The Fingo (or Mfengu) as Colonial Military Allies during the Cape-Xhosa Wars, 1835–1881', in Miller (ed.), Stephen M., *Soldiers and Settlers in Africa, 1850–1918* (Leiden and Boston: Brill, 2009).

Stearn, Roger T. 'Lanyon, Sir (William) Owen (1842 –1887)', *Oxford Dictionary of National Biography* (Oxford University Press, 2004; online edition, January 2011). <http://www.oxforddnb.com..libproxy.wlu.ca/view/article/16060> (accessed 20 August 2015).

—'Macdonald, Sir Hector Archibald (1853–1903)', *Oxford Dictionary of National Biography* (Oxford University Press, 2004; online edition, January 2011) <http://www.oxforddnb.com.libproxy.wlu.ca/view/article/34702> (accessed 20 August 2015).

Theron, Bridget. 'Theophilus Shepstone and the Transvaal Colony, 1877–1879', *Kleio*, 34 (2002), pp. 104–127.

Trapido, Stanley. 'Reflections on Land, Office and Wealth in the South African Republic, 1850-1900 ', in Marks (ed.), Shula, and Atmore (ed.), Anthony. *Economy and Society in Pre-Industrial South Africa* (London: Longman, 1980).

Turner, Thomas. 'Lawn Tennis Shoes for Men and Women, c. 1870 –c. 1900' <www.academia.edu/3542656> (accessed 3 December 2015).

Tylden, George. 'The Development of the Commando System in South Africa, 1715 to 1922', *Africana Notes and News*, 13 (March 1958–December 1959), pp. 303–313.

Van der Waag, Ian. 'South Africa and the Boer Military System', in Dennis (ed.), Peter, and Grey (ed.), Jeffrey. *The Boer War: Army, Nation and Empire* (Canberra: Army History Unit, Australian Department of Defence, 2000).

Van Jaarsveldt, Kaptein A.E. 'Pretoria gedurende die Eerste Vryheidsoorlog', *Scientia Militaria: South African Journal of Military Studies*, 1: 11 (1981), pp. 48–56.

Visser, Kaptein G.E. 'Die Eerste Vryheidsoorlog: Enkele Aspekte met die Britse Siening van die Boere en die Verskille tussen Boer en Brit', *Scientia Militaria: South African Journal of Military Studies*, 1: 11 (1981), pp. 69–75.

Von Moltke, Kaptein R. 'Wapentuig van die Eerste Vryheidsoolog', *Scientia Militaria, South African Journal of Military Studies* , 11: 1 (1981), pp. 8–29.

Unpublished Theses

Grobler, J.E.H., 'Die Eerste Vryheidsoorlog, 1880–1881: 'n Militêre-Historiese Benadering' (unpublished PhD thesis, University of Pretoria, 1981).

Paterson, Hamish. 'The Military Organisation of the Colony of Natal, 1881–1910' (unpublished MA thesis, University of Natal, 1985).

Pitout, D.N. 'Die Slag van Amajuba, 27 Februarie 1881' (unpublished M.A. thesis, University of Pretoria, 1980).

Theron-Bushell, B.M. 'Puppet on an Imperial String: Owen Lanyon in South Africa, 1875–1881', (unpublished D.Litt. et Phil. thesis, University of South Africa, 2002).

Index